MICHAEL HARRINGTON

AMERICAN RADICALS
A SERIES EDITED BY HARVEY J. KAYE
AND ELLIOTT J. GORN

Also available in this Routledge series:

WILLIAM APPLEMAN WILLIAMS
The Tragedy of Empire

BY PAUL M. BUHLE AND EDWARD RICE-MAXIMIN

MICHAEL HARRINGTON

Speaking American

ROBERT A. GORMAN

ROUTLEDGE
New York and London

Published in 1995 by

Routledge
29 West 35th Street
New York, NY 10001

Published in Great Britain by

Routledge
11 New Fetter Lane
London EC4P 4EE

Copyright © 1995 by Routledge
Series design by Annie West
Printed in the United States of America on acid-free paper

Library of Congress Cataloging-in-Publication Data

Gorman, Robert A.
    Michael Harrington—speaking American / Robert A. Gorman.
    p.   cm.
    Includes index.
    ISBN 0-415-91117-6 (hb). — ISBN 0-415-91118-4 (pb)
    1. Harrington, Michael, 1928–1989
    2. Socialists—United States—Biography.
    3. Radicals—United States—Biography.
    I. Title.
    HX84.H37G67   1995   95-19421
    335.5'092—dc20   [B]   CIP

Contents

To Colin and Jesse, and to a hopeful future

PREFACE

SOME THINGS, THEY SAY, ONLY INTELLECTUALS are crazy enough to believe. For many in the U.S., foremost among these are the inferences that Marxism is democratic and socialists are patriots. The center and right in America have always equated progressive social change with totalitarianism, and condemned leftism as un-American and undemocratic. The Old Left, on the other hand, played its bad-guy role to perfection. Like cheap gravy on an aged filet, orthodoxy annihilated the specificity of American life, reducing every activity to an impersonal law. Subjectivity, politics, science, gender, race, religion, and family—the flesh of everyday life—were reduced to class and then pulverized beyond recognition. It was as if, by fiat or perhaps through a few decades of Marxian political education, orthodoxy would eradicate an entire culture.

While mainstream Marxists doggedly backed an orthodox party or faction, early in this century other leftists quietly reformulated Marxian theory and practice. They have, in effect, molded Marxism to U.S. liberalism, producing a corpus of theory and strategy that I have recently called "Yankee Red." These socialists have co-opted the nation's rock-bottom sense of individualism, its faith in political activism, its commitment to empirical science, and its tolerance of deep, powerful non-economic associations. Mass culture, which historical materialists neither fathomed nor tolerated, became a vehicle for progressive change, the body wherein Marx's radical spirit materialized. By acknowledging what orthodoxy wouldn't, that is, the dynamic linkages between base and superstructure, these socialists evoked what for liberals was the frightening specter of a home-grown, popular radicalism. Neither liberal nor orthodox, these indigenous outcasts were unconditionally ignored by liberals and censured by the mainstream left.

Michael Harrington is certainly America's preeminent non-orthodox socialist. In socialism he calls the "unknown" Marx a "reformist with a revolutionary purpose . . . [who] saw an alliance with trade-union gradualism as a step toward the abolition of classes." This characterization could also be applied to himself. Socialism, for Harrington, eliminated the social division of labor and democratized significant decision-making processes, rather than merely redistributing wealth or nationalizing factories. Inequality, not markets, was his enemy. Without inequality, markets, even in socialism, could be progressive. Socialism thus empowered people politically and culturally as well as economically. If people thought and acted differently they could reclaim a nation long ago stolen by wealthy insiders. This enlightened subjectivity grew by contesting injustice everywhere. Harrington believed that congressional power was an indispensable weapon for such ideologically engaged citizens. He tried hard to realign the U.S. party system in order to turn electoral politics leftward.

Harrington's revolutionary pragmatism testified to both the capitalist state's power to improve proletarian lives and the mass appeal of reformism. And it bet the barn that higher living standards and increased political power behind other struggles would fortify a democratic socialist impulse among voters.

Harrington was thus a quintessential American theorist: practical, eclectic, and infused with U.S. popular culture. He squeezed the radical potential from capitalism without obliterating our everyday experiences by creatively fusing orthodox materialism, liberalism, and neo-Marxism. Unless the economy magically heals, this kind of project will soon occupy a growing number of our intellectuals and activists.

Michael Harrington: Speaking American takes Harrington's major ideas one at a time, and examines each against a background of pertinent orthodox, neo-Marxian, and liberal concepts. It also speculates about socialism's role in a perplexing post-communist world where even victorious nations are in economic trouble.

We begin, in the Prologue and in Chapter 1, with an account of the major events, institutions, and personalities that shaped Harrington's world view from childhood through his encounters with Dorothy Day, Norman Thomas, Max Schachtman, Irving Howe, the Socialist Party, the New Left, the Democratic Socialist Organizing Committee, and finally the Democratic Socialists of America. The hub of Harrington's socialism is a unique dialectical vision wherein he departs from both liberalism and orthodox Marxism. Chapter 2 outlines Harrington's dialectics and rejects conventional views that he is actually a "radical liberal" or a mainstream Marxist. Harrington nudges dialectics into everyday life in order to help explain our experiences. In Chapter 3 we examine Harrington's early radicalism as he tentatively stretched beyond economism toward a more innovative left identity. *The Other America*, Harrington's most popular but also his least understood and most superficial book, stunned a complacent nation and also taught Harrington some surprising lessons about being famous, wealthy, and socialist in America. Chapter 4 shows how Harrington, almost single-handedly, legitimized for bereft leftists America's romantic infatuation with political heroes like the Kennedys,

Martin Luther King, Jr., Eugene McCarthy, George McGovern, and Jesse Jackson. If, as Harrington implied, politics really did matter, then hitching onto rising liberal stars could brighten the prospects for an eventual move leftward. Henceforth, political engagement became radical as well as chic, and many activists soon felt that capitalism could be contested through leftist rear-guard actions that chipped into the nation's pecuniary bourgeois soul. This chapter compares and contrasts liberal and orthodox theories of the state, retraces the origins of democratic socialist political theory, and recreates Harrington's view of when, where, and how legitimate politics fuses with revolutionary activism.

What events would transform an apparently placid nation into a cauldron of crisis and dissatisfaction? Chapter 5 examines Harrington's multifaceted crisis theory, which depicted capitalism's economic as well as political, ideological, cultural, and foreign-policy contradictions. With the socialist Harrington at least partially committed to a political strategy, he was forced to reconceptualize both the revolutionary agent and process. In Chapter 6 we see how Harrington redefined the U.S. class structure, monitored the birth of what he called a New Working Class, and tackled the difficult question of how New Class Theory would be operationalized. Party realignment, he argued, was the answer, because it could mobilize a multi-class progressive coalition that might win elections. Harrington eventually learned that U.S. parties were dealigning, not realigning, and that socialists needed to impact a lot more than elections. Most radicals were lost somewhere in left field while capitalists were circling the bases. Reformist tactics had thus hardened into reformism. In short, socialism was still a foreign language in the U.S. Chapter 7 describes Harrington's "New Socialism," which tied a nineteenth-century utopian socialist ethic to Marx's revolutionary politics. By recovering socialism's forgotten past, Harrington compensated for modern leftism's meager values and its mindless addiction to welfare-state capitalism. Anchored in the ancient republican ideal of the citizen, where public and private blended, Harrington argued that a real synthesis of individualism and collectivism was now materially, ethically, and politically possible. He called this synthesis Socialist Republicanism, and found it catalyzing every progressive U.S. movement that stressed individual dignity and power and the importance of equal participation in public decision-making. Harrington felt that socialists had to dip into the nation's everyday popular culture—once contemptuously called the superstructure—and gently open the floodgates of democracy.

Our nation is now perilously close to economic disaster. Innovative ideas are certainly needed, and the final chapter evaluates Harrington's contributions. Politicians come and go, but good ideas and strategies, like fine jewels, are always in demand. Harrington's is a democratic, patriotic message of renewal, hope, and change. With people today searching for alternatives to business as usual, it just might sell in what is now a paltry market for solutions.

I am indebted to Harvey J. Kaye, Elliott J. Gorn, and Ray Franklin for their invaluable advice, guidance, and encouragement during the agonizingly long months between first reviews and final product. They can take credit for making this book better than it would otherwise have been, even though I must shoulder the blame for its defects. The office staff here at the University of Tennessee Department of Political Science—Sue Howerton, Phyllis Moyers, and Debby McCauley—couldn't have been more efficient or friendly. Peter Filardo, at New York University's Tamiment Institute Library, helped me plow through the unpublished letters and manuscripts of the Michael Harrington Correspondence in the records of the Democratic Socialists of America. I am grateful to him and his fine staff. The excellent photographs of Michael Harrington are courtesy of Bob Adelman. David Glenn, at the DSA headquarters in New York City, supported this project with timely information and help. Thanks also to Cecelia Cancellaro and Claudia Gorelick at Routledge for their assistance in turning a manuscript into a published book. My sister, Malka Gorman, with many more important things to do, somehow managed to ask the right questions, give great advice, and render support just when I needed it most. She also had the good sense to settle in beautiful San Francisco. Jesse Paris Gorman and Colin Matthew Gorman, my sons, have made me prouder and happier than I ever thought I could be. They also know just when to leave the old man alone. I am dedicating this book to them. And Elaine, as always, has shared the best and worst with me through all these years. She sparkles brighter than ever.

R. A.G.

Knoxville, Tennessee

PROLOGUE

FROM PORT HURON TO POSTERITY

ON 12 JUNE 1962, 59 EAGER RADICALS—mostly students, but also some veterans from the civil rights movement in the South, some trade union activists, and several leftist political leaders—convened in Port Huron, Michigan, intent on drafting a platform for the fledgling movement known as the New Left. Four days later they ratified a manifesto subsequently called "the Port Huron Statement." The troubling events that followed drastically altered America's political landscape for years to come. They also affected the personal lives of several key participants, but none more so than the thirty-four-year-old socialist Michael Harrington. Port Huron became the central event in Harrington's life. It destroyed his reputation and credibility among heretofore sympathetic young, non-communist radicals, and also unexpectedly purged his socialism of Old Left shibboleths.

A war-weary nation had just spent the 1950s blissfully consuming goods and basking in prosperity. The economy was growing. Jobs, particularly for college-bound students, were plentiful. Nonetheless, by the early 1960s, many young people grew restive. They discovered racism, sexism, poverty, and neo-colonialism. They also noticed indifferent parents and politicians, and irrelevant socialists who were constantly bickering with each other. Some college students eventually decided to take matters into their own hands by creating an alternative, iconoclastic radicalism: a New Left. The times, Bob Dylan testified, were indeed changing.

The term "New Left" originated in England in the late 1950s, when disgruntled Marxian intellectuals from the British Communist Party joined anti-nuclear activists to form "New Left Clubs" that were based at university campuses. In 1960, two journals—the *New Reasoner* and *Universities and Left Review*—merged into the *New Left Review*, the intellectual organ of the New Left Clubs. At about this time in the U.S., a group of activist socialists broke with the Socialist Workers Party and created the magazine *American Socialist* to introduce New Left radicalism into America. Thus, the term "New Left" was in use among American radicals during the early 1960s.

Harrington was a member of the Socialist Party (SP) and the head of its youth wing, the Young People's Socialist League (YPSL). He was also the heir apparent to Norman Thomas, whose long and distinguished career as SP leader was winding down. Harrington and Thomas both felt that the SP was flirting with irrelevance. Most of its time and efforts were spent addressing abstract sectarian questions that had once fascinated hard-core socialists but that were light-years removed from the needs and interests of young Americans in 1962. The New Left, with its vigorous, anti-sectarian leaders, was perceived by both men as more viable than the YPSL. They decided to cast their net for this nontraditional constituency.[1]

Harrington was officially invited to attend the Port Huron Conference as the representative of the League for Industrial Democracy (LID), the parent body of an organization called the Student League for Industrial Democracy (SLID), which had recently changed its name to the Students for a Democratic Society (SDS). "I was there unofficially as a personal friend of the young activists who engineered that transformation," Harrington pointed out. "Together we were going to put some very new wine into a very old bottle."[2] Among these young SDS activists was a charismatic leader named Tom Hayden. In the spring of 1960, at an Ann Arbor meeting of socialists celebrating May Day, Harrington had met Hayden and asked him to join the YPSL. According to Harrington, "his attitude was that he agreed with me on almost all practical and political questions . . . . He'd say, 'I agree with you. But where I disagree with you is that you use the word 'socialism,' which is a European word, which simply cuts off your American audience.' And what he was essentially telling me was that he wanted to have a different language. He wanted to speak American."[3] A year later, Hayden wrote in *Mademoiselle* that his generation trusted only three people over thirty: C. Wright Mills, Norman Thomas, and Michael Harrington.

This mutual affection between Hayden and Harrington set the stage for what both believed would be a cooperative and fruitful meeting at Port Huron. Harrington assumed that, under Hayden's leadership, the conference would meld the New Left and the SP into a formidable force. Hayden looked forward to receiving financial and political support from the left's old guard for his own movement. No one anticipated that this hopeful meeting would quickly deteriorate into bitter name-calling and suspicion. Only years later did Harrington fully appreciate Hayden's desire for a unique, indigenous radicalism. By then Harrington's bridge to the New Left was already burned; nonetheless, he devoted the rest of his life to articulating a socialism that spoke directly to Americans.

Harrington's friendship with Hayden was, in fact, a house of cards built on wishful thinking. Theoretical and personal conflicts, always latent, materialized suddenly in Port Huron's charged atmosphere. Hayden and the New Left felt that the "evils" of communism were caused by capitalist mistrust and provocation. They questioned the "policy-making assumption that the Soviet Union is inherently expansionist," and suggested that "the savage repression of the Hungarian Revolution was a defensive action rooted in Soviet fear that its empire would collapse."[4] Anti-communism was therefore as foolish as pro-capitalism. Radicals had to end injustice by any means imaginable, even cooperating with communists or adopting certain communist practices. Anti-communist left-wing intellectuals had created a climate of popular hysteria that made a reasonable appraisal of the Soviet threat impossible. "While the older radicals are indispensable for information and advice," Hayden conceded, "and while our sympathies parallel theirs on nearly every other domestic issue, they tragically coalesce with the less informed, conservative and even reactionary forces in performing a static analysis, in making Russia a 'closed question.'"[5]

Hayden saw the escalating conflict in Vietnam as an internal struggle between two indigenous forces, the nature of which was unaffected by communist support for the freedom-fighting rebels. He demanded that America immediately withdraw its troops. Harrington, on the other hand, thought history had proved unequivocally that communism was inhumane and reactionary: socialists had to oppose it as forthrightly as they did capitalism. The SDS, in Harrington's view, was thus foolishly "anti-anti-communist,"[6]: failing to distinguish the left critique of communism from McCarthy's. Communist support for Vietnamese insurgents, moreover, had altered the guerrilla movement, transforming the war in Vietnam into a spiritless struggle between wealthy landlords and communist dictators. Harrington wouldn't endorse Hayden's call for unconditional U.S. withdrawal. Hayden also lumped liberals and trade unionists into what he called "an undifferentiated mass of old fogies and sell-outs"[7] who were rigidly capitalist. Labor, in particular, had grown "too rich and sluggish" to lead, and "the general absence of union democracy," Hayden added, "finalized worker apathy."[8] Radicals could no longer trust the proletariat, and must depend on America's youth, especially college students, to lead the nation as the vanguard of progressive change. Hayden later expanded this vanguard to include feminists, blacks, minorities, and the "underclass," (i.e. the powerless, poor, criminal, and addicted).

Harrington strongly disagreed with this minimalization of the workers' role. He saw students, minorities, and the underclass, as atomized and fragmented, while workers were united by shared conditions.[9] Socialists, he believed, had no choice but to identify with the humane values of trade unionists and liberals—the left wing of American politics—who represented a potential electoral majority. By mocking them and the welfare state they struggled to create, Hayden antagonized the heart and soul of progressive America. SDS, Harrington warned, threatened to trivialize the left.

These intellectual conflicts were fundamental, but something more perplexing was also at work. Port Huron was as much a rite of passage for a new generation of radicals as it was an attempt to chart the course of American socialism. Hayden admitted as much in 1984: "It was a setup. There couldn't be a more perfect setup. We were giving birth to some new force in American politics. And Michael, purely by virtue of being older and having other attachments, was being an obstacle in the delivery room . . . . To the extent that you want to get Freudian about it, and there was some element of that there, he was the perfect guy for everybody to overthrow."[10] Harrington also experienced a difficult emotional transformation: "Here I was: I was thirty-four. I'd been a youth leader for so long that people were joking that I was 'the oldest young socialist in America.' It's personal autobiography: I'd always been the youngest at everything I'd ever done . . . . Now I'm in this Oedipal situation. Up comes this younger generation. I think that they are ignoring my honest, sincere, and absolutely profound advice. And this struck at my self-image . . . . I interpreted this as an Oedipal assault on the father-figure."[11] These dense conflicts made the schism unavoidable, although its fury would have diminished had someone understood what was happening.

Harrington had read the SDS Manifesto's working draft, crafted by Tom Hayden, before arriving at Port Huron and was comfortable with what he called its "larger political vision." But as he meticulously pored over it ("I can almost see specific places where I marked it up"[12]), Harrington grew troubled. Hayden had simply disavowed the SP's pro-labor and anti-communist traditions. Offended, Harrington wrote an angry letter, which has since been lost, to the SDS offices in New York City.[13] When he arrived in Port Huron as an invited speaker, Harrington was seething. Supported by a reputation as America's brightest and most promising young leftist, and by the resources and prestige of organizations like the SP and LID, he presumed that his own viewpoints would be adopted.

Harrington's companion speaker at Port Huron was Donald Slaiman, a disciple of the socialist and anti-communist Max Shachtman who had joined the staff of the AFL-CIO because he admired its hawkish leader, George Meany. Slaiman bitterly opposed the Hayden draft, and urged Harrington to challenge it.[14] He was also angry that SDS had granted "observer status" to a teenage member of a communist youth-front group. The tension increased among SDS members, who anticipated trouble and anxiously awaited Harrington's arrival.

Harrington didn't remember clearly his initial dialogues with SDS leaders. He vaguely recalled discussing a wide range of topics, including anti-communism, liberalism, and the labor movement. "The whole question of historical agency," Harrington reflected, "I'm sure that came up at Port Huron. I would have been very critical about the idea that students were the vanguard." Apparently someone accused Slaiman of red-baiting. He reacted by screaming, defending George Meany, and depicting Hayden and his cohorts as "Stalinoids," the pejorative term Shachtmanites applied to communist sympathizers. The debate quickly polarized as Slaiman and Harrington became angry outsiders in a hostile crowd.

The group eventually adjourned to a dining room stocked with beer and cigarettes. Harrington, who admitted having an "enormous capacity for drinking beer and talking about politics," was now flanked by his friend Harry Fleischman. Hayden's debating partner was Roger Hagan. Hayden shocked everyone by insisting that he had put *too much* anti-communism into the Manifesto in order to appease left-wing bigots and cold warriors, including, presumably, Harrington. Harrington recollected this barroom debate as "not unfriendly,"[15] but the young students who watched were stunned by Hayden's insult and the pervasive hostility.

After the nighttime confrontation with Hayden, Harrington departed Port Huron for another speaking engagement, convinced that the draft Manifesto was profoundly mistaken. Back home in New York City, he heard from Rachelle Horowitz, a friend and ally in SDS, that an all-night meeting of SDS leaders had failed to satisfy Harrington's demands. "On the substantial issues," she related, "we went down the tubes."[16] Harrington decided to punish SDS. On 28 June 1962, The League for Industrial Democracy—the parent organization and financial sponsor of SDS—threatened to cut off financial, printing, and mailing privileges, and to discredit SDS among liberals. On 6 July, Harrington accused SDS of "accepting reds to your meeting . . . . You knew this would send LID through the roof." He then declared "There is no SDS as a functioning organization with a political life. It does not exist . . . ." A defensive Hayden pointed to the values section of the draft Manifesto, which rejected communism. "Documents shmocuments," replied Harrington, "Slaiman and I said that this was antithetical to the LID and everything it stood for."[17] Harrington and the LID board then invalidated all formal decisions made at Port Huron. They also fired Hayden and Al Haber, censured all SDS materials leaving the central office, and appointed a new, more sympathetic "student secretary." SDS Field Secretary Steve Max, an ex-member of the communist Labor Youth League and the son of a former managing editor of the *Daily Worker*, was taken off the payroll. "We knew we weren't communists," an SDS activist complained, "but the idea that our parent organization thought we were was Kafkaesque."[18] Finally, on 7 July 1962, LID changed the lock at the SDS national offices in downtown Manhattan, forcing SDS officials to pick the new lock in order to reclaim important documents.

In meetings held during the second week of July, SDS decided to compromise with Harrington by modifying the Hayden draft. It sent the final version to LID, accompanied by a detailed clarification of SDS positions. SDS accused LID of "falsehood, exaggeration and slander," and pointed to newly revised passages dealing with communism based on the "excellent discussion . . . held with Mr. Harrington."[19] SDS also reworked passages to emphasize the progressive values it shared with LID.

Under pressure from democratic leftists, including Norman Thomas, who were embarrassed by the gutter-fighting, Harrington and the LID board backed off. In September, 1962, a negotiated settlement was completed that provided for a joint "Statement of Principles," a qualified loyalty pledge by Hayden, a letter by Harrington deploring the "confusion on all sides," and a revised SDS Manifesto that was circulated uncensored. Steve Max was allowed to remain as field secretary, but LID refused to pay his salary. LID agreed to continue subsidizing SDS to the tune of $8,000 to $10,000 a year. LID also insisted on censoring Hayden's 1962 "President's Report," deleting several objectionable passages including a reference to "the smearing effects of the [LID] charges."

Socialism's civil war had ended, but the wounds would never fully heal. A disillusioned and embittered Casey Hayden, Tom's wife, complained, "I know now what it must have been like to be attacked by Stalinists."[20] Tom Hayden taunted Harrington: "[Port Huron] taught me that Social Democrats aren't radicals and can't be trusted. It taught me what Social Democrats really think about civil liberties and organizational integrity."[21] "This situation," Hayden added, "created a sense of 'them'—the old leftists —and 'us': Now we were embattled. They—not the right wing—were trying to prevent the growth of a new radical force. The names they called us reinforced our new left identity."[22]

At first Harrington denied the significance of Port Huron, replaying his own struggles against red-baiting and McCarthyism.[23] Soon, however, he realized the full horror of what had happened during, and immediately after, the 1962 meeting. He had lost the confidence and trust of young U.S. radicals at a time when, in different circumstances, he might have become their leader. Moreover, in June 1963, John F. Kennedy initiated a thaw in the Cold War by declaring in a speech at American Universtity, "Let us re-examine our attitude toward the Soviet Union." Within a year the Manifesto's analysis of communism had become common within the political mainstream. Once America's most promising young socialist, Harrington had foolishly settled in a right-wing neighborhood of Cold War bullies. He was embarrassed and humiliated.

Harrington belatedly conceded that his behavior at Port Huron was irrational and stupid.[24] He admitted to ignoring the moral appeal that communism held for decent people, especially during the depression and the civil rights struggles. "I should have had the maturity to understand that young people groping toward a political ideology were not to be treated as if they were old Trotsky faction fighters following a line."[25] After what seemed to liberals and leftists an interminable decade, Harrington applied this logic to Vietnamese peasants as well, and called for the immediate unconditional withdrawal of U.S. troops from what was, he finally realized, an internal struggle. He regretted leaving Port Huron before the completion of the Manifesto's final draft, which incorporated many of his criticisms, and later following a conservative old-guard in LID that, he discovered, "did not really share my basic attitudes." Harrington also apologized for his intemperate reaction (he later called it a "middle-age tantrum"[26] to the "ungrateful youths who had rejected my wise advise"[27]. "When I came to my senses," he wrote in 1989, "the damage had been done and, as far as many in the New Left were concerned, I was one more horrible example of the untrustworthyness of people over thirty."[28]

New Leftists didn't rush to forgive and forget. Fifteen years after Port Huron, Hayden still characterized Harrington's actions as "paranoid, hysterical, anti-communist mud-slinging . . . . [I]t was more anti-communist than it was socialist."[29] Even former SDS leaders like Steve Max and Richard Flacks, who knew from firsthand experience the germ of truth in Harrington's anti-communism, rejected the apology. Emotions cooled somewhat during the reactionary Reagan years. Thanking Harrington in 1981 for a critical but "very fine review" of a published monograph, Hayden added, "At last, I guess we're all learning how to disagree constructively."[30] In a 1986 speech at Hofstra University, Hayden "regretted" his naiveté regarding "the cynical motives of the Soviet Union," as well as the "hostility" that angered others and inadvertantly "compounded the pain of many Americans who lost sons and loved ones in Vietnam."[31] Later he conceded that if SDS had consistently applied its moral principles in 1962, "those of us who were aroused about a cigarette butt being put onto the neck of a black student in the South would have been equally concerned about an ice pick being put into Trotsky's brain."[32] In former leader Bob Ross's words, SDS saw the history of communism as "unfruitful, uninteresting and irrelevant . . . . We wanted to be ignorant of all that."[33] The organization paid a horrible price for its ignorance. In 1969, when SDS had already run out of gas and its leaders were foolishly peddling "authentic" Marxism-Leninism, it was infiltrated and captured by the Progressive Labor Party, a disciplined cadre of Leninists, and handed to urban guerrillas who were called Weatherpeople. Harrington's abrasive mini-course on the history of communism, held during one beer-filled Michigan night in 1962 and reinforced by events seven years later, had taken almost a quarter of a century to sink in.

There were no winners at Port Huron. Hayden and SDS forfeited an institutional base with the political and financial resources to organize for the long haul. Traditional socialists, on the other hand, merely confirmed history's negative judgement: they were dinosaurs to radical young Americans who weren't obsessed with, or even particularly interested in, the turmoil surrounding Russia's Revolution.

Harrington earned the dubious honor of being the biggest loser. Psychologically, he was devastated, his self-image shattered. Having spent over a decade cultivating an image and a constituency, he destroyed both in one foolish night and its aftermath. Professionally, Harrington was now a man without turf. Stereotyped as a strident anti-communist, anti-capitalist, and anti-New Leftist, he was simply ignored altogether by scholars. No significant books on Harrington, and surprisingly few serious articles, were published until 1995. And politically, Harrington was left in isolation. Communists would have nothing to do with him. New Leftists never fully accepted his apology, and questioned his slow about-face on Vietnam and his tolerance of Cold War hawks. Harrington's mushy support for U.S. intervention in Southeast Asia transformed liberal discomfort into outright hostility. The electoral center and right were alternately enchanted by Harrington's independence and dismayed by his radicalism. As long as he remained marginalized, the articulate leftist was occasionally hired as a media commentator. His television and radio editorials harmlessly reaffirmed corporate America's democratic credentials, and probably boosted ratings as well.

But something had changed for Michael Harrington: he had decided to confront Hayden's challenge to "speak American." In 1962, Harrington thought like a traditional Old Left socialist because every social problem was reduced to class conflict between workers and capitalists. New Leftists realized that economism could not explain all of social life in the 1960s, or mobilize a vanguard. With their incomes rising, U.S. workers didn't think in terms of class, even though capitalism exploited them. Bereft of critical ideas, however, New Leftists ended up discarding the socialist baby with the Old Left bathwater. Harrington's painful apology to Hayden enabled him to rethink socialist politics and theory. The resulting theory neither reduced life to economics, nor assumed, like New Leftism, that unhappy interest groups could spontaneously build socialism. It spoke directly to Americans in a language drawn from everyday experiences, and its message was socialist.

This was not an easy or quick transition for Harrington. Stubborn remnants of the early reductionism still lingered when he died in 1989. Nor was it an original project, because others in America and Europe had already done the spadework. Moreover, Harrington, wasn't entirely successful: most Americans either refused to listen or did not understand. Harrington felt that this would change as social problems worsened, and only history can prove or disprove him. Until that judgement is in, however, we can admire the audacious project. Who else has tried to anchor socialism in America's idiosyncratic individualism? Port Huron ignited this effort; Harrington's personality, background, and training equipped him to complete it.

1

A Yankee Radical

EDWARD MICHAEL HARRINGTON WAS BORN in St. Louis on 24 February 1928. He grew up among a warm, loving family in a pleasant middle-class Irish Catholic neighborhood.[1] His father was a patent attorney who had fought in France during World War I, and his mother was a teacher. Like most of their neighbors, the Harringtons were New Deal progressives touched by the traditional teachings of Roman Catholicism.

Harrington attended parochial school in St. Louis, and then enrolled in a pre-law curriculum at Holy Cross College, a Jesuit institution in Worcester, Massachusetts. The dogmatic, highly intellectual training he received served him well during a lifetime of debate and contestation, even though his confidence in the Catholic Church's teachings disintegrated once Vatican II, in 1965, encouraged Catholics to think critically. After graduating in 1947, Harrington briefly challenged his family's Irish Catholic New Dealism by becoming a Taft conservative. At Yale Law

School, however, he engaged older, more radical students returning from military service. These nocturnal marathons purged most of Harrington's middle-class ambitions, as well as his conservatism. Within a year he had dropped out of Yale and rejected his father's profession. "The day I left law school," Harrington recalled, "I switched from Taft Republicanism to democratic socialism without even bothering to tarry a while in the liberal camp in between."[2] Harrington enrolled at the University of Chicago to do graduate work in English literature, where in 1949 he earned an M.A.

Even as a child Harrington knew that someday he would write. He was sports editor of his high school and college newspapers, and, in 1944, a copyboy at the St. Louis *Post-Dispatch*. After his short stories were rejected by several literary magazines in 1947, Harrington became a poet. "For the next seven or eight years, I worked on my poems every single day."[3] It was lackluster poetry, often depicting his own private epiphanies. In his spare time, Harrington read Marx and demonstrated against Spanish fascism and the Korean War. But poetry, Harrington believed, should not be infected by social issues or by ideas like Marxism or Freudianism. "For the most part I explored private emotions in the laid-back style that was then in vogue."[4] During these literary years between 1948 and 1950, "there was a distinctly aesthetic and elitist dimension to my Leftism," Harrington recalled. "Capitalism was not so much cruel and exploitative as crass and vulgar: the bourgeois was hated as a boor rather than as a thief."[5]

Only five of Harrington's poems were published, and none of these appeared in distinguished literary journals. New York City, he decided, was the place to be. He financed the trip by finagling a job in the Pupil Welfare Department of the St. Louis Public School System, and was assigned to the Madison School, in an Arkansas sharecropper district near a "Hooverville" slum. One rainy day in 1949, Harrington entered a dilapidated house near the Mississippi River, which, he remembered, "stank of stopped-up toilets, dead rats, and human misery. It was a terrible shock to my privileged, middle-class nostrils. I had come there as a temporary and opportunistic social worker trying to save up enough money to go to New York and be a poet and a Bohemian. An hour or so later, riding the Grand Avenue streetcar, it dawned on me that I should spend the rest of my life putting an end to that house and all that it symbolized."[6] Harrington decided to stop wrestling the Muses, and instead confront social reality. What he called the "contradictory, sloppy processes of hearts and minds"[7] had shaken this upwardly mobile, Midwestern, Catholic poet to his roots.

The journalist Dan Wakefield still recollects a "lanky, straightforward guy with freckles, a boyish grin, and broomstraw hair, speaking in a strong Missouri twang," exploring Greenwich Village in late 1949. "In looks, voice, and manner he could have passed for an older version of Huck Finn, or even

Jack Armstrong, the All-American Boy."[8] Harrington wrote poetry in the day, and spent boozy evenings with bohemian literati at the White Horse Tavern, where he became the convivial host of an on-going seminar on culture and politics. He earned a living writing for the *Columbia Encyclopedia*, apprenticing as a writer-trainee at *Life* magazine, soda-jerking, operating machines at a shop owned by socialist friends, helping run the New York City branch of the Workers Defense League, and freelancing as a researcher and writer for the Fund for the Republic, where he reported on blacklisting in the entertainment industry. The twenty-six weeks of unemployment insurance Harrington received were, in his words, "the joys of socialized bohemianism," and his "Thomas E. Dewey Fellowship."[9]

The glamour of Village life in the early 1950s was irresistible, but Harrington still was haunted by that St. Louis slum. Living on 5th Street between Avenues C and D on New York's Lower East Side, Harrington volunteered to work for the American Friends Service Committee if it agreed to cover his living expenses. It couldn't, so he turned to Dorothy Day's Catholic Worker on Chrystie Street. After swearing an oath of voluntary poverty, he stayed for one year and then served on the staff of St. Joseph's House of Hospitality, a settlement house serving Bowery derelicts. Harrington also helped edit the *Catholic Worker*, a monthly newspaper. These two years serving the "pathetic, shambling, shivering creature who wandered in off the streets with his pants caked with urine and his face scabbed with blood"[10] powerfully reaffirmed Harrington's socialism.

When the Korean War began in 1950, Harrington enlisted in the army, received a conscientious objector classification, and prepared for two years of non-military service. Instead, he was unexpectedly ordered to attend bi-weekly training sessions, to which he hesitantly agreed. During the annual two weeks of mandated active duty he was reassigned from the medic corps to the infantry, where he refused rifle and hand grenade instruction. Sympathetic officers returned him to the medics and blocked a court martial, but Harrington nonetheless quit the army in disgust. As fate would have it, a bungling military bureaucracy handed Harrington an honorable discharge.

Eager to engage America's capitalists and fed up with extreme personal sacrifices, in 1952 Harrington decided to enter the political arena. He found a confused and splintered left. FBI agents had infiltrated the Moscow-controlled Communist Party. Trotskyists were factionalizing. The Industrial Workers of the World was an ineffectual rump organization led by one Sam Wiener, a house painter. Max Shachtman's Independent Socialist League (ISL) was evolving from Trotskyism to democratic socialism. And the Socialist Party (SP), outflanked on the left by F.D.R.'s New Deal and on the right by Cold Warriors, lacked vision or even a *raison d'être*. Although Harrington had joined the YPSL, the SP's youth branch, immediately after converting to socialism, and already had impressed SP leaders, he was now looking elsewhere.

As early as 1953, Harrington faced a central problem of Marxism. The young Marx saw a short, violent, and inevitable transition from capitalism to socialism, but later he suggested that clever leftists could influence capitalist politics. "How then should radicals," Harrington asked, "who seek nothing less than a new civilization, act when they could preside over increments of power?"[11] Should they merely improve living conditions, or dogmatically oppose everything the bourgeoisie stands for?

Harrington admired pragmatists like Walter Reuther and Norman Thomas—"the genuine, and utterly sincere and militant, Left-wing of American society"[12]—and was intrigued by the anti-communist Max Shachtman. He thus chose efficacy over extremism, and joined the little known Youth Socialist League (YSL), an anti-communist organization of about 200 students and young workers that was fraternally linked with Shachtman's ISL until 1954, when they were formally merged. Here, Harrington was pulled into socialism's turbulent orbit as he debated doctrinal questions with Bayard Rustin, Dave Dellinger, Norman Thomas, Paul Goodman, Dwight Macdonald, and A. J. Muste.

In September 1958, YSL-ISL members, led by Harrington and Shachtman, entered the SP as a bloc. The SP was America's largest non-communist socialist party. Its political potential, and the chance to work with Thomas and Shachtman, inspired democratic socialism's heir-apparent. Harrington became editor of the SP's official journal, *New America*, and in 1968 was selected as national co-chair. A terminally-ill Norman Thomas had already informed friends and colleagues that he hoped Michael Harrington would succeed him as leader of America's democratic left.

During the 1960s, the socialist Harrington went public. He rebuilt the League for Industrial Democracy (LID), established in 1905 as a progressive educational and training organization, into a coalition of trade unionists, blacks, and intellectuals. He was active in the civil rights struggle, writing speeches for Martin Luther King, Jr., organizing freedom marches—including the March on Washington in 1963—and, with Shachtman, working in the A. Philip Randolph Institute, an alliance of labor and the black community, to promote minority rights.[13] After *The Other America* was published in 1962, Harrington consulted with Sargent Shriver in the federal government's War on Poverty and provided the only pro-labor commentary in the major print media with his column for the *New York Herald-Tribune*. At his peak, Harrington delivered over one hundred public lectures each year to students, professionals, workers, and grass-roots organizations. His speeches combined serious analysis and moral passion; listeners learned and were inspired to action. Even years after he died, people who knew and worked with him immediately recalled his almost magical ability to capture an audience with his frenetic oratorical style: "Harrington works himself into a furious sweat. He bangs the dais, prods his finger at the air and pulls at his forelock till his tousled hair makes him look wild and distracted. He is overcome by a fierce epileptic energy that wrings out his eloquence, then leaves him spent."[14]

Harrington's popularity came amidst the factionalism of the 1960s. New Leftists had soured on traditional socialist parties, including the SP, and Martin Luther King Jr.'s assassination created a moral vacuum on the left. The pendulum of black liberation soon swung toward racial nationalism rather than economic justice, and the civil rights coalition of blacks and whites split into feuding factions. At the heart of all this upheaval was Vietnam. The war drained resources from America's urban and rural ghettos to finance the military, gutting the federally-funded Great Society programs. Meanwhile, emotional appeals for and against U.S. involvement splintered blacks and whites, workers and intellectuals, liberals and radicals. The war's political fallout eventually ruined what was left of Harrington's liberal, worker, and minority coalition.

The SP in 1968 was fractured into three groups: Shachtmanite Cold Warriors who supported U.S. war efforts; the militantly anti-war Debs Caucus; and Harrington's Realignment Caucus, which opposed both the war *and* unconditional withdrawal—goading one SP partisan to complain "I am unable to ascertain what the position of the 'Harrington faction' really is."[15] Harrington couldn't cobble a consensus on this crucial issue, and he became more dovish. He left the Realignment Caucus and in 1971 organized the Coalition Caucus, which backed George McGovern's anti-war presidential candidacy. Sounding a lot like Tom Hayden at Port Huron, Harrington now felt "obliged to put up a fight against the SP becoming a party of Cold War socialism at that point in history when the Cold War is coming to an end."[16] He also tried to pry open the hawkish, union-dominated SP to include liberal and radical members of the middle class, the so-called "new politics" constituency.

In November 1971, the Coalition Caucus requested a referendum of the Party on a motion demanding that the U.S. set an early date for withdrawal from Vietnam, but it was denied by the National Action Committee, violating the SP constitution. In March 1972, the SP once again snubbed Harrington and merged with the conservative Democratic Socialist Federation (DSF), a splinter group that had left the Social Democratic Federation after it merged with the SP in 1957. In July, the SP-DSF became the Social Democrats, USA (SDUSA), and joined AFL-CIO leaders in refusing to endorse McGovern. Harrington considered this tantamount to endorsing Nixon.

Clearly isolated in his own party, upset by vicious internecine haggling (e.g., "I got involved in this [factional quarrel] with the greatest reluctance given both my personal predelictions toward writing and speaking rather than organizing and a sense of weariness that, after all these years, one more internal hassle is necessary"[17]) and disillusioned with the war in Vietnam, Harrington resigned as co-chair in October 1972, two months before leading 250 followers out of the party to found, in February 1973, the Democratic Socialist Organizing Committee (DSOC). Shachtman's winning faction turned the SDUSA into perhaps the most right-wing socialist party in the world.[18]

Harrington now completed the process of contrition begun ten years earlier. In his resignation letter Harrington endorsed every major New Left position. Still staunchly anti-communist, Harrington nonetheless conceded in his resignation letter "that the strategy of supporting reactionary anti-communists as an alternative to communism . . . only helps communism by wrongly identifying it with the struggle for national liberation and social justice."[19] American troops had actually *promoted* the spread of communism and trampled democracy in Vietnam. Harrington's decade-long opposition to unconditional withdrawal was thus immoral and counterproductive: immoral by supporting capitalism; counterproductive because a U.S. victory would have legitimized communist claims throughout the third world and sunk the nation deeper in guerrilla quicksand. Harrington saw that unconditional withdrawal was good politics as well. By disregarding a young, educated, idealistic, and progressive anti-war movement the SP had committed a "historic error somewhat analogous to the mistake of those craft unionists in the 1930s who disdained the opportunities for industrial unionism."[20]

Harrington's letter also criticized George Meany. Socialists, Harrington warned, no longer could be "uncritical apologists for one wing of the movement," especially when it was isolated from "some of the most vital tendencies in the labor movement itself."[21] Unions, in short, are not necessarily progressive, although progressive movements will fail without unions. "I think," Harrington told his supporters, "we should begin to discuss the possibility of a socialist . . . organization which would bring together socialists, minorities, intellectuals, and trade unionists, have no political line (other than a broad social democratic approach), and act primarily as a center for the discussion and deepening of ideas."[22]

DSOC jumped into the political mainstream with practical economic strategies that New Deal liberals could endorse.[23] It was a "committee," not a political party. "We have retained the 'organizing committee' in our name since we have defined our task as reaching the vast majority of socialists in the United States who are outside of organized socialist tendencies," explained Harrington. "We want to work with them in the creation of a viable, relevant socialist center for thought and action—a center geared to the everyday experiences of activists in the trade unions, in the women's movement, in the struggles for minority rights, and in all the movements of the democratic left."[24] Thus DSOC represented the Democratic Party's left wing, but also promoted socialism. Harrington used DSOC to lobby Democratic Party officials, defeat unfriendly Democrats, and extend New Deal reforms. He hoped to attract liberals, minorities, and feminists whose economic interests were shared by blue-collar workers, and nudge their Democratic Party to the left. "We wanted to win our rights as socialists to legitimately participate in mass debates on programs within the councils of the Democratic Party. We succeeded magnificently in that goal."[25]

Harrington promoted DSOC's agenda in 1974 by taking matters into his own hands. "At the ripe old age of forty-six," Harrington decided to enter bourgeois politics as a Reform candidate for delegate from New York's seventeenth congressional district to the special Democratic Party mini-convention.[26] He won, but wasn't inspired. "I could probably have been a pretty good campaigner," Harrington mused, but "when people say 'Cut out this socialism crap and become Ted Kennedy II,' they just don't understand. It wouldn't have been me."[27] This was Harrington's first and last run for public office.

The "first Left organization in history not to lie about its membership figures,"[28] DSOC had recruited more than 4,000 people at its peak in 1980. *Dissent* magazine, although not quite an "organ" of DSOC, became its liaison to intellectuals. Harrington described it as "enormously valuable" and deserving "our enthusiastic support in every way."[29] Established as a radical quarterly in early 1954, with Lewis Coser and Irving Howe as editors, from the beginning *Dissent* reexamined the socialist tradition, challenged McCarthyism, and was inflexibly, even vindictively, anti-communist. Like Harrington, *Dissent* wanted to use the Democratic Party to pry open social welfare programs that could genuinely improve the lot of poor Americans, and it cynically rejected the fads and fashions that popped up among university radicals. But with Howe in charge, *Dissent* was as concerned with the arts as with politics, and thus at least until the late 1970s was also popular with Harrington's target group of young, radical intellectuals. By then, however, the predominantly economic nature of DSOC's program had alienated many non-traditional leftists concerned with cultural empowerment. They were disappointed that trade union officials ran DSOC, while blacks and women made up less than 5 percent of its membership.[30]

Harrington set his sights on those New Leftists who, in 1972, had formed the New American Movement (NAM) to succeed SDS. Bruised and humbled by the Weatherpeople in 1969, NAM members were still in no position to resist, so formal negotiations between DSOC and NAM began in 1979. The two sides quickly agreed that socialists needed to work inside the Democratic Party, that communism was not socialism "as we defined the term,"[31] and that two states—one representing Jews, the other Palestinians—should exist in the Middle East. Although a radical minority within NAM resisted, a unity convention was held in Detroit in 1982. The following year, DSOC and NAM were merged into the Democratic Socialists of America (DSA). With more than 6000 members, DSA became the largest democratic socialist organization since the SP of 1936. Unlike the SP, it endorsed candidates for public office rather than fielding its own slate. Its agenda combined DSOC's realignment tactic with NAM's more urgent struggle for cultural change. Harrington became its first chair, and retained this post—which he later shared with Barbara Ehrenreich— for the remainder of his life. "On a personal level," he commented, "I had finally expiated my stupidity in SDS [Students for a Democratic Society]. In terms of the United States of America, we had either created an important bridge to a future Left or mobilized an ineffective remnant. Only time will tell."[32]

Harrington was also active in the Socialist International (SI), a coalition of socialist parties from around the world that was established in 1951 with headquarters in London.[33] He suspected that Shachtman and SDUSA had sponsored an international "conspiracy" against DSOC membership in SI beginning in 1976.[34] DSOC was nonetheless fully admitted in 1978, despite SDUSA's furious opposition, and DSA later took over its seat. Known among socialist leaders as an eloquent speaker and writer, as well as a practical thinker, Harrington influenced politicians like Olaf Palme, Willy Brandt, Michael Manley, and others around the globe who were busy redefining socialist politics in their own nations. At the SI's Sixteenth Congress held in Albufeira, Portugal, in 1983, he was chosen Secretary of the Resolutions Committee and Coordinator of the Committee on a New Declaration of Principles. Drafted by Harrington and adopted unanimously by the SI, the "Manifesto of Albufeira" summarized the state of affairs of contemporary democratic socialism. Harrington also penned the first draft of a new declaration of socialist principles, which was approved some years later. It defined socialism as "an international movement for freedom, social justice and solidarity . . . [whose] goal is to achieve a peaceful world where these basic values can be enhanced and where each individual can live a meaningful life with the full development of his or her personality and talents and with the guarantee of human and civil rights in a democratic framework of society."[35] Although Harrington is best known for Americanizing socialist theory and politics, during the 1970s and '80s he also challenged socialists to think and act globally. He realized that socialism's fate, in the U.S. and elsewhere, was bound to the fate of humanity.

More than anything else, Harrington's belief that socialists needed to organize themselves for the long haul, rather than go it alone as rebels or intellectuals, defined his public life. Socialism to Harrington meant working together for justice, whereas liberal politics meant standing up for narrow interests. An unorganized socialist wasn't a socialist at all. So from the moment Harrington engaged the left and entered the YPSL until he died as head of the DSA and an international socialist leader, he was part of a formal movement committed to working cooperatively for the common good.

Harrington realized that sectarianism had helped destroy the Old Left, and that the New Left's collapse in the late 1960s was at least partially due to its self-conscious *dis*organization. The New Left's useful critique of bureaucracy had gradually evolved into an anti-hierarchical polemic that made even democratic organization impossible. While the New Left in the early 1960s was an irreverent and important political force, in barely a decade it became irrelevant, passing quickly into obscurity. The avalanche of post-New Left ethnic groupings such as the Black Panthers, Chicano farmers organized by Cesar Chavez in the Southwest, urban Puerto Ricans called Young Lords, and Asian American groups on both coasts never aligned with each other or with larger constituencies. They competed for scarce public resources, while hurting themselves with internal factional disputes. Black politicians like Richard Hatcher in Gary, Indiana, Coleman Young in Detroit, Harold Washington in Chicago, and Ron Dellums in California took their radical backgrounds into the electoral mainstream but couldn't unite progressive voters into larger political organizations. They won elections, but lost their ideals in the give and take of liberal politics, confirming what Harrington already knew: socialists had to organize nationally or perish. He felt this could be done within America's two-party system by purging the Democrats of conservatives and the Republicans of liberals, thereby realigning both parties along distinct ideological lines and creating an electoral home for socialists inside the Democratic Party. But he also handled every internal socialist conflict as a pragmatic conciliator trying, in Harry Fleischman's words, "to bring people together."[36] After the fateful lapse in Port Huron, Harrington always worked to create consensus rather than majority opinions, even when this meant yielding on important issues. His inability to keep the SP's warring factions together was thus a significant personal calamity, and his leadership in negotiating the DSOC-NAM merger his greatest success.

But everyday living involved much more than organizing socialists. Harrington's international reputation and a modest income from lecturing and writing removed him from the "Bohemian poverty" in which he had lived for fifteen years.[37] However, even socialists had to prepare for catastrophes, and in capitalist America that meant either paying exorbitantly high health-care premiums or finding a full-time job with adequate fringe benefits, something the overworked Harrington had neglected. Until 1972, he was covered by the medical plan that his wife, the former Stephanie Gervis, received as a journalist for the *Village Voice*. This coverage ended when Stephanie chose to freelance and spend more time with their two young sons. Ironically, Harrington wanted nothing more than to live as a freelance writer. "Once you freelance," he told his friend Dan Wakefield, "I can't imagine ever going back to a regular job."[38] Now he had to do just that.

Harrington had published seven books by the age of forty-five, including the acclaimed *The Other America*, but his highest degree was an M.A. in English Literature from the University of Chicago. He briefly held an endowed chair at the University of Illinois in 1970. "But I had been nominated to that post by the law school," Harrington later admitted, "and had lectured in almost every department of the university without teaching a single course. I was an irregular, an exotic star brought to campus precisely because I did not fit into the standard academic slots."[39] Harrington had taken only one course in economics at Yale, and one course in sociology at Holy Cross. Joseph S. Murphy, the President of Queens College in Flushing, New York, who in 1972 was searching for stimulating teachers whose lives outside the academy were somehow the equivalent of a Ph.D., appointed Harrington to be Visiting Professor of Political Science. Harrington casually walked into class in the winter of 1973 and, as he described it, "taught the first political science course I ever attended."[40] He was granted early tenure in 1974, with no dissenting votes, and was then appointed to the graduate faculty of the City University of New York.

By the mid-1970s, then, Harrington was solidly established as a socialist intellectual, writer, organizer, political activist, lecturer, and professor. He somehow found the time and energy to do many things, the ability to excel in each one, and the drive to continue forever. This breathless pace lasted another decade. Then, on a November morning in 1984, as he was idly waiting for a traffic light, Harrington thoughtlessly touched his neck. The lump he felt was later diagnosed as cancer. After several successful rounds of surgery and radiation, his battle had apparently ended in victory. A new set of tests in late 1987 proved otherwise. He had inoperable cancer of the esophagus, and doctors gave him from six months to two years to live.

Harrington once compared himself to Odysseus's wife, Penelope, who avoided unwanted suitors only as long as she continued weaving a shroud. "As long as I have a new book," he told a *Newsweek* reporter, "maybe I can stave off death. I can come up with new books forever. Maybe I've discovered the cure for cancer."[41] For nearly two years after the final diagnosis—consuming only liquids, enduring numbing pain— Harrington wrote two excellent books, continued teaching at Queens College and was appointed a CUNY Distinguished Professor, lectured at home and abroad, administered DSA, conferred with European and third world socialist leaders, and passionately discharged his duties as husband and father. His sense of humor never flagged. Informed that DSA would host a party at Roseland, the Manhattan dance hall, Harrington commented: "When my friends at DSA started talking about having this party for me, I told them I wanted to wait until I was dead for my memorial service. So it will be gemutlich. But we need to raise some money for DSA, and I'm sort of under the gun."[42] And his sense of decency was equally undiminished. In the terminal stages of his own painful illness Harrington comforted a friend who also tragically was stricken with throat cancer. Eyewitnesses still fondly remember this difficult act of sympathy and compassion, and salute the essential nature of the dying man who executed it.[43]

Myths endure longer than men. Harrington died in his home in Larchmont, New York on 31 July 1989, leaving his wife Stephanie, his sons Alexander Gervis and Edward Michael III, his friends and associates, and a legacy that keeps pace with America's accelerating problems.

POETRY, RELIGION, AND SOCIALIST POLITICS

In the best of circumstances, that is, in societies with rich leftist traditions, Marxian theory usually confuses people. America is not the best of circumstances. A complex of factors, including capitalist intimidation, have made working-class Americans devout individualists drawn toward capitalism. Socialists thus confront the formidable task of criticizing exploitation that is nourished by everyday experiences. Traditional leftists often scandalized meaningful institutions along with an unjust economy. They failed miserably in mobilizing discontent, which was real and widespread, and came to lead a movement without many followers.

Public figures like William Haywood, Eugene V. Debs, and Norman Thomas, who were primarily activists, tried to popularize socialism. Their oratory was felicitous but lacked philosophical substance. The philosophers Louis Boudin, Louis Fraina, and Sidney Hook tried to humanize socialist theory, and were generally misunderstood or ignored. With one foot in public culture and the other in theory, Harrington knew that political success couldn't grow in philosophical quicksand, nor could socialist theory survive without popular support. So he tackled the gigantic task of redefining socialism to speak directly to Americans. More than others on the democratic left, Harrington was uniquely qualified to succeed.

Harrington once confessed that aspects of his psyche "strike me as inexplicably, even mysteriously, individualistic and unhistorical, a consequence of my inner self rather than of the times in which I live."[44] This child of middle America, by most socio-economic standards an "insider," was always unexpectedly rebellious. He rejected his father's profession, his family's religion and politics, his class's ambitions, his generation's conservative ideology, and the expectations of his socialist peers, all because, in his words, "the self I did not choose, the self I was before I knew it, has shaped much of my life, even its accidents."[45] As a young man he admired the eccentricity of great poets, even those of questionable character. "I profoundly admired the poetry of T.S. Eliot, some of Pound's work, and Yeats's," Harrington admitted. "So I knew very well that a fascist could write great poetry, even an anti-semitic fascist." Harrington found eccentricity in himself as well. The years he spent writing poetry and living as a bohemian in Greenwich Village indelibly marked his outlook. "The poetry of my [later] socialism . . . [is] the vision not simply of an economic or political program," Harrington, the frustrated artist, wrote, "but of the potential for beauty concealed in the ordinary lives of suffering humanity."[46] Harrington always remained a poet. Socialism was a means of bringing beauty back into a world that was mistakenly reduced to market, empirical, or materialist laws.

Harrington's iconoclasm, his background as a poet and literary critic, and his scrupulous honesty and intelligence, created multifaceted interests. "Remember," he commented in 1988, "the original Marxist ideal was really this nineteenth-century idea of the intellectual. Someone interested in economics, history, sociology, art. Marx, for heaven's sake, read novels."[47] Always guided by complex perceptions of the world, not by formulas, Harrington therefore abhorred zealots, particularly leftists who reduced everything to economics. In an early essay about the former communist Granville Hicks, he conceded Hicks's central point: abstract thoughts are realized in the often unpoliticized, surprising lives of real men and women, and these, not obsessions, are grist for the philosopher's mill.

Harrington's religious beliefs fueled his eccentricity. Raised as a devout Catholic, and educated by Jesuits to think carefully and argue persuasively, in college he still found it difficult to reconcile God's existence with humanity's earthly suffering. His faith was rejuvenated somewhat when he read Pascal and Kierkegaard after joining the CW, but flagged again, after a long internal battle, in the stench of urban misery. The question of God's existence had evolved into a question of God's guilt, which was too momentous for faith alone to resolve. Harrington became an atheist, but never fully escaped the early training. "Taking a religion very seriously while

I was growing up was a critical part of the destiny my childhood packed into me," he confessed in 1988. "It meant, above all, that I accepted the idea that life was a trust to be used for a good purpose and accounted for when it was over. I have been an atheist for about thirty years, yet in this fundamental conception of the meaning of existence I am as Catholic as the day on which I made my first communion."[48]

This bow to Catholicism wasn't just rhetoric. Harrington once returned $500 of a $700 fee for debating William Rusher at Lehman College because $200 was, he believed, "a reasonable academic honorarium."[49] He also returned more than $10,000 worth of royalty checks prematurely sent to him by a publisher. "Please tell the royalty department," Harrington politely asked, "not to tempt my virtue again."[50] Harrington always measured his behavior and beliefs by Catholic standards. "As I grow older," he once told Sargent Shriver, "I think of myself as a non-Catholic Catholic . . . I remain very much outside of the Church but within its orbit."[51] Christ's suffering on the cross symbolized the incarnation of God's power in humanity's aching masses. For Harrington, this became such a compelling irony "as to have revolutionary potential for atheist and Christian alike."[52]

Instilled with a Jesuit's feeling for life's paradoxes, and motivated by Christian morality, Harrington certainly wasn't cut out to be a communist minion. Socialism was anchored in the defining principles of his life, not in dogma, and these were reinforced by the organizations Harrington selected to mediate his inner self and the outside world, beginning, of course, with the Catholic Worker Movement.

A series of anti-Marxian papal pronouncements, beginning with Pope Leo XIII's *Rerum Novarum* in 1891, had severely restricted what American Catholics could study, and had thrown the Church's moral weight behind the popular, loosely defined cause of anti-communism.[53] Moreover, aside from its influence on the socialists Monsignor John A. Ryan and Father Edward McGlynn, the largely Protestant Social Gospel movement had bypassed Catholics. But Pope Leo's poignant depiction of industrial poverty also awakened millions of Catholics to working class suffering in capitalism. Many believers resolved this tension between faith and injustice by helping the poor, often through neighborhood associations or clubs that catered to the needy and lobbied for public aid. Pope Pius XI's *Quadragesimo Anno* (1931) revisited the evils not of capitalism as such, but of the concentration of economic power in capitalism. Its corporatist "middle course" between socialism and laissez-faire capitalism was polluted by fascists, and quietly abandoned. By the late 1940s and 1950s, then, mainstream Catholic theology in America remained anti-socialist but also sanctioned the formation of reformist action groups. On the left fringe of these groups, somewhere between socialism and apostasy, organizations like

Dorothy Day's CW began to appear. Many Catholics, Harrington included[54], got involved in these organizations and were inspired to pursue radical objectives on the secular left, outside the canon.

French emigré philosopher Peter Maurin and Dorothy Day—a Brooklyn-born feminist and socialist before World War I, a Greenwich Village bohemian with Eugene O'Neill and Hart Crane, and a communist sympathizer who converted to Catholicism in 1927—founded the CW on New York's Lower East Side during the depression days of 1933.[55] The pragmatic Day, who Harrington once said looked like a mystic out of a Dostoevsky novel, gradually became the dominant force, blending the radical secularism of her early life with the Christian devotion that characterized her conversion experience. Day realized that secular activism was essential to the struggle for Christian justice. As a Catholic Worker she challenged civil injustice in the streets, and became the publisher, editor, and chief writer for the *Catholic Worker*, which now has a circulation of over 100,000. Almost from the beginning, St. Joseph's—the CW House of Hospitality in New York City where Day lived—attracted famous artists and writers, like Harrington, who for short periods lived anonymous, spartan lives devoted to charity. Many agreed when Harrington eulogized in 1980 that "Perhaps the Church will make her a Saint."[56]

CW's daily activities were anchored in four principles: voluntary poverty as a means of bonding with the oppressed; achieving social justice through nonviolent activism; pacifism; and personalism, that is, improving society through direct, personal engagement. CW Houses of Hospitality sprang up throughout America, especially in urban areas with large Catholic populations in the Northeast and Midwest, where many still operate. Closely scrutinized by Rome and by J. Edgar Hoover's FBI, CW managed to survive and instill its unique brand of Christian radicalism in generations of followers and sympathizers, and also to help thousands of poor homeless people.

CW was an antidote to Harrington's post-academic moral predicament. With its Catholic-inspired radicalism, it linked Harrington's religious past with his activist future, and also stiffened the non-scientific dimensions of his socialism. He learned from living and working with Dorothy Day that the Christian God was immanent to this world, not something to be feared in an afterlife. Religion had to inspire actions that realized God's kingdom on earth, such as ending capitalist exploitation and establishing a moral socialist community. But Harrington's impatience with what he saw as an insensitive, uncooperative Church deconstructed his faith, and highlighted the CW's hands-on, practical social activism. Religion, he concluded, should avoid dogma, while inspiring people to resist injustice. "It inspires, it defines values which must be realized in this world," he noted, "but tactics are not a function of the eternal." When God ordains one kind of activity, "that," for Harrington, "is usually the prelude to intolerance and messianism" because it establishes "a supernatural legitimacy for a human choice of means to an end."[57] In other words, religion justifies activism, but humans choose tactics. The decision on how far one can go to support social change is thus the same for believers and atheists: the choice must be made in terms of present politics, not divine advice. Harrington's critique of messianic communism was thus incubating as he aided Manhattan's downtrodden. Democratic socialism was the secular equivalent of atheistic Catholicism.

The YPSL was the first secular organization that Harrington joined after breaking with the Church and leaving CW. From its inception in 1915, it had travelled the full breadth of America's left searching for a home.[58] YPSL voted to join the worldwide communist movement in 1919. By the mid-1920s it had affiliated with the more moderate SP and became its most dynamic and popular branch, especially on college campuses where its intellectuals debated socialist theory. It later supported SP radicals, opposed U.S. participation in World War II, and was eventually taken over by Trotskyists. After the war YPSL decided to train union leaders. Harrington, who was then a New York-bound social worker, joined and pitched in. In 1953, Harrington led YPSL supporters into the YSL, a branch of the ISL (formerly the Workers Party), whose predecessors had recruited another generation of YPSL members into Trotskyism in 1936. When the YSL rejoined the SP in 1958, it set up a larger, reconstituted YPSL under the leadership of Harrington, Bayard Rustin, David McReynolds, and Bogdan Denitch, and enlisted in America's civil rights and peace movements during the 1950s and '60s. After Port Huron, YPSL grew resentful and conservative, whereupon Harrington—by then head of both the SP and YPSL—took his supporters into the DSOC. YPSL officially disbanded in 1977, because with so many former members now in DSOC it, and later the DSA, became lineal successors to the old YPSL. Harrington's eclectic political theory, we shall see, borrowed ideas and tactics from the various stages of YPSL's rambunctious passage through this century.

Harrington also joined the LID, an organization of young socialists whose down-to-earth ideology mirrored, and helped sustain, his own pragmatism. Originally known as the Intercollegiate Socialist Society, from its beginning in 1921 LID tried to mobilize students around popular educational, political, and economic reforms. After the depression, LID fractured into the new Student League for Industrial Democracy (SLID), and the parent LID, which educated workers and minorities outside the academy. Six years after merging with the ill-fated, communist-led National Student

League in 1935, both LID and SLID reaffirmed their traditional pragmatism and anti-communism.[59] By the 1950s they were funded primarily by trade unions and appealed to liberals as well as radicals.

YPSL focused on scholastic, intellectual issues while SLID, led by Harrington and Norman Thomas, lobbied for concrete liberal and labor-oriented reforms. This two-pronged anti-communist student critique of capitalism represented the two aspects of Harrington's radicalism. In YPSL, he engaged great socialist thinkers, and ultimately reconstructed Marxian theory. In SLID, Harrington tried to improve life for working class Americans through coalition-building and practical reforms.

In the Socialist Party, Harrington became interested in dialectics and capitalist state activities. He was also influenced by the SP's pragmatism, its moderate politics, and its anti-communism. And like so many other Americans, Harrington was inspired by the idealism and morality of Debs and Thomas.[60] Socialists and American patriots, they both had plugged into the bread and butter values of mainstream, working class Americans, but neither explained how patriotism and reformism, normally cultural weapons for exploiting workers, created socialism. The Jesuit in Harrington needed to justify this anomaly, and the disillusioned social worker chose Marxian, not biblical, exegesis. But the SP lacked a solid, coherent critical theory; electoral conquests and the growth of a powerful middle class soon turned reformism from a means into its sole objective. Political activism, particularly for Thomas, became the only acceptable revolutionary tactic, and state power the only measure of democracy. Thomas's SP reduced everything to electoral success, mimicking, on a political level, orthodoxy's economism. Harrington resolved to relight the revolutionary spark in democratic socialism.

It was the Trotskyist Max Shachtman, rather than Thomas or Debs, who, other than Karl Marx, most influenced Harrington intellectually. Leon Trotsky had inspired democratic radicals who believed in the 1917 Revolution but were deflated by its unexpected totalitarianism. Since Stalinism *and* Trotskyism were based on a materialism that, by the early 1950s, had been directly linked to the rise of the Soviet state, most Trotskyists, including Shachtman, soon abandoned Marxism altogether. They often became liberals or even conservatives.[61] Harrington, on the other hand, remained a loyal socialist, unhinging critical theory and politics from its materialist anchor.

Born in 1929, after Stalin's bloody Moscow purges, as the Communist League of America (CLA), Trotskyism was continually reincarnated in organizations that appeared, splintered, and dissolved, in Max Eastman's playful metaphor "like an onion trying to commit suicide."[62] It nonetheless remained both unintelligible and uninteresting to most workers. Trotskyists believed that Russia's socialist revolution would collapse without communist insurrection everywhere. They also felt that the Soviet workers' state had degenerated into a dictatorship, but could be salvaged; that backward nations, governed by the theory of combined or uneven development and directed by communists, needed to forcibly telescope the development process; that communist parties should "bore from within" existing trade unions and parties rather than create parallel institutions, and steer any cooperative alliances leftward; and that communists, if necessary, had to tell peasants what to do. In brief, Trotskyism took a hard-line or leftist position on most political issues, but also condemned Stalinism and socialist bureaucratization. Left Trotskyists emphasized confrontation, while right Trotskyists highlighted the critique of socialist bureaucracy.

A Polish immigrant to New York City who joined the Communist Party (CP) while still a teenager, Shachtman moved to Chicago and was selected by CP leader James Cannon to edit *Labor Defender*, which he turned into the American left's first photographic magazine. With Cannon, Martin Abern, and others, Shachtman became a Trotskyist in 1929, and soon emerged as a spokesman and leader, editing the movement's major newspaper, *The Militant*, and journal, *New International*, and founding Pioneer Publishers. He also served as Trotsky's trusted aid in charge of diplomatic and international affairs.

The CLA merged with A. J. Muste's American Workers Party in 1934 to form the Workers Party of the United States (WPUS). When WPUS was expelled from the SP in 1938, only two years after joining, it reorganized as the Socialist Workers Party (SWP) and became a member of the newly created Fourth International, a worldwide organization of Trotskyists. A dispute between Shachtman and Cannon split the SWP in the Fall of 1939, and caused Shachtman to take his supporters into a new Workers Party (WP), which turned into the ISL and YSL in 1949, and ten years later dissolved into the SP.

The schism in American Trotskyism was ostensibly caused by Shachtman's refusal to defend the Soviet Union during World War II. Equally important, however, was the famous "Russian Question," which concerned the class nature of the Soviet Union. Shachtman agreed with his ally James Burnham that a new class had taken power in the Soviet Union. He initially felt that the new "bureaucratic collectivist" system was better than capitalism. By 1941, however, Shachtman claimed that there was nothing worth defending in the new collectivist social order, and formed a "Third Camp" that was neither capitalist nor bureaucratic socialist. After Stalin's ruthlessness was fully revealed to the world in the 1950s, Shachtman conceded that Third Camp socialism was untenable. He then backed anti-communist witch-hunts and the Bay of Pigs invasion, and eventually became a Vietnam hawk as well as a patron of Richard Nixon. Still a self-proclaimed social democrat, in practice Shachtman abandoned socialism altogether. Cannon stayed with Trotsky's "degenerated workers' state" position, for which Soviet leaders were an undesirable bureaucratic caste, an aberration, that deserved to be abolished even as the Soviet economy was defended and democratized. Shachtman also favored a pluralist party structure, while Cannon wanted it centralized. Right Trotskyists were soon called "Shachtmanites;" left Trotskyists, "Cannonites."

Shachtman became the leader of America's non-communist radical intelligentsia, and profoundly influenced young socialists like Michael Harrington. In a new version of the old "bore from within" strategy, Shachtman wanted socialists to use the existing two-party system rather than create a Labor or Workers party. His strategy was based on the theory of "realignment," that is, transforming the Democratic Party into a coalition of liberals and socialists by expelling racist and conservative "Dixiecrats." Realignment was to become a centerpiece of Harrington's theory also, particularly during the 1960s and '70s. Shachtman also considered organized labor the engine of any feasible democratic left, and he was compulsively anti-communist, rejecting both Stalin and communist sympathizers, the so-called "Stalinoids."

Harrington believed that Shachtman had identified the central feature of 20th-century Marxism: democracy was the indispensable means by which the base could control its superstructure. Socialism without democracy turned into the nightmare Shachtman called bureaucratic collectivism: in the name of materialist science, communist officials created a totalitarian state. Democracy without socialism rationalized another kind of bureaucratic collectivism ignored by Shachtman in his later years: wealthy people, governed by the free market, used the liberal state to exploit workers and maximize corporate profits. Workers, Harrington concluded, must control both the base and the superstructure. They must own *and* control social resources. "These extensions of Shachtman's theories," he suggested in 1972, "have led me to a basic proposition: that the future is not going to be a choice between capitalism, communism, and socialism, but between bureaucratic collectivism advantageous to both executives and commissars, and democratic collectivism, i.e. socialism."[63] Shachtman's theory of bureaucratic collectivism, in short, gave Harrington an idea that was democratic, socialist, and non-traditional. It was also applicable, as critique and praxis, to communist, capitalist, and third world societies.

Harrington felt that Shachtman's decision to abandon Third Camp socialism was the result of traumatic personal experiences in Russia during the 1930s and 1940s,[64] when Shachtman became convinced that Marxism was monolithic. After the war he equated Stalinism and barbarism, and concluded that the entire Marxian package was defective. Marxism, materialism, and totalitarianism congealed into one deplorable entity. With nowhere to go but right, Shachtman and his disciples fled first to liberalism and then conservatism. Instead of following them, Harrington redrew the ideological map, providing a sanctuary for democratic socialists.

Harrington was aided by a close friend and mentor, Irving Howe. Only eight years older than Harrington, Howe's socialist credentials included membership in the YPSL, SWP, WP, and ISL, where he lamented Shachtman's conservatism and, in 1952, resigned. Howe later went with Harrington into DSOC and DSA. His affiliations, in short, paralleled Harrington's. For a time in the 1950s and '60s, Harrington looked to Howe for political guidance.[65]

Howe's influence on Harrington was problematic. Like Harrington, he was an independent thinker, continually attacking McCarthyism and bourgeois cultural conformity as well as the communist left, and staunchly supporting America's anti-communist foreign policy objectives. As the preeminent radical literary critic of his time, Howe uncovered the aesthetic dimension of socialism, and confirmed Harrington's inchoate critique of scientific Marxism. Howe also became something of a role model for the young Harrington, whose first love was literature. Dozens of literary reviews that Harrington published in the 1950s—many in *Dissent*, the journal of democratic socialism that the New York City born and educated Howe launched in 1954—were probably solicited by Howe. During these early years Howe helped discipline Harrington's thinking and work habits, and smoothed the rough edges on his prose. And Howe's friendship and support, particularly during difficult times associated with Port Huron, the Vietnam War, and SP factionalism, helped keep the young Harrington on his chosen path. His concern for Harrington was almost paternal. "I have been worrying a little," Howe advised Harrington during the 1972 struggle with conservatives to control the SP, "over what does seem to me the extent of the burdens you have . . . . [Y]ou really ought to try to shake off some of the smaller burdens, the occasional items that don't contribute much to mind or purse."[66]

On the other hand, Howe always stayed a few steps to the right of Harrington, and probably delayed Harrington's belated break with the SP. Particularly after *Dissent* appeared, Howe focused his energies on raising Yiddish literature to a position of dignity among educated Jews. Consequently, his politics, always second fiddle to literary pursuits, often flapped aimlessly in shifting ideological breezes. A preoccupied Howe, for example, once asked Harrington for "one piece of information for a speech I have to make: your stuff refuting the idea that vast amounts of money were spent/wasted in the sixties without good results."[67] It was not unusual for Howe to side with liberals or even conservatives in order to obstruct worldwide communism. Thus, in the 1960s, Howe's caustic literary essays delegitimized New Leftists, especially those who had criticized Israel, as well as activist blacks and feminists. A decade or so later, Howe enlisted in the extreme right edge of liberalism that supported both conservative Contra forces trying to unseat Nicaragua's socialist Sandinistas, and the hawkish *New Republic*, owned and directed by Howe's former student and friend Martin Peretz. *Dissent* finally discarded the "socialist" label in the early 1980s, and became "democratic leftist." Neo-conservatives like Nathan Glazer and Hilton Kramer often praised Howe's anti-communism, while radicals became disillusioned with Howe's literary methods and heroes, which were outdated and ethnocentric. Feminists were aggrieved at Howe's "contempt and derision" for the women's movement.[68]

But as Howe watched the orthodox left self-destruct abroad and at home he also followed Harrington into the DSOC and DSA, resisted overtures from the right, abandoned anti-feminism, courted younger radicals, and even criticized Israel. In short, the vague term "democratic socialism" permitted Howe to define its political content differently throughout his life. This opportunism cut both ways for Harrington. During the 1950s and '60s, when Howe's influence was strongest, Harrington was pulled toward the right edge of leftism—what Arnold Kaufman, its leading advocate, termed "radical liberalism"[69]—where democratic socialism meant anti-communism, political reformism, and widening the capitalist welfare state. Harrington later turned these principles from political objectives into tactics, but they nonetheless remained central to his thinking. As Harrington discovered a singular voice, and as the Old Left disintegrated, Howe was pulled left. Once the student, Harrington now became the teacher. Like Shachtman, then, Howe inspired Harrington to rethink the theory and praxis of democratic socialism. Especially in the early years, however, Howe's dominating friendship likely suffocated the creative impulse that eventually set Harrington free.

Except for Marx, whose imprint is on everything Harrington wrote, the signposts that guided Harrington through tangled leftist theories all hang in the narrow corridor of democratic socialist history from Debs to Thomas, Shachtman and Howe. Harrington nonetheless read widely and always engaged public culture. In the 1950s, C. Wright Mills shook lethargic post-war intellectuals into committed action, and in a series of popular books challenged them, Harrington included, to reformulate orthodox Marxism.[70]

In *White Collar* (1951), Mills showed how America's prevailing capitalist ideology was undermined by a "new" middle class of hired employees who barely resembled their creative, risk-taking nineteenth-century predecessors. Individualism had gradually become a mystification, and middle-class Americans were morally confused and politically impotent. In *The Power Elite* (1956), he argued that America, and by implication other capitalist societies, had polarized into a small elite of powerful actors and a mass of powerless, isolated, vulnerable individuals. And in *The Sociological Imagination* (1959), Mills dared intellectuals to support informal local associations that one day might control public decision-making.

Retail Clerks (1962), Harrington's first book[71] and one in a series of studies of comparative union governments sponsored by the Center for the Study of Democratic Institutions, verified Mills's account of a new, bureaucratized middle class. Moreover, Harrington's democratic socialism, born in great debates with socialist legends and nurtured by Shachtman's theory of bureaucratic collectivism, was certainly toughened by Mills's critique of pluralism and his faint praise for what the New Left later dubbed "participatory democracy."

Although Mills helped catalyze Harrington's thoughts on key issues, he was never a major influence. Mills's *New Men of Power* (1948) criticized the U.S. labor bureaucracy, a needless attack that Harrington feared could weaken the union movement. To steer clear of communism, Mills purged class from his analysis of elitism. *The Power Elite* stated that America's supposedly classless society was, in fact, controlled by a fairly large, self-perpetuating group, but it also rejected Marxian conceptions of class in favor of a theory of elites. "Class," to Mills, was an economic term; "rule" a political term. He wouldn't accept the Marxian theory that the former causes the latter. Instead, capitalism represented a division of power between political leaders, big-business executives, and military chiefs—the so-called power elite—and the masses. Mills chose to describe how each elite controlled the masses rather than uncover the bonds that made them one class. Harrington, on the other hand, always felt that class was central to understanding America, even if it didn't determine everything. Mills, moreover, was an iconoclastic, existentialist, bohemian biker who did things his own way, while Harrington cherished working class organization and was pledged to the socialist movement. Mills, in short, interested Harrington but didn't significantly shape his thinking or his politics. Indeed, Harrington surely felt that Mills's influence on New Leftists was much greater than it should have been given his plucky but seriously deficient theories.

Throughout the 1960s, '70s, and '80s, popular intellectuals—on the left and right—stimulated Harrington, like Mills did in the 1950s, to enrich and expand his own work. Louis Althusser, Daniel Bell, James O'Connor, Immanuel Wallerstein, Antonio Gramsci, Alvin Gouldner, Eric Olin Wright, liberation theologians, feminists, market socialists, and others all touched Harrington with words or deeds. So did the Vietnam and Cold Wars, the collapse of communism, privatization, and the crisis of capitalism. Harrington used many ideas and situations to ferry the general concept of democratic socialism to specific ports, some heretofore off-limits to traditional socialists. Harrington told us clearly what it means to be a democratic socialist. His actions and words, however, were inspired primarily by socialists from the past. Academic stars came and went, but Harrington was always wedded to a century-old socialist legacy.

THE CRASH

His personality, background, affiliations, and close associates all bespoke Harrington's non-traditional agenda. The anomalies were wicked, almost schizophrenic. Harrington pledged to work inside of the system in order to transform it; to convince liberals that socialism fulfilled their capitalist principles; to distinguish true democracy from all the pretenders; to espouse public ownership of major industries while decentralizing public institutions; and to dissociate Marxism from every existing Marxian state.

Added to these unorthodox politics was Harrington's paradoxical personal life. Here was a socialist who, in his twenties, swore an oath to voluntary poverty, and a decade later—following the publication of *The Other America*—was honored with money, fame, and even some power. Harrington's lecture fees tripled almost overnight to $1500, "but," he blushed, "I will occasionally speak for less, depending on the occasion. If you were strapped, I would be willing to speak for $1000 plus expenses."[72] He became a darling of the liberal media, often appearing on television talk-shows, and courted by mainstream publishers and journalists. Repudiated by young radicals who remembered Port Huron and by traditional socialists, Harrington was sheltered from capitalist approbation primarily by Stephanie and his two sons. This, however, proved a mixed blessing. "The nuclear family," he mourned, "is unquestionably a miserable, privatizing, anti-socialist, and selfish social form."[73] The bourgeois character of the family, "that institution which I regard as reactionary and yet better than any other present system for the propagation and care of children,"[74] insidiously infected parents and children. Harrington found that the idealistic, self-sacrificing role he assumed as father and husband almost imperceptively evolved into greed and competitiveness. Yet the alternative, sacrificing the material well-being of his family to a collectivist ideology, was unthinkable in America's laissez-faire environment.

Caught between socialist ideals and material success, an aging Harrington became defensive, guilt-ridden, and anxious. During the 1960s, when his public visibility peaked, even the simplest everyday activities—

watching a son play soccer, talking with neighbors, attending PTA meetings—were fraught with difficulties. His well-known radicalism estranged everyday acquaintances, who feared even small differences, without really endearing him to angry colleagues on the left. Success and public exposure made him a magnetic target, and Harrington felt besieged at every turn. Whenever possible he hid his identity as the foremost U.S. socialist.

During a March, 1965 speech in San Diego, Harrington crashed. As he began a standard talk on poverty, he grew faint and dizzy, and grasped the lectern for support. "I cut the question period short and went back to my motel," he remembered. "By the time I reached the room I was sweating profusely and there were tremours in my back and chest. I wondered if I was having a heart attack." It was, of course, a breakdown—in Harrington's words "a fearful case of social vertigo"[75]—not a heart attack. All the internal pressures and contradictions of being socialist and successful in capitalist America had exploded. The psychological cost of remaining radical even when acceptability beckoned was painfully high. Perhaps a concern for their own mental health as much as ideology pushed Shachtmanites into the mainstream. In any case, Harrington underwent psychoanalysis for four years, and during this period lecture halls, a natural environment for so long, became frightful. He curtailed his schedule, but, primarily for financial reasons, didn't cancel it entirely. "I would have to go into training for three days to give a speech," he later admitted. "Nobody would know that I'd be gripping the podium and that my fingers would be going white from the emotional effort of maintaining my equilibrium. But I have this Irish gift. I would keep rattling on as if nothing was happening."[76]

In some ways, things just got worse during the 1970s and '80s. When, for example, "after some years of soul-searching and mainly because of our two kids,"[77] the Harringtons in 1979 moved from the inner city to the suburbs—travelling a path already beaten by his accusers—the story was picked up by the *New York Post* and the *Wall Street Journal*, and used to humiliate Harrington. He responded aggressively, and at length, calling these dailies "scurrilous rags" that "had reduced a complex ethical and social issue to a dirty little piece of nasty gossip."[78] Then he rationalized the move (he was not opposed to the pleasures of life, only to how they were distributed in our society; his new house in Larchmont was middle class, not a mansion), before noting the pain and defeat he felt leaving Manhattan, in effect legitimizing the attacks. In another instance in 1986 he was asked by a high-school student at a talk he gave in Charleston, South Carolina why a radical receives a substantial honorarium. Harrington responded testily that U.S. socialists must play by capitalist rules whether they like it or not. "I was, and am, absolutely right—and uncomfortable."[79] Eventually he decided to give two free speeches for every paid one. In short, Harrington's popularity made it difficult to defend himself without appearing to be self-serving. He started doubting himself, and pining for the days spent at the Catholic Worker, "the happiest time of my life. For one thing," he realized, "there were no contradictions. No one could say I was a hypocrite . . . . I was totally happy."[80]

Harrington never entirely resolved these contradictions, the offspring of an unlikely union of patriotism and socialism. By the mid-1980s, however, he had finally learned to live with them. But even at the end, in 1988, as he dispassionately surveyed the past, there was a special poignancy to the recollection of these difficult years that betrays an unresolved *guerre á mort*.

The breakdown and its emotional residue were unforeseen outcomes of intellectual, political, social, economic, and psychological factors fusing in Harrington's life-project. The misadventures at Port Huron certainly catalyzed the entire process, and the conundrums of democratic socialism were rooted in Harrington's post-conference decision to formulate a new, indigenous radicalism that engaged liberals. Immediately after Port Huron, Harrington was a lonely figure on the political landscape, alienated from every major progressive constituency. A new generation of radicals had arisen, and Harrington had silently plunged into middle age. The whiz-kid of American socialism was no longer a kid. His aura of invincibility had also evaporated in the furnace of taunts and insults that heated the chilly Michigan evenings. Almost overnight, Harrington became a rejected, isolated, aging, maverick socialist. With unanticipated material success tossed in, the wonder is not that he crashed and then struggled throughout the 1970s and '80s to get back on course, but that he eventually recaptured most of his reputation as America's leading socialist.

Dogma and Dialectics

Port Huron was central to Harrington's professional life. He emerged scarred emotionally and politically, but determined to redefine socialism in an American dialect. Harrington henceforth steered a middle course between communism, which was un-American, and New Dealism, which was anti-socialist. His personality, background, affiliations, and mentors prefigured this eccentric project.

Dialectics, always essential to Harrington's socialism, also became a canon for measuring his actions. Although these occasionally came up short, Harrington never diluted the standards. He steadily widened his targeted constituencies beyond male, white unionists, and his last books finally exhibit that sweeping dialectical vision he originally discovered in the late 1960s.

What were Harrington's core values? From that moment in St. Louis when he became a socialist, he continually wrestled with Marxian texts, explained Marx to disbelieving Americans, and outlined a new, authentically Marxian theory and politics. Karl Marx was unquestionably the most important influence on Michael Harrington, and *Socialism* (1970), Harrington's philosophical account of Marxism, is certainly his finest book. It is the most accessible Marxian text ever written by an American, and it established Harrington's reputation around the globe as a preeminent thinker and scholar.

Harrington wanted to write a book like *Socialism* in the early 1960s, but for political and personal reasons was unable to. It was still too close to the McCarthy years, and to the anti-ideological decade that followed, to expect that Americans would read a book about Karl Marx. Harrington, moreover, officially exited the Socialist Party in 1973, but he began questioning Old Left socialism a decade earlier, and the glacial ideological change progressed steadily thereafter. Like a ripe fruit, then, *Socialism* was ready to drop in the mid-1960s. After 1962, however, Harrington had real input into the nation's War on Poverty. The author of *The Other America* was a political player during the liberal 1960s, whereas the author of *Socialism* couldn't have entered the ballpark. Harrington nonetheless was uncomfortable with *The Other America's* startling success, and relieved when Norman Thomas, terminally ill in a nursing home in 1968, finally encouraged him to write about socialism, not poverty.[1] Thomas's injunction psychologically freed Harrington, and by 1968 the political climate had also changed.

In the late 1960s, Students for a Democratic Society (SDS) and the New Left were demoralized by organizational failures, a shrinking base of supporters, and shattered dreams. Campus activism had not ended the Vietnam War. The nation had lost its fight against poverty, and the economy was sputtering. Fearful whites were becoming conservative and racist. Despite a decade of demonstrations, capitalism was alive and well. And economic imperialism was punishing dependent third world nations like colonial soldiers once did. Hard-line factions were sprouting in SDS, offering old Stalinist wine in new bottles, and promising success by any necessary means. New Left syndicalists, utopians, anarchists, and liberals angrily reacted, ridiculing the traditional left. "Participatory democracy" was a vague enough term to unite everyone in the short run because it rationalized what was happening in the early and mid-1960s on university campuses. But in the long run it neither preserved the loose New Left coalition nor offered Americans a plan of action.

Some New Left intellectuals and graduate students who had studied European Marxism became socialist philosophers during the 1960s. SDS established a Radical Education Project in 1966 to spread their non-traditional ideas among the nation's undergraduates, but it fizzled without adequate resources or the support of grassroots activists. An SDS convention in 1967 acknowledged the organization's poverty of ideas and, for the first time, openly discussed Marxism. A year later black (anarchist) and red (communist) flags were posted on the convention stage, but SDS—and the New Left generally—were already dying and these excursions into radical theory were too little and too late.

As their political hopes waned during 1968–71, many activist students and faculty who had struggled for racial, ethnic, and gender equality; had opposed poverty, war, and imperialism; and had supported the labor movement, changed their tactics. In what Paul Buhle called "the last intellectual burst of the New Left, an outgrowth and a celebration in the face of widespread political collapse,"[2] radical activists became scholars, the number of leftist journals increased dramatically, and social history exploded into areas as diverse as feminism, the family, sexuality, madness, deviance, psychology, play, even proctology. This was history and scholarship "from below:" it evinced a sympathy for and an interest in victims, average people, laborers, and popular culture. Journals such as *Radical America*, *Radical History Review*, *Studies On The Left*, *Liberation*, and *Politics and Society* became popular on campuses, and opened the academy to Marxian studies even as the nation as a whole was slamming the door on leftists.

With nothing to lose politically in 1970, with a receptive audience of former activists and radical scholars waiting, and with leftists needing a theoretical hanger for all those critical studies, Harrington finally wrote <u>Socialism</u>, and, six years later, *The Twilight of Capitalism*. Examining these and related texts, as well as pertinent historical commentary, one can see why Harrington was both a democrat and a Marxist, and what the word "dialectics" actually means.

ORTHODOX MARXISM

"Classical," or orthodox Marxism, which for most people defined what Marx said and what Marxism was, is anchored in philosophical materialism and the science of historical materialism. Orthodox Marxists believe that humans alone have the ability to make tools, and thus in the struggle to survive have a distinct advantage over subhumans, who can only find and use nature's own tools. Uniting first into organized groups, then tribes, and finally societies, humans eventually produce more than they consume, and then fight over how to share the surplus. Human history, in the orthodox reading of Marx, is the totality of those actions by which we produce in the material world to satisfy changing needs.

Oppression originates when one group appropriates the excess goods produced by others. The forms of this appropriation, what Marx called the "relations of production," characterize society's material base. Relations of production reflect the technical level of productive forces: as technology—

e.g., equipment, productive forces, technical skills, and the division of labor—develops, entirely new forms of appropriation become possible. Forms of social oppression are thus linked to productive technology.

For orthodox Marxists, relations of production comprise three connected phenomena. First are property relations, essentially the legally protected powers to control raw materials, instruments of production, and products of labor. Second is the social division of labor, separating citizens into one materially productive segment and another involved in functions such as government service, management, and entertainment. Intellectual labor appears when appropriation is refined to such an extent that leisure time expands, and materially non-engaged people begin abstractly speculating. The rise of the arts, sciences and philosophy—what today we call culture—characterizes a particular form of social inequality. Idealists, orthodoxy warns, have ignored the requisite material factors that permit intellectuals the leisure to ponder first principles. Finally, productive relations are the method of socially exchanging and distributing products, the capitalist version of which Marx described empirically in his later works. In sum, a "base," or substructure, comprises the technical level of productive forces and the relationships involved in production. The latter includes property relations, the social division of labor, and methods of social distribution and exchange.

The position and role occupied in the base determines class, which in turn conditions the way one perceives and understands reality. Class membership, in other words, determines ideas and beliefs. The dominant economic class owns and controls raw materials, instruments, and products of labor, appropriating excess goods and distributing them to maximize its own interests. Because it has accumulated excess leisure time and resources, the dominant class can rationalize its own material interests. A dominant culture comprises the ideas and institutions by which a society defines itself—in Marx's terminology, the "superstructure." The level of productive forces and relations of production therefore shape a society's self-image. The dominant economic class is also the society's ruling intellectual force.

The primary aim of orthodox Marxists in formulating this materialist conception of history is to explain periodic large-scale social change. Productive powers expand at a greater or lesser rate depending on historical circumstances, including the pertinent social relations of production. Eventually, however, a given set of social relations of production are outgrown or rendered obsolete by the productive powers. The prevailing relations either make it difficult to employ the existing powers or else fetter the further development of these powers. Powers and relations of production thus come into conflict or "contradiction," and social revolution begins. This conflict transforms the relations of production, realigning them with the productive powers, which can then resume expanding. Changes in the superstructure, including its political and legal institutions, are explained by these changes in the base.

The mechanism by which this realignment occurs, orthodoxy claims, is the class struggle. Social relations of production divide society into groups distinguished by their degree of control over production. These groups become classes as soon as they are organized and represented by a political movement that defines and promotes their class interests. Class interests depend on the common situation of a class's members, and especially their hostile relation to other classes, which arises because the social relations of production assign effective control over production to some at the expense of others. Those who have this control have a common interest in retaining it, and those who are excluded have a common interest in acquiring it. A class's interests are ultimately identified with the establishment and defense of a particular set of social relations that elevate its members to social dominance. At any given stage of history, the class that establishes production relations that best suit the extant productive powers is victorious. In this manner history has evolved from pre-feudal to feudal to capitalist stages, and cultural hegemony has passed from tribes to landlords to entrepreneurs.

The state, for orthodox Marxists, is superstructural: its form and its actions correspond to economic structures. Similarly, the state is a tool of the ruling class: it is a mechanism by which that class controls society and legitimates its own economic relations. Religion, morality, philosophy, and art are "ideological" because they promote class interests. A class ideology distorts reality by seeing everything only from one class's perspective, and presenting the conditions for that class's rule as the preconditions for social peace and justice.

While orthodox Marxists occasionally apply this materialist conception of history to pre-modern societies, their main concern—and, they claim, Marx's as well—is with capitalist development. Driven by the quest for profits, individual capitalists continually modernize the instruments of production, and in so doing create wealth hitherto unimagined. In the course of this process, capitalism needs and acquires more labor, ultimately commodifying the entire labor force. Craft workers and peasants are transformed into wage laborers who are bought and sold on the market because selling one's own labor is the only means to survive. On the job, workers produce more value than they receive, with the difference, or "surplus," going to the employer. This economic exploitation ripples through the superstructure, where workers are promised liberty but are actually alienated because capitalist social relations dispossess the vast majority of producers and frustrate their collective self-determination. As machinery and factories become larger and more sophisticated, capital congeals in a few enormously profitable enterprises, and the conditions for organizing workers concentrated in these factories improves. Capital, in short, has created the very forces that might negate it. Sooner or later, orthodox Marxists believe, organized labor will become a potent political force that during one of capitalism's periodic breakdowns will seize state power, most likely through insurrection. This upheaval, however, can take place only when productive forces are developed to the point where they negate capitalist social relations and also efficiently fulfill workers' material needs. Although Marx himself rarely speculated about the post-capitalist future, orthodox Marxists believe that classes, the division of labor, private property, and commodity production all will disappear as empowered workers socialize production and distribution, and engage in socially useful labor. Marx called this communism.

Historical materialism is thus a program for orthodox Marxian research as well as a weapon in the hands of the proletariat, and social change means becoming part of a class movement that is controlled by material development. All social ideas, institutions, and activities—revolution included—can be reduced to economics. The economic base, moreover, has a built-in mechanism of conflict and change, culminating in the abolition of classes altogether.

Marx described material production concretely, for the most part rejecting abstract theories. Friedrich Engels connected materialism to a useful social theory. Dialectics, for Engels, embodied three universal laws that governed matter in motion: the law of the transformation of quantity into quality, and vice-versa; the law of the interpenetration of opposites; and the law of the negation of the negation. These three principles functioned impersonally and explained all of reality. They also made class struggle and worker rebellion, as well as the economic contradictions of capitalism, inevitable. The Second International (1889–1914) eventually recognized Engels as Marxism's official philosopher, and his "dialectical materialism" became the philosophy of orthodox Marxism.

The transformation of quantity into quality meant that as quantities of matter increase or decrease they alter qualitatively. A numerical increase in atoms, for example, transforms a molecule into a substance with new properties. A change in temperature produces melting or freezing; the accumulation of cooperative human labor alters the environment; an increase in workers and a decrease in capitalists inevitably yield a qualitatively new form of social life.

Nature, for Engels, consists of bodies in motion, constantly interacting through attraction and repulsion. From these two subforms of matter—attraction and repulsion, positive and negative—various qualities present in the universe (for example, heat, electricity, light, magnetism, sentiments, and so on) are derived. The world is therefore a unity of opposites. According to the law of the interpenetration of opposites, each perceived item is a tense amalgam of antagonistic, interpenetrating motions, which at any one time are empirically invisible. Revolution, then, is as true and inevitable as a morning's sunrise or a subway ride to work, even though it is empirically nonverifiable at that particular moment in an apparently peaceful society. Everything contains its own opposite which, as a result of laws one and three, emerges and is negated.

The law of the negation of the negation held that it is absolutely certain that every object, thought, or condition will turn into its opposite. This negation is then negated, producing a new reality synthesizing primary qualities of the first two stages and preserving them in a more perfect, or progressive, form. A seed, for example, develops into a plant (its negation), and the plant produces new seeds or dies. These new seeds, the negation of the negation, propagate the original's most useful or strongest traits but also introduce new ones that increase the second plant's life chances. Similarly, property relations evolve from common ownership in primitive society, to private ownership in capitalism (the negation), to the common ownership in socialism (the negation of the negation). Socialism is thus heir to the residual best from both previous stages of history.

Orthodoxy, however, still lacked a politics. V. I. Lenin transformed dialectical materialism from a frozen formula into dynamic activities. Revolution, he argued, consists of creative, goal-oriented actions by knowledgeable and organized agents triggering history's objective mechanisms. Leninists thus self-consciously directed history toward its preordained socialist future, even if this meant bypassing Marx's capitalist stage of development and preempting workers as the agents of proletarian rebellion. Lenin's activism and his secretive, hierarchical Party were adopted by communists everywhere, and became a permanent feature of orthodox Marxism. Until recently, orthodox philosophy and politics have directed mainstream communist parties throughout the world.

A "NEW" KARL MARX

In spite of successes, orthodoxy proved a mixed blessing especially to Westerners because it was neither democratic nor individualist. Turning Marx's weakest link, that is, an incomplete and often ambiguous philosophical anthropology, to his own advantage, Harrington discovered in Marx the roots of a compassionate, non-materialist dialectic.

Human beings, Harrington claimed, aren't puppets manipulated by impersonal laws. The orthodox Marx and Engels, he noted, were "fathers of totalitarianism," "materialistic simpletons" who taught that economics determines everything. For as long as this false image prevailed—and when Harrington died, orthodoxy was still a state religion throughout the communist world—"the graven images of Marx and Engels are among the greatest obstacles to the socialist future."[3] The critique of orthodoxy was justified because it unearthed what Harrington called a "new" Karl Marx, until now "the most misunderstood single thinker in the history of human thought,"[4] and also cleared the path for progressive change.

"Communism," Marx wrote in a short attack on Proudhon, "must free itself from all the 'false brothers' of the fashionable socialism of the time."[5] Marx had discovered that ostensibly socialist movements, such as those led by Bismarck and Napoleon III, often served the needs of feudalists, shopkeepers, and entrepreneurs, who collectively disguised their interests in vague abstractions. Even in this century, the word socialism was disingenuously appropriated by communists, fascists, welfare state capitalists, and petty dictators, all hitching their own narrow interests onto trans-historical laws. Stalin, for example, used it to build a totalitarian cult of personality; Clement Attlee to build the British welfare state; Hitler to build fascism; and third world leaders to justify authoritarianism. Genuine socialism, on the other hand, was democratic, humane, and true to Marx.

Marx realized that by the mid-nineteenth century two events that could dramatically alter history had occurred. First, the forces of economic production had developed to a point where abundance was a real possibility. In economic scarcity, even successful democratic movements crash into a wall of poverty, and thereafter promote economic growth rather than democracy. This is why capitalism, the most dynamic economic system, flourishes in certain historical epochs. With abundance, however, societies can pay for democracy by redistributing an ample bounty from the few who have more than they need to the many who don't. Second, at this precise moment large numbers of workers concentrated in highly mechanized factories finally noticed their own incredible productive power. They also read about, heard, and saw where, and to whom, the enormous riches they had created went.

These two events, in Marx's view, created the conditions necessary for socialism, but did not create socialism itself. That required workers actually taking control of their productive power. Socialism thus depends on deprived workers in a society of abundance deciding to unite and change this society.

This commitment to democracy and self-emancipation, in Harrington's view, is the heart of Marxism. Marx always rejected the anti-socialist socialisms of the radical left (e.g., the elitist Blanquists and Millenarians) and the radical right (e.g., the reformist Tory Socialists, Christian Socialists, and Louis Blanc's State Socialists), and insisted that socialism represented the common good as defined by empowered, self-conscious workers. Marx's democratic credentials, Harrington concluded, are thus "well over a hundred years old and quite new."[6]

All of Marx's writings, for Harrington, are democratic in this sense, although his strategy gradually changed. The early work described how reflective freedom was alienated by capitalism, and later Marx described the actual dynamics of capitalism. A conflict exists only when these two projects are separated, which was not Marx's intent. The theoretical unity of Marxism, that is, the principle that people create their own futures, inspired each specific book.

Harrington also claimed that an "unknown Karl Marx," who envisioned a nonviolent electoral proletarian politics, emerged during the years from 1850 to 1883. This mature Marx was "inherently revisionist,"[7] because he identified socialism with the labor movement. Henceforth, in Harrington's view, Marx favored plugging into the peaceful struggles of unions and workers parties. Workers, Marx suggested, could sponsor a successful democratic united front with liberal capitalists against aristocrats by supporting reforms such as universal suffrage and the ten-hour work-day. "In Marx's perspective," Harrington wrote, "it was the democratic self-organization of the proletariat that was the truly radical act—even if it initially took reformist forms. The aim remained utterly revolutionary . . . . The strategy was now social democratic."[8] This long, slow reformist contest trained workers in the art of self-government, and also prevented a postrevolutionary bureaucracy from usurping power.

Why, then, did Marxism become totalitarian? Harrington's answer begins with a "scandalous assertion" that Marx and Engels occasionally misrepresented Marxism. These misstatements were coopted by power-hungry bureaucrats and then foisted on workers. Destroying them, Harrington felt, "is the first step in bringing to life the new Karl Marx."[9]

The problem, for Harrington, originated in *The Communist Manifesto* (1848), where Marx and Engels proposed an alliance of workers and reformers that would transform the economically distressed petty bourgeoisie into workers. With society rapidly polarizing into a few wealthy capitalists and many exploited workers, the transition to socialism would then take place immediately. The growth of both wealth and immiseration would ignite a mass rebellion.

Marx soon realized, however, that neither reformers nor workers were radical, the middle class was growing, the proletarian–petty bourgeois alliance was unstable, and capitalism was healthy. He became angry and confused. "For two bitter disillusioned years after that turning point," said Harrington, "Marx was indeed in a sullen, ultra-Leftist mood, and this period is a classic source for the Bolshevik, and then the Stalinist, version of Marxism . . . . It brought Marx as close to anti-democracy as he ever came."[10] It was during these years, from the Fall of 1848 until the middle of 1850, that Marx discussed Permanent Revolution, secretive working class parties, and the unmitigated treachery of the bourgeoisie—all latently totalitarian ideas.

Also during these years Marx used the phrase "dictatorship of the proletariat," which actually originated when Marx and Engels, with Blanqui, signed the statutes of the World Society of Revolutionary Communists in 1848. Article One declared that "The aim of the association is the overthrow of all privileged classes, their subjugation by the dictatorship of the proletariat which will maintain the revolution in permanence until communism, the last organizational form of the human family, will be constructed." Two years later, with the Blanquists now enemies, Marx and Engels denounced the statutes. The phrase nevertheless became identified with Marxism, and later communism.

Harrington suggested that Marx did not use the term dictatorship in its traditional sense.[11] In *The Class Struggles in France* (1850), Marx explained how all states—republics or monarchies, democratic or non-democratic, capitalist or socialist—are dictatorships because one class only dominates. "Wherever we find a state," Sidney Hook has commented on this issue, "we find a dictatorship."[12] Dictatorship, then, defined society's class configurations, not its political content. Marx, therefore, did not say that a proletarian dictatorship necessarily represses civil liberties, anymore so than a bourgeois democracy necessarily backs them. In a democratic dictatorship the majority's will is realized in and through the dominant class, and this, of course, is how Marx defined socialism. How else, asked Harrington, can one understand Marx's depiction of the Paris Commune as a dictatorship characterized by universal suffrage, equality of wages, and the immediate recallability of all officials? Property relationships now favored workers where they once, in France's liberal democracy, had favored peasants or capitalists. "So 'dictatorship,'" Harrington concluded, "does not mean dictatorship but the fulfillment of democracy."[13] Harrington conceded that most people never deconstructed primary texts, and thus defined the word literally. The Marxian phrase "dictatorship of the proletariat" has thus subverted Marx's actual view of socialism.

Harrington believed that the foreword to Marx's *A Contribution to the Critique of Political Economy*, published in 1859, worsened matters. Society's material base, Marx seemed to say, shaped the entire culture, even though Marx did not clearly explain what the base was. People usually interpret this to mean that every thought and act is determined by social production, i.e. when economies change in history so do cultures. Marx's post-1846 empirical studies, in this view, reduced subjectivity to class, and turned actors into puppets. Harrington admitted that this reading of the foreword can be supported by Marx's ill-chosen comments in the *Critique* and in *Capital* that depict society as a mechanical model of base and superstructure lunging toward socialism.[14]

Harrington nonetheless rejected this materialist reading of the foreword as false and dangerous. Marx, after all, had also equated "material relations of life" to the totality that Hegel termed "civil society." Marxian economics thus denoted, in Harrington's words, "the whole world of laissez-faire, its pleasures and poverty, its human interrelationships and its needs, as well as its material goods and machines. It was, even in its greed, suffused with a specific humanity, with precisely that which made man greater than the animals."[15] Surely, Harrington concluded, Marx meant that civic culture, consciousness, and class were internally related, and collectively comprised "economics." Why else would he have discussed the linkages between concrete and abstract, and among such entities and concepts as class, population, value, money, wage-labor, price? Marx himself, in *A Contribution to the Critique of Political Economy*, defined society as "a rich totality of many conceptions and relationships,"[16] rather than a predetermined lump. Although Marx was unclear and occasionally misleading on this issue, his indolent readers must also share some of the blame.

Marx's sloppy reductionism certainly contributed to the excesses of Soviet-style communism, but Harrington emphasized that it was "only episodic and counterbalanced by a huge corpus of intellectual work that put matters rightly."[17] Perhaps, Harrington guessed, Marx wanted to simplify complicated material. Jürgen Habermas has suggested that Marx was momentarily confused about what all the data meant. Since Harrington saw Marx's economic reductionism as an aberration, he left the causality question unresolved.

Engels presented another, more difficult problem. A brilliant scholar and historian, Engels was also the creator of dialectical materialism, the scientific theory—"not to be found, even as a momentary indiscretion, in the writings of Marx"[18]—that sanctioned orthodoxy. Moreover, Marx had read, approved, and even contributed a section to Engels's militantly reductionist *Anti-Dühring*. If, as Harrington claimed, Marx was not a reductionist, why didn't he publicly or privately protest?

Harrington gave two reasons for this tolerance. First, Engels was a polemicist. Marx tolerated the intellectual double standard in order to mobilize workers who needed justice, not science. Engels himself suggests this in several letters he wrote after Marx's death. Thus, *Anti-Dühring* was regarded by Marx as a polemic, not a work of theory. Marx and Engels ordinarily would never have engaged in such mechanical thinking.

Second, in the late nineteenth century many European scholars sought universal social laws resembling Charles Darwin's theory of evolution.

Harrington believed that Marx was affected by Darwin's enormous popularity. Marx's unsolicited praise for Darwin in the afterword to the second German edition of *Capital* thus implies that he tolerated Engels's sweeping generalizations because they resembled Darwin's,[19] as does Engels's testimony, in Marx's obituary, that Marx had explained the development of human history with Darwinian precision. Engels must have known Marx's professional ambitions and the obituary served to cement Marx's legacy as the Darwin of social evolution.

Why, Harrington then asked, did the reductionist Engels so easily subvert the democratic Marx? Because every major political actor preferred Engels's Marxism, although for different reasons.

Workers were struggling in a cruel nineteenth-century free-market world, and dialectical materialism was an easier intellectual fix than democratic Marxism. It also more accurately reflected their need for quick, dramatic changes in economic relationships. Finally, Harrington suggested it was a new, simple, and comprehensive creed to replace the religious faith that industrial life was annihilating.

Leftist intellectuals were empowered by dialectical materialism. As Communist officials they later exploited workers and transformed Marxism into just another elitist ideology. Harrington believed Engels's Marxism false under any conditions, but in the nineteenth century at least it expressed the real needs of workers. It was a progressive ideology that stood for proletarian dignity. Contemporary dialectical materialism, on the other hand, is a bureaucratic ideology that controls, rather than helps, workers.

Finally, capitalists wanted the simplistic version of Marxism to mock and repudiate, and they happily discovered that dialectical materialism was empirically unverifiable. Capitalism was thriving, often through innovative state planning that Marx and Engels didn't foresee. Factory conditions were improving and wages rising, so proletarian rebellion seemed unlikely. Political authorities easily goaded leftists back into the mainstream and, the battle won, convinced intellectuals to equate Engels and Marx, thereby assuring a permanent victory. It would have been politically foolish to unearth the real Marx, even if they had known he existed.

THE MARXIAN UNDERGROUND IN AMERICA

Harrington was neither the first nor the only one to expose a "new," democratic Karl Marx. "[Marx] has been recognized for over fifty years by a sort of Marxian underground," Harrington admitted, "by a handful of political and academic thinkers, all of them on the margin of power, the brilliance of their Marxian theory in an ironically inverse relationship to the impotence of their Marxian politics." He wanted to raise this underground from history's catacombs by translating what he called its "mysterious hieroglyph-ics"[20] into a language Americans could understand.

Orthodoxy accepted unquestioningly the laws of historical and dialectical materialism. Critical Marxists accepted only what explained a world where joy, suffering, love, and anxiety—not merely economics—touched workers' lives. Consciousness was real and important for them, and the price materialists paid for ignoring subjectivity was irrelevance. Harrington also believed this price too high.

The subjectivist reaction to orthodoxy appeared simultaneously in the U.S. and Europe at the turn of the century. Whereas Americans devised apt tactics, however, Europeans reformulated Marxian epistemology. This division—U.S. and third world leftists concentrating on practical policy, Europeans on abstract theory—has, with several notable exceptions, persisted throughout this century. In dealing with the thorny problem of subjectivity, European neo-Marxists relied primarily on Hegel and Husserl[21], and offered American radicals philosophical reasons for taking subjectivity seriously. Where orthodoxy stamped its reality on the social world, Hegelian and phenomenological Marxists described the irreducibility of consciousness and the importance of translating economics into reflection. The message from Europe to America was clear: the subjective component of freedom could not be imported from abroad, but instead had to be rooted in real problems and meaningful solutions.

Harrington's dialectic comprised a philosophical package never before seen on the U.S. left, but he didn't work in a vacuum. An inchoate, unsophisticated, and at times incoherent Marxian underground did exist in America, and Harrington tapped it.

In 1901—14 years after Antonio Labriola, in the *prelezione* of his *Problemi della filosofia della storia*, had first summoned Hegelian Marxism—the Socialist Party (SP) was founded in America. Although its leaders pledged allegiance to Engels' scientific socialism, SP members nonetheless disagreed sharply when analyzing U.S. conditions and formulating tactics. By its 1904 convention, the party had split into left, center, and right factions, each with its own leaders and programs.

The right was led by Victor Berger and, like European social democrats inspired by Eduard Bernstein, it was reformist. The center and left factions were virtually indistinguishable until 1907. Leftists, however, courted only blue-collar workers and spoke in simple colloquialisms, while the Morris Hillquit-led center embraced intellectuals as well as workers, and fashioned abstract monographs that eluded most workers but kept several radical presses busy. A broad center–left coalition constituted a large majority of SP members and guided SP policy from the party's founding in 1901 until about 1907. It also produced the most popular SP leaders during this period, including Eugene V. Debs, William (Big Bill) Haywood, and Algie Simons, editor of the *International Socialist Review*.

The center–left coalition, particularly its left, encountered a serious dilemma: materialism clarified the social and political power of capital, but was superfluous in a land of immigrants and individualists. U.S. workers didn't understand or appreciate impersonal laws that ignored everyday problems. SP leftists could not legitimately represent real American workers and also speak a foreign ideology, so they decided to simply disregard the theoretical problem. Marxism was justifiable because it explained everyday reality and, in practice, improved proletarian living conditions. SP leftists neither confirmed nor denied historical materialism. Since materialism, in any case, wasn't defensible in U.S. factories, the SP sensibly sided with workers rather than philosophers.

In the SP's hands, Marxism changed workers' attitudes by plugging into and expanding meaningful grassroots struggles. Working class consciousness, heretofore taken for granted, was now worth fighting for. The right's reformist proposals, such as public ownership of utilities, might benefit workers in the short term, but the center–left coalition also favored worker struggle, emancipation, and self-government, all through socialist electoral activity. By voting for socialists, workers on their own initiative realized historical necessity and completed a revolutionary process that capitalism's own internal contradictions had begun.

SP success was measured by the size of the socialist vote and the number of SP candidates elected to office. Consequently, SP activities during these years were primarily in the areas of electioneering, public demonstrations and lectures, and publishing mass-circulation socialist literature and journals. The party became popular by sharing workers' experiences and communicating information through neighborhood channels—abstract theories and vague prescriptions weren't needed. Debs once suggested eliminating intellectuals altogether from leadership positions in the party. He felt that knowledge arose from the critical awareness one achieves when confronting everyday problems and solving them through struggle, and that this kind of knowledge could not be memorized.

SP activism left its mark on socialists like Harrington, but it still needed a rational foundation. Even innovative tacticians eventually were co-opted by materialists, leaving radicals who resisted to search for new institutional homes.

When this happened in 1906, some SP leftists became members of the Industrial Workers of the World (IWW), or the Wobblies. The IWW was an indigenous U.S. workers' organization that stressed common sense and citizen autonomy. Proletarian power was the Wobbly pot of gold, and Wobbly leaders knew that Americans' love for family, land, and freedom somehow had to be translated into socialist economics. Revolution was inevitable, but from a practical, thoroughly Wobbly point of view, workers had to coalesce into a force powerful enough to challenge capital. Power required class solidarity, bonding self-conscious actors into a cohesive group. Where the SP's left simply ignored theory altogether, Wobblies picked over orthodoxy, Darwinism, and syndicalism, salvaging something from each. Putative logical contradictions were irrelevant to them because logic was for intellectuals, not workers.

The materialist Debs focused on the practical question of why, given its inevitability, socialism had not yet appeared in the U.S. His answer, like the Wobblies', was direct and simple enough for the average American to grasp: although the Constitution was, in his words, of "everlasting benefit to mankind,"[22] it had also deified self-interest and blocked popular democracy. Narrowly conceived, individual rights trivialized the idea of majority rule by creating a hegemonic class of wealthy entrepreneurs who held power, prestige, and the ability to shape the nation's agenda. Workers condoned their own horrible exploitation because each "free" individual felt alone, isolated, and powerless.

More than twenty years before either Harrington or Tom Hayden was born, Debs translated Marxian theory into an American vernacular in order to touch the dispossessed emotionally, working through, rather than around, powerful patriotic sentiments. If workers knew that exploitation was not only wrong but un-American, then their shame would become anger, their guilt, pride, and their isolation, rebellion. This raised awareness, not knowledge of objective laws, was what Debs called Marxism's "supreme demand," and Debs hoped inspiring oratory would prove an apt means to raising it.[23]

Debs's point, which Harrington later endorsed, was that workers had to "cultivate the habit of doing . . . [their] own thinking."[24] As people gained a measure of self-respect, they appreciated their own value, and realized that one person's livelihood was linked to everyone's. Proletarian consciousness thus preceded democracy. When people became reflective, activists were no longer needed.

Whereas the Wobblies saw struggle as a practical means of improving conditions and empowering workers, Debs believed struggle was its own reward, regardless of the outcome. The act of resisting capitalist injustice explained, illustrated, and confirmed Marx's theses, making opening a book unnecessary. Therefore, like the SP left, Debs felt politics was an educational tool that fueled workers' burning anger. Political success created knowledgeable workers who pushed the system to its limit, and then beyond into rebellion. Although struggle was its own reward, successful struggles were even better because, by improving factories and reforming society, they reinforced the will to continue struggling. Eventually, workers would grasp the truth: the inevitability of socialism.

Like Harrington, Debs was thus an indigenous revolutionary who the historian David Shannon has characterized as "American enough for the most prejudiced cultural nationalist and red as flame."[25] He defended the Constitution because other Americans did, not because it was necessarily good. Two decades before Gramsci wrote about "cultural hegemony," and more than 60 years before Harrington celebrated Gramsci, Debs concocted his own organic socialism, self-consciously experienced by workers whose lifestyles and beliefs were worth more than volumes of socialist rhetoric. If workers trusted electoral politics, Debsians would turn the ballot into a powerful weapon of change that transformed the state into the political equivalent of industrial unions. Then it could legislate proletarian hegemony.

Although they wouldn't do so themselves, SP leftists, Wobblies, and Debs challenged Marxists to re-think the delicate balance between democracy and objective truth. Harrington adopted their reformist tactics, but he also substantiated their politics. Armed with a unified theory and praxis, Marxism then could successfully compete in the political arena.

Harrington wasn't the first American to tackle this difficult task. Anti-intellectual Marxian subjectivism was first noticed by two sophisticated radicals, Louis Boudin and Louis Fraina, who hoped to explain it philosophically. Both men were Marxists and colleagues of Debs on the SP left. Both, moreover, joined the Communist Party (CP) in 1919, and neither survived very long among historical materialists. Their brief, ill-fated intellectual experiments, too esoteric for workers and too radical for mainstream Marxists, reinforced among socialists the belief that in the U.S. practical results, not theories, count. Harrington surely knew their work and learned from their mistakes.

Boudin admitted that ideas are economically determined, and classes rationalize practical interests. Once unleashed by economic development, however, ideas become class weapons that, he explained, "play a distinct and quite important role" in transforming society.[26] They develop independently, generating changes even before economic conditions became untenable. At certain times in history, Boudin believed, economics, consciousness, and actual social struggles crystallized into rebellions. By entering factories and ghettos, Marxists cultivated the kind of meaningful class struggle that united thoughtful workers into a powerful revolutionary force. Economics determined when and where socialism was born, but only workers willing to fight and die for a cause they believed in could deliver it.

The more practical Fraina also wanted to elevate and intensify what he called the "moral, intellectual, and class consciousness of the proletariat,"[27] not just reiterate platitudes. Marxism, he claimed, needed a psychology of human potential to complement its economic analysis of social potential.[28] Fraina saw popular culture as the bridge to this psychology, connecting economic laws and proletarian consciousness. By engaging capital in popular arenas such as religion, music, sports, dance, and avant-garde theater, socialists could write, sing, pray, choreograph, and play their way directly into public culture.[29]

These inchoate syntheses of subjectivity and materialism were overdue but shallow. The logical problem of reconciling free actors and material laws was eliminated by redefining freedom to include necessity, rather than replacing materialism with a philosophy that wove cognition into the fabric of history. What happens if thoughtful workers choose passivity, or act at the wrong moment? Should historical materialists accede to popular opinion, or lose faith in the masses? When the CP chose the latter, Boudin, always an unrepentant materialist, philosophically had nowhere to go. In order to remain a democrat *and* a materialist he relinquished the core of his Marxism, working-class consciousness, and in 1924 became a Kautskyist.[30] The German materialist Kautsky felt that socialism was inevitable, so workers needn't be coerced, even by a vanguard party, to rebel prematurely. In a similar fix, Fraina declared that subjectivity "must be directed" away from "proletarian suicide."[31] Directed, of course, by the Leninist Party, which Fraina joined in 1919. The contradiction between Fraina's subjectivism and materialism, which had also proved Boudin's undoing, festered during the 1920s and '30s. A disillusioned Fraina abandoned Marxism altogether in 1942.[32] These attempts to subjectively revitalize Marxism had both failed.

The *theoretical* synthesis of Marxism and subjectivism had indeed failed dismally. Harrington later realized that Marxism first had to be philosophically redefined, which the materialists Boudin and Fraina couldn't do. Orthodoxy reduced subjectivity to economics, so materialist dreams of reconstituting reflexivity were doomed from the beginning. The lesson for Marxists was simple: the non-theoretical project of raising proletarian consciousness solved the logical dilemma by avoiding it, and in the long run would fail. But it also preserved Marxian credentials and provided an institutional base to work from. Given the immature state of radical theorizing in the U.S., anti-intellectualism was theoretically justifiable.

Sidney Hook was a notable exception who proved the rule. A brilliant intellectual who had studied phenomenology in Germany, a student of John Dewey, and for many years an engaged Marxian radical, Hook anchored his Marxian critique in the pragmatist claim that science, "naturalistic, historical and empirical throughout," is objectively true, regardless of personal values or society's class character.[33] Authentic Marxism therefore was not a science. By transforming Marxism from a critical theory of social change into an objective science, orthodoxy had erased consciousness from history.

"Neither a science nor a myth," Hook explained, Marxism was actually "a realistic method of social action" that directed us to act reflectively rather than wait for history's laws to unfold mechanically.[34] Consciousness was the foundation of authentic Marxism, and social change, not knowledge, its goal. Hook thus accepted most of Marx's economic theories *not* because they were scientific, but because they expressed theoretically workers' practical interests and activities. In Hook's view, workers had to make the appropriate value judgments themselves and take the personal risks of rebelling. Science could verify the accuracy of these judgments and the actual utility of worker activism, but could not, however, determine the beliefs or actions of reflective workers.

Hook's *Toward the Understanding of Karl Marx* (1933) was the most important work of philosophy yet produced on the U.S. left. It took the first step of deconstructing materialism, opening the door to a meaningful theory of subjectivity. But rather than entering a room filled with working class inauthenticity, Party organization and tactics, and post-revolutionary socialism, Hook suddenly stopped. Possibly the Marxian establishment's unusually hostile review of *Toward the Understanding of Karl Marx* was to blame or perhaps the left's warped, factionalized world disengaged Hook's razor-sharp intellect. Certainly, the irrepressible professor simply could not tolerate Stalinism. In any case, after 1936 Hook withdrew into Dewey's pragmatism.[35] Like Fraina, Hook equated materialism, Marxism, and totalitarianism, and urged scientists and democrats to reject them all. Capitalism, despite its problems, permitted empirical experimentation, and hence encouraged scholars to verify the consequences of social action. For Hook, science became the prerequisite of democracy. Marxism had created closed societies where dogma replaced science, and the democratic spirit was purged by Party bureaucrats. The task of philosophically defining an open, contentious, egalitarian society, which Hook had enthusiastically tackled as a Marxist, was left to the Europeans and, later, to Harrington.

DIALECTICS

The ill-fated Marxian underground was handcuffed by cultural biases, especially the unconditional U.S. faith in empirical science. Philosophical presuppositions such as our autonomous, non-social human nature, the separation of fact and value, and the non-political quality of science, all justified empirical social science but weren't empirically verifiable. Harrington concluded that the vaunted "neutrality" and "impartiality" of empirical scientists disguised bourgeois values, embodied the material interests of entrepreneurs, and rationalized capitalist institutions. "Every account of society involves a vantage point," said Harrington, "a choice of the relevant data, definitions which are given and not taken."[36] The bourgeois assumptions of empirical science determined what questions scientists asked and what variables were relevant. The notion that data could be value-free was false.

Empiricism, for Harrington, transformed a dynamic, fluid, complex social structure into snap-shots that froze the status quo. Facts, he noted, were mistakenly conferred "the dignity and solidity of a natural force."[37] Life's organic wholeness was shattered into disconnected parts, with each really an internally related concept rather than a simple fact.

Harrington believed that Marx also viewed life in this non-empirical manner. One therefore had to know the totality of Marxism to understand the meaning of any single Marxian text, which was a problem in America's hyper-empirical culture. Isolated passages and texts, mistakenly pulled from the totality, gave readers the linear causes they wanted, and then were inflated into economic science. Even "underground" Marxists who were disillusioned with orthodoxy wanted to reduce life to a single factor.

Harrington reclaimed the dialectical soul of Marxism. Empiricists believed that consciousness, like a moving billiard ball, reacted predictably to perceived external objects. Rather than beginning with one small, isolated fragment and then building empirical connections, Harrington began with the whole and then clarified how each part worked. Where empirical science presumed that life's fragments were independent and self-enclosed, Harrington depicted life's irreducible complexity. Objects were thus linked to, and defined by, the processes that created them, and the broader environments that conditioned these processes. Each separate item transcended the immediate empirical world because it was bound to history, to other parts and processes, and to the future. Dialecticians acknowledged the reality and importance of concrete specifics, and empiricists recognized interrelationships. It was a question of emphasis, that is, how to best organize reality and communicate knowledge. To Harrington, dialectics reflected the actual quality of social life ("an organic whole filled with internal movement;" "a rich totality of many determinations and relationships"[38]), and thus explained the origin and meaning of social facts. Empiricism was valid and useful primarily for natural scientists and technicians but didn't convey the richness of everyday life. As social science, it manufactured mundane explanations of thoughtless behavior.

In his early writings, Marx had defined the human species as free *and* determined, creators *and* creatures of circumstance. Subject and object, actor and world, spirit and matter, all interpenetrated. Perceptions were thus part of complex wholes that embodied biography, social history, international relations, socio-economic structures, values, and everyday activities. Each defined, and was defined by, the whole. Harrington called this "spiritual materialism," and distinguished it from both idealism and materialism.[39] Spiritual materialism combined Marx's youthful ideals with his mature economic writings, and viewed the isolated social fact dialectically, as an artificial and profoundly conservative product of the status quo that obscures rather than illuminates interrelationships which might incite change. Dialectics penetrated these empirical deceptions by rebuilding the fact's web of relationships. Empirical science thus sustained the bourgeois world that created it, whereas dialectics depicted the real experiences of workers in capitalism.

In short, Harrington claimed Marx defined society as a dynamic totality where separate parts interpenetrated. Society was thus fractured into levels ranging from the psychological to the communal, each stuffed with a totality of intersecting parts. Although Marx's "magnificent insight" into the conflict between means and relationships of production is, to Harrington, "one of the most usable truths of the twentieth, and the twenty-first, centuries,"[40] the economic base where this contradiction originated is forever linked to social, political, and cultural events. What Marx called "economics" was actually consciousness, social classes, public culture, and human artifacts, as well as means and relations of commodity production. In other words, Marx's mode of production is our mode of life.

Since productive relationships govern how we eat, drink, and find shelter, for Harrington they were primordial, "providing a society," in his words, "with its pervasive lighting, its special atmosphere . . . . [They] do not infuse every aspect of cultural and political life with a single underlying content. They bathe the superstructure in that pervasive light, they touch and color the totality, but that leaves room for relative autonomies. Art, science, and politics all have their own rhythms."[41] Since the survival of our species depended on means and relations of commodity production, Harrington believed they played the unique role of allocating rank and influence to other kinds of production. Empirical inquiry explained precisely how each form of production impacted the totality. In other words, art, science, politics, sports, and economics each had its own history and influenced society in its own special way.

Influenced by Louis Althusser, Harrington claimed that the way a society organizes its relations of production will explain the roles played by non-economic factors.[42] In ancient Greece politics was decisive, whereas in the Middle Ages religion played the central role. Only in capitalism does economics as such play the leading social part in its own name. Here, it enjoys the unusual role of being both determinant and dominant, primarily because only capitalism expresses human relationships exclusively in a cash form. "Within the historically specific context of capitalist society," Harrington wrote in *The Twilight of Capitalism*, "social relationships are thus necessarily turned into things. Everything, even honor itself, is said to have its price."[43] Since Marx focused on nineteenth-century capitalism, economics—narrowly defined as commodity production—was decisive. Had he studied feudalism it would not have been as important. Harrington, focusing on the twentieth century, believed modern capitalism had evolved to the point where an expanding state, not economics, was the trip-wire for progressive change.

Marx's seminal economic theories thus provide "not a pass key to the ages, but a paradigm that can help us understand the tumultuous transition in which we live."[44] They are pivotal in capitalism, but less relevant to the pre-capitalist past and the post-capitalist future. Orthodoxy mistakenly universalized the unique case of capitalism.[45] Economics *is* basic to every society, but it doesn't function identically everywhere. It is primary or predominant or determining, even when subordinate to other factors, because it decides which will dominate. And economics is always in a fluid, organic whole. It is defined by what it isn't.

"Economics," then, does not really exist. Nor, for that matter, do sociology or politics. The so-called disciplines are contrived paths into the multidimensional whole, and represent their creators' interests. The academic definition of economics, according to classical political economy, arose when "civil society" became autonomous, at the moment when private pursuit of wealth became honorable and fashionable. Economics explained and justified this world by establishing scientific laws of the marketplace that also sanctified commerce.

This same dynamic is at work within a discipline. Economics, for example, means different things to different people. If we concentrate initially on the buying of labor power and material, then on how these are consumed in production, and finally on how commodities are sold for a profit, we highlight capitalist exploitation. If instead we emphasize how labor power and material are consumed in production, then examine how commodities are profitably sold, and finally see how profits are used to buy labor power and material, we accent capitalist economic growth. Each separate economic factor is linked to others, but cannot be reduced to them. Each also impacts the process in its own special way, just as the economic process impacts the totality. "Even a single social fact, then, exists in a web of relationships," Harrington pointed out. "In the organic whole there are relative autonomies, different historical times."[46]

Any explanation of social life is partial and one-sided, illustrating some phenomena and occluding others. Economism clarifies objective economic structures, even as it conceals race, gender, and religion. Subjectivism accents ideas and decision-making but obscures pertinent structures. By focusing on the state, moreover, the panorama of relevant non-political factors is lost. The subject matter of each explanation, in short, is internally related to what it ignores. Conversely, each explanation illustrates one dimension of social life better than others, so distortion is unavoidable. Therefore, hypotheses are selected, not based on their correctness—they all distort—but on how well they isolate the desired knowledge.

Consciousness and ideas aren't reducible to anything else, including economics, but they also are inseparably linked to the whole. Thinking is therefore affected by production. Capitalism glorifies the cash value of human relationships, turning people into things. It makes us ignore linkages and believe in independent actors and disciplines, and it obscures precognitive assumptions such as an item's worth being equal to its monetary value, or a person's worth depending on his status and salary. It tells us that monetary value is governed by invisible laws, and that economics stands outside society and history. Capitalism, in short, conceals its prejudices. Dialectics, however, clarifies our assumptions, "that often elusive lighting," Harrington commented, "that is the setting for the crudest of facts."[47] It liberates humanity from unquestioned, uncontrollable abstractions that often make life miserable.

Economism and reformism were equally misconceived: one reifying economics, the other politics. Both, for Harrington, are "one-sided categories which abstract from the living totality."[48] Harrington conceded that Marx viewed "the organic whole of capitalism from the perspective of its economic relationships,"[49] and orthodoxy clearly explained capitalist exploitation. "There was, and is, a class struggle in the United States," allowed Harrington, "and indeed it has been bloodier and more violent here than in Europe."[50] However orthodoxy also trivialized everything but class and sanctioned dictatorship. Reformists discerned the state's crucial role in stabilizing capitalism, but ignored workplace injustice. Meaningful activism, for Harrington, was part of a broad campaign of economic, political, and cultural emancipation, and had to be dialectically linked to the real world. By severing this link, the Communist and Socialist Parties became reductionist.

Capitalism survives because it facilitates commodity production and distribution at today's level of economic development.[51] But reflective workers were tending the plows and looms, and selling commodities. Their commitment was provisional, related to, not dependent on, existing production. Social change requires that objective and subjective conditions be at complementary levels, and neither is epiphenomenal. Since socialism is based on cooperative, not competitive, production and distribution, it depends on there being enough material goods, when equally distributed, to keep everyone living comfortably. No amount of wishful thinking cancels the need for material abundance. Conversely, capitalist wealth, like a cocked gun, realizes its socialist potential only when citizens are willing to pull the revolutionary trigger.

Harrington believed the marriage of material wealth to revolutionary commitment was still unsettled in the U.S. Americans didn't understand socialism, or see the socialist possibilities inherent in capitalism. Socialists often assumed that poverty, suffering, and especially struggle would change this. Harrington, however, thought socialist consciousness would grow as conditions improved because a rising standard of living, "that mood of rising enjoyments and declining satisfactions,"[52] outperformed poverty in marshalling workers into a better future. Even Marx, Harrington noted, after his "romantic and unrealistic"[53] remark that from extreme degradation will come total emancipation, finally realized that, for socialists, rising wealth was more effective than deepening poverty.[54] Thus, restraint and moderation were Harrington's revolutionary slogans. As the welfare state incrementally raised living standards, it also raised worker subjectivity to the level of capitalism's objective productive capacity. Eventually people would want as well as need socialism.

By eliminating objective laws, Harrington's open dialectic also purged certainty, and we now know that it is much easier to build a socialist economy than to create socialist culture. History is unpredictable, even for Marxists, and workers can as easily turn right as left. On the other hand, with capitalist welfare states approaching bankruptcy, some kind of fundamental change seems likely. Harrington's political theory explains this crisis dialectically and points us toward a democratic socialist future. No one knows when or even if we will arrive.

A MARXIAN PARADIGM

Harrington framed what he called a "Marxian paradigm" for guiding social inquiry. It was not a testable model, like a theory in natural science, but merely suggested that Marxian questions and answers existed, and they could help us understand and improve society. Academic sociology, especially functionalism and systems theory, already incorporated several Marxian insights. Sociologists, however, had substituted empirical for dialectical presuppositions, and mostly disregarded Marx. In contrast, Harrington's eight-step paradigm was derived from Marx's critique of capitalism.

The first step is Marxism criticizing its own definitions and data. Marxian facts are selected because they are relevant and important; each fact's meaning is class-based; and common-sense values and vocabularies often conceal as well as communicate, and always rationalize the status quo.

"Marxism," for Harrington, "is a 'critical' theory in the Kantian sense of the term—it probes its own concepts and terms as well as those of its opponents; it seeks to articulate the unstated assumptions of an era and regards their unstatedness as eloquent clues to what a society really means."[55]

Second, Marxism is rigorously scientific but not value-free, because social analysis is always biased. A ruling class, for instance, creates sciences that reinforce the status quo, whereas subaltern classes choose subversive methods. Sciences, moreover, are either empirical or philosophical, depending on the sponsor's needs. Empirical science is thus correct only from the dominant class's viewpoint, even though empirical evidence can also confirm the interests of any group and the theories of any science. Workers in capitalism are culturally "sold" on alienation, in part at least through their belief in empiricism. Harrington felt that some intellectuals and workers can penetrate deceptions and articulate new, more progressive ideas. These survive if reflective workers accept them, perhaps during a crisis when old recipes fail. "In effect, then," Harrington concluded, "the Marxist paradigm argues that all theorists who do not make their social class perspective explicit to themselves and to their audience are operating on the basis of the unstated premises of their time and place."[56] Not all Marxists are correct or even intelligent, but a Marxian paradigm is linked to proletarian interests and employs any efficacious method, empirical or non-empirical.

Third, Marxists believe that behavior is consciously chosen, and also limited by what can be done at a given moment in historic time. "There is," for Harrington, "a dialectic of necessity and freedom, and it constantly leads to consequences influenced by the given circumstances at least as much as by the individual actors."[57] Harrington's paradigm is a dialectical net that captures praxis and objective conditions. It isn't materialist or idealist, and does not advocate determinism or absolute freedom, presuming instead that freedom is internally related to the world's objective limits. This blend of freedom and necessity, whose details vary in space and time, makes history fascinating and, ultimately, unpredictable.

Fourth, in Marxism, history is indeterminate, but not haphazard. Economic relationships allow humanity to materially reproduce. Societies ostensibly can exist without a state, art, sports, laws, music, or even explicit mores, but never without economics. Thus, economics is central to Harrington's paradigm. Even economics, however, is infused with subjectivity, and embodies the totality of the experienced world. It cannot determine culture because it is internally related to it, but because it is primordial (both chronologically and in terms of importance), economics decides the relative significance of other relationships, thus defining and embodying the social world. Economics choreographs social life, determining which groups dance the lead and what steps work best.

Fifth, Marxists believe that contradictions affect history, even though no universal contradiction exists. Empirical inquiry determines how contradictions influence specific societies during specific periods of upheaval. Marx showed that capitalism is structurally contradictory, or in Harrington's words, "that the conflict between its increasingly social way of working together and its still private mode of decision-making and allocation of resources is a basic fact of life of the system, the origin of its 'law of motion'."[58] In non-capitalist societies—for example, nineteenth-century India—contradictions were perhaps less significant. But in twentieth-century America, Harrington felt that contradictions, prudently used and factually verified, help explain social change.

The economy takes social form in the shape of classes. Class is essential for Marxian analysis, and comprises the sixth step in Harrington's paradigm. In capitalism, classes coalesce around a production process where workers sell labor power to entrepreneurs. Marx concluded that capitalism creates two opposing classes, workers and capitalists, whose conflicts eventually cripple production and transform the entire system. Even Marx, however, couldn't explain the many intermediate groups that identified with neither workers nor capitalists. An empirically-based class theory must aid socialists in understanding and changing capitalism.

Class formation is affected by technology, the seventh step of Harrington's paradigm, but technology is internally related to a society's level of intellectual development. In practice, specific socio-economic formations merely use technology selfishly, so it is important, but not determining. By linking technology to other social structures, Marxists learn its system-maintaining and system-changing functions.

Crisis is the eighth and final step. Marx showed that the possibility of crisis is inherent in capitalist structures. By expanding productive capacity beyond the market's ability to absorb production, capitalists create all the well-known symptoms of a contracting economy. This kind of crisis occurs only sporadically, and cycles of recovery and growth usually alternate with crises. Marxists must explain why crises appear at specific moments and not at others—why, in other words, the possibilities of crisis are only realized in certain contingencies. This, wrote Harrington, "requires scrupulous attention to the actual workings of the system at a given moment, not generalities about its structural . . . iniquity."[59] Capitalists usually ignore crisis altogether, and communists reduce everything in capitalism to a simplistic, built-in tendency toward crisis. Harrington wanted to clarify crises' possibilities, symptoms, and causes, and thus help frame an effective working class political program.

Harrington's dialectical method, crystallized in this paradigm, blends subjects normally treated as independent variables. It reflects everyday living, which capitalists and communists falsely reduced to one primary factor. Harrington credited Marx with uncovering the dialectical quality of experience, and blamed capitalism for its inscrutability. Inspired by America's Marxian underground, Harrington directly engaged capitalists with a systematic, thoughtful, and feasible methodology that endorsed worker emancipation. Ignored by most Americans, its real value is nonetheless joined to the knowledge and worker benefits it produces.

3

THE OTHER MICHAEL HARRINGTON

HARRINGTON'S DIALECTIC BYPASSED the lifeless Old Left and gave New Leftists some food for thought. *Socialism* and *The Twilight of Capitalism*, the most theoretical of Harrington's early and middle works, were completed by 1976, twenty-five years into his radicalism and over a decade after he began to seriously publish. His major publications during these years—*The Other America* (1962), *The Accidental Century* (1965), and *Toward a Democratic Left* (1968), as well as dozens of political and literary articles—illustrate the ambivalence of a socialist who had soured on both the Old and New Lefts, and hadn't yet fully discovered his own voice.

Harrington's popular and influential studies of American poverty[1] convinced a dreamy nation to finally notice impoverishment, revealing it to be more hideous and widespread than anyone had imagined. Keynesianism was no longer the cure for the hole in the heart of U.S. capitalism, but economism did not work either because U.S. workers, unlike those in Europe, were individualists. If an exceptional U.S. culture made organizing workers difficult, it also proffered surprising opportunities. In the late

1960s and early '70s Harrington handed Old Leftism to the historians by redefining the link between base and superstructure.

POVERTY THEN AND NOW

Harrington's one and only commercial success was *The Other America: Poverty in the United States*, published during the Kennedy era in 1962.[2] He was always embarrassed by its remarkable performance, particularly because the text mentions neither Karl Marx nor the word "socialism." He had, moreover, published many articles during the 1950s and early 1960s in popular journals such as *Commonweal*, the *New Republic*, and the *Nation*, and none were explicitly socialist. Aside from suggesting that not all Marxists were vulgar determinists and that America needed a more radical democratic left,[3] they tackled abstract literary questions, totalitarianism in China and the Soviet Union, poverty, and American unionism. Harrington never explained why, when he was intensely engaged with factions of the democratic left, he hid his full political agenda from the public.

In fairness to Harrington, *The Other America* was never intended as a socialist critique. The bland Eisenhower years had convinced people that mass culture was homogenizing the nation. Peace, economic growth, and a glittering technology were welcome prizes for war-weary Americans. The nation's traditional social cleavages—wealth, prestige, status, race, and ideology—seemed to be disappearing in a frantic rush to get rich and blend in. Poverty and conflict, the argument went, no longer stained the social landscape. Harrington had travelled the length and breadth of America during lecture tours in the 1950s, and knew that these fantasies were "dangerous half-truths."[4] He decided to quantify his experiences with the help of official government statistics and interviews with outcasts who lived a million psychological miles from the beaten tracks of white, middle-class, suburban America. Harrington wanted to deflate the nation's complacency by "evoking" poverty, suggesting, in his words, "its look, its smell, its often twisted spirit, with just a few rudimentary references to the underlying trends." In the "Father Knows Best" mentality of the 1950s, Harrington realized that "the American people are much more receptive to dramatic moments and vignettes than to accounts of macroeconomic structures."[5] The result was *The Other America*.

The book's title referred, in Harrington's own words, "to what was negative in the economy and social structure."[6] Anything "negative" during these years would likely have bombed commercially, so *The Other America*'s success was actually serendipitous. "It could very easily have been the shot heard in the immediate vicinity," Harrington confessed in 1988, "with nice little reviews" in mainstream journals.[7] But Dwight

THE OTHER MICHAEL HARRINGTON

52

Macdonald published a glowing 30-page review in the *New Yorker*, and the floodgates opened.

It was a book for the times. Liberal intellectuals used it to catalyze public aid programs. Tired of eating goldfish and piling into Volkswagons, but still unable to locate Vietnam on a map, students stumbled on a cause worth fighting for. The book is said to have inspired President Kennedy to initiate the reforms that became the War on Poverty. Martin Luther King, Jr. once laughingly told Harrington, "You know, we didn't know we were poor until we read your book."[8] The *Boston Globe* editorialized in 1987 that medicaid and medicare, food stamps, and expanded social-security benefits are all "directly traceable" to *The Other America*.

The book's incredible popularity shocked Harrington: "I can remember sitting in a trattoria in Rome and an American—a minister on vacation—coming up to me to shake my hand. And I wondered what the heck it was all about."[9] His life was permanently altered. "I was thirty-five when it came out," he remembered in 1988, "and up until then I'd never made any money in my life. Earning a living as a writer in this country sucks, as my son would say. But all of a sudden there were all these lecture invitations, and they paid quite well, and it freed me to write my subsequent books."[10] Harrington resisted mining the journalistic vein opened by *The Other America*, although he wouldn't have been shocked if *The New American Poverty*, published twenty-two years later by "the author of *The Other America*" and stuffed with facts and figures about poverty during the Reagan era, had refilled the coffers.

The Other America conveyed the pain that poor Americans quietly endured every day. Poverty had been merely a statistic, a crossing beyond which an uncertain number of people were in some vague way rendered invisible. Harrington added flesh and feelings, turning an abstraction into a painful experience. He took readers into ghettoes, barrios, dilapidated apartments, empty hamlets, sweatshops, and migrant shelters, exposing a nation of fifty million suffering people that lived, largely unnoticed, down the road a ways. The message and style were accessible to the target population of normal, decent, compassionate people living average lives in isolated middle class neighborhoods.

If poverty was merely an income level, as the government suggested, than poor people could only blame themselves because they were losers where others had won; they simply didn't play hard enough to compete successfully. Harrington showed how the descent into poverty was often uncontrollable, and how poverty created disadvantages that inhibited and demoralized the players. In such conditions anyone would lose. Poverty, then, was a way of life that slowly destroyed those in its grip, and all were potential victims.

Poverty, Harrington concluded, was a culture that began when income fell to a point—what British economist Peter Townsend called the "threshold of deprivation"[11]—below which one could not partake of socially sanctioned activities, customs, and diets, and also could not purchase the minimal levels of health, housing, food, and education that, in Harrington's words, "our present stage of scientific knowledge specifies as necessary for life as it is now lived in the U.S." Psychologically, the impoverished, Harrington felt, were "those whose place in society is such that they are internal exiles who, almost inevitably, develop attitudes of defeat and pessimism and who are therefore excluded from taking advantage of new opportunities."[12] They were often unmotivated, depressed, and isolated, which only worsened an already bleak situation. Poverty was thus a constellation of miseries that comprised an indissoluble whole. "Being poor is not one aspect of a person's life in this country," Harrington pointed out, "it is his life . . . . These are people who lack education and skill, who have bad health, poor housing, low levels of aspiration and high levels of mental distress. They are, in the language of sociology, 'multiproblem' families. Each disability is the more intense because it exists within a web of disabilities. And if one problem is solved, and the others are left constant, there is little gain."[13]

Highly visible anti-poverty public-relations campaigns that didn't supply jobs, food, housing, education, and hope were useless. Poverty had to be attacked head-on, with enough material resources and new ideas to emancipate fifty million victims. Welfare-state capitalism, Harrington suggested, was not the answer. New Deal liberals wanted to help but didn't really understand the problem, and they were tied to big business. Poor people thus received meager benefits and weren't ready when opportunity finally knocked. "The parents are anxious for the children to go to work," observed Harrington; "the pupils are pent up, waiting for the moment when their education has complied with the law."[14]

The Other America had such dramatic impact that Harrington was solicited by Sargent Shriver to help shape the nation's response. Through the Economic Opportunity Act, passed in 1964 when unemployment was declining and prices were stable, Lyndon Johnson launched the nation's "official" War on Poverty. This act set in motion community action programs, VISTA (the domestic Peace Corps), and legal-aid programs. Politicians believed that prudent fiscal and monetary policies, and ambitious social programs, would skim some of America's expanding wealth to rescue the poor, and also cure the economy of recessions. During the Kennedy and Johnson administrations, Congress created the Occupational Safety and Health Administration, the Equal Employment Opportunity Commission, the Consumer Product Safety Commission, and the

Environmental Protection Administration, and also passed the Equal Rights Amendment. Johnson's Great Society program created more than 200 new social and economic programs, most with a strong urban emphasis. Between 1960 and 1970, federal aid to the states increased from $7 billion to $24 billion, and the percentage of federal funds going to urban areas increased from 55 percent to 70 percent. Federal programs were also begun to help the poor and provide added security for others. In 1965 alone, Congress passed legislation designed to provide medical care for the elderly, the disabled, and the indigent, through medicare and medicaid; offer aid to public schools and loans to college students; supplement rents for poor people; establish grants, loans, and training programs for health professionals; and support development efforts in Appalachia. The federal Job Corps and food stamps programs helped sustain many who had fallen on hard times, while Head Start redistributed educational opportunities for children in poor neighborhoods.

Idealistic students—many after reading *The Other America*—moved from campuses to slum neighborhoods to help wipe out poverty by struggling for black equality and empowering local communities. Organizations like the Student Non-violent Coordinating Committee (SNCC) and the Students for a Democratic Society mobilized urban neighborhoods in many of the nation's large cities. Black activists in SNCC were more effective than whites because they had stronger bonds with black communities. In contrast, activist whites, who often came from privileged backgrounds, could mobilize on specific issues but lacked shared interests with working-class whites. Together, however, blacks and whites catalyzed grassroots support for the Civil Rights Act of 1964, which gave the attorney general the power to file desegregation lawsuits and prohibited federal aid to school districts that remained segregated. The Voting Rights Act was passed a year later, enabling federal officials to register voters and to suspend literacy tests in areas where less than 50 percent of the voting-age population was registered for, or had voted in, the 1964 national election. And the Community Action Programs actually brought political experience and leadership skills to unprecedented numbers of black and other minority residents of poor and isolated communities.

Poverty, however, stubbornly refused to go away, especially in Northern ghettoes where riots often broke out. The left lacked a coherent, rational program and attractive leaders, and the liberal center was pledged to helping the poor, not eliminating poverty. When the civil rights and community empowerment struggles failed to wipe out entrenched poverty, even amidst a torrent of meliorative social programs, student activism exploded around the nation. Activists wanted their wealthy universities to materially upgrade nearby communities and the nation; to upset business as usual and destroy what Mario Savio—the Berkeley activist and leader of the Free Speech Movement—called the "bureaucratic manipulation of life"; to help dismantle authority structures; and to advocate a fair redistribution of the nation's wealth. Their frenzy was inflamed by the escalating Vietnam War and the emerging conviction that America contained a permanently impoverished class which was disproportionately black.

Meanwhile, many members of the white middle class and the ethnic working class became less tolerant during the late 1960s and early '70s. Never really comfortable with student activists, they were disgusted that New Leftists, after 1969, had apparently been taken over—on several campuses at least—by left-wing extremists and black-power advocates, and some pined for order, traditional values, and Republican politicians. Taxes, as well as the cost of living, were rising faster than their incomes, and impoverished welfare recipients appeared to be ungrateful. The word "poor," which had connoted sympathy, compassion, and care, was supplanted gradually by the word "welfare," suggesting that poor people were lazy and cheating. The Republican Nixon administration came to power in 1968 on a conservative platform that appealed to these disgruntled Americans.

When the Watergate scandal drove Republicans from the White House in 1976, an "unofficial" war on poverty was initiated by the new Democratic Carter administration during a time of chronic high unemployment and inflation, but it was crippled by the financially strapped middle class, who chafed at rising taxes. Government officials simultaneously gave up and declared victory. A 1977 Congressional Budget Office (CBO) study expanded net income to include in-kind goods and services.[15] Overnight, the CBO eliminated 3,628,000 from the poverty roles, and doubled the rate at which poor people entered the middle class.

Harrington noticed the incongruities. Why did government count non-income for poverty and not for personal taxes? Why did it ignore the undocumented poor? Did it know that the single largest portion of in-kind income went to elderly people waiting to die in nursing homes? And why, fifteen years after *The Other America*, did officials insist that poverty began when income dropped one cent below some arbitrary statistical floor? Harrington estimated that the number of impoverished Americans in the 1970s was about what it was in 1962.[16] Why did poverty persist? Why did sincere, motivated, educated activists fail so dismally? Why was an angry middle class being economically squeezed? Harrington, believing the New Left had to shoulder some but not all of the blame, decided to revisit the problem of poverty in a new book, *The New American Poverty* (1984).

"The poor are still there,"[17] declared Harrington. Inflation, recession, high unemployment, a widening income gap, and suburbanization had even made matters worse. Americans once believed that the War on Poverty was a patriotic national mission, but by the early 1980s a humbled nation had lost its will and its generosity. Progressive middle classes, the backbone of Kennedy's reformism, faced unemployment and huge debts. Compassion had become unaffordable, and threatened people needed to understand, not just feel, the economic crisis, so Harrington now accented structures rather than images.

"There is no such thing as poverty," Harrington decided, "there are poverties."[18] Nineteenth-century poverty existed in a corporate-dominated, early capitalist economy flexing its productive muscles in an unregulated market, whereas depression poverty represented capitalism's internal contradictions. Overproduction had fueled a cycle of growth, crisis, and contraction that convulsed the economy and jolted public officials into bailing out unemployed workers. Post-World War II poverty, until about 1970, was anomalous in a robust welfare state that employed fiscal and monetary regulations, and safety-net social services. It hid in depressed pockets of an otherwise affluent society, and led to meliorative programs that also expanded domestic markets.

Until the early 1970s, poverty could usually be fixed by fine-tuning the system. What Harrington called the "New American Poverty" was different. It was a product of processes that couldn't easily be altered, and prefigured an economic crisis the likes of which Americans had never before faced.

First, a large number of wealthy multinational corporations had internationalized capital and prioritized world trade. National economic health was now linked to a world market dominated by large, borderless, acquisitive enterprises.

This transformed the division of labor worldwide as well as in America, because these multinationals invested in the most profitable markets. Advanced capitalist nations supplied them educated workers commanding high salaries for skilled work, and also poor, undereducated but trainable labor. Industrializing nations, on the other hand, were overstocked with semi-skilled workers whose moderate living standards and salaries were very attractive. Skilled, high paying jobs thus remained in America, and so did unskilled, menial, and service jobs. Semi-skilled industrial work had stimulated Western economic expansion for decades, and now it relocated to what scholars called the semi-periphery: industrializing third-world nations that were near economic take-off, but not yet airborne. The U.S. was left with educated, trained workers at the top, an unstable middle with steadily declining wages, and a growing number of unskilled, marginalized people.

The total number of new jobs rose during the 1980s, but most (almost 65 percent) were in the service and retail sectors, with low wages and few benefits. The average weekly wage in manufacturing in 1983 was $478.98; in services, $238.71; and in retail, $171.05.[19] The annual retail wage was actually below the official poverty line for a family of four, and the service sector was barely above that. Women and minorities made up a disproportionate share of this nearly impoverished workforce. The total of desirable high-tech jobs increased somewhat, but at a rate slower than the increase in service jobs, and less than the loss in blue-collar manufacturing. The percentage of employed blue-collar workers dropped from 35.3 percent of the workforce in 1970, to 29.7 percent a decade later.

With the addition of increasing automation, this situation becomes volatile. Automation closed obsolete factories in the U.S., and substantially cut the number of semi-skilled, mid-level factory jobs. The pool of workers competing for high-tech positions rose, and many were forced into unskilled jobs at salaries lower than those to which they were accustomed. Others remained unemployed. According to government statistics, in 1984, 60.1 percent of workers dismissed since 1980 had found other jobs; 25.5 percent were still unemployed; and 14.4 percent left the labor force. Most re–employed workers took a pay cut. The loss of income thus affected about 59 percent of the more than 5 million workers whose jobs had disappeared. The CBO estimated that about 30 percent of America's manufacturing jobs would be lost in the years from 1984 to 2000. Seven million workers will need to be relocated and retrained, and over 21 million people, including families, will be affected.

Unlike previous poverties, the new poverty formed structures of misery that didn't respond to populist rhetoric or reformism.[20] Despite governments actions, poverty and unemployment continued expanding, the middle class slowly dissolved, inequalities in wealth and income grew, and frightened Americans watched politicians blame it all on the welfare state.

Even America's "labor aristocracy," the traditionally secure upper stratum of labor that includes smokestack industry workers from the heartland, joined the decline. Many were laid off, or anticipated economic disaster for their families if the economy went sour. These were middle class workers ("a sociological contradiction and a psychological fact," Harrington commented, "in a country where the working class exists but cannot say its own name."[21]). They were unionized, disciplined, willing to borrow from relatives or expend savings, and often far too proud even to apply for public assistance. Because most were home-owners, they wouldn't relocate. Virtually none were eligible for medicaid benefits. The economic downturn not only wreaked havoc on them as individuals, it also devastated their communities, where teachers, white-collar workers, lawyers, doctors, and small-business owners were caught in poverty's backlash. The new poverty, Harrington concluded, had entered America's suburban, middle-class neighborhoods. Sleepy, tree-lined streets were jolted by economic trends that once dwelled in ghettos.

Middle-class anxiety may have upped the political ante of poverty, but it didn't improve life for those who had always suffered. A large number of the vagabond poor of the 1950s and early 1960s were non-violent alcoholics who lived in flophouses. They, too, were uprooted from "normal" lives by the new poverty and sent unprepared into a changing world, becoming homeless "street people," or taking up residence in adult homes, single-occupancy hotels, city shelters, or psychiatric wards. Largely uneducated and lacking essential skills, the uprooted were unemployable in an automated, internationalized job market. As a result of this increasing marginalization, they became demoralized and prone to outbreaks of nihilistic violence, often turning cities into zones of random terror.

Blacks who had migrated to the North when Southern agriculture was mechanized in the 1940s and '50s faced a diminishing supply of high-paying blue-collar jobs, due to the concurrent automation of Northern factories. A fraction found secure factory work and entered the middle class, and their educated children improved black communities by working in schools, welfare agencies, and other public-sector employment—the areas hurt most by Reagan-era cutbacks. Most blacks, however, were caught in a spiral of substandard work and unemployment. Even in "good" times, black unemployment was almost twice that of whites, and among black teenagers unemployment was five times the overall rate. Blacks in the steel and auto industries, where lay-offs were heaviest, usually suffered more than whites because often they were hired later. Harrington thus noted that two black Americas existed in 1984: one middle class, fearful, and predictably self-centered; the other unemployed, hopeless, drug-oriented, and violent. Violence has always accompanied poverty and disintegrating neighborhoods, and now it was also being started by retributive blacks realizing that they had been victimized all along by the same kind of irrational violence that whites now feared. Blacks, in short, were marginalized by an automating, internationalizing, polarizing labor market. "There is an economic structure of racism," Harrington concluded, "that will persist even if every white who hates blacks goes through a total conversion .... [I]t is not a state of mind but an occupational hierarchy rooted in history and institutionalized in the labor market."[22]

In the past, immigrants to America were predominantly poor, searching for a path to middle-class respectability. An expanding economy was the safety-valve for simmering ethnic antagonisms, but the safety-valve now was locked shut. New immigration rules raised the number of Latins, Caribbeans, and Asians permitted to enter America. These often uneducated and unskilled immigrants were tossed, with blacks, into the shrivelling job market. Some from backgrounds and cultures that empha-sized economic success, such as Koreans and Indians, managed to succeed. Farms and sweatshops, however, played poor immigrant groups against each other to keep wages low. Thus the prospect of intra-class ethnic and racial violence increased steadily throughout the 1980s.

Women, especially black women, suffered from these new structures of poverty even more than men. With the number of out-of-wedlock and teenage births both skyrocketing, Harrington estimated that the feminine percentage of adult poverty in America had doubled in the years since 1962.[23] Many diverse psychological and cultural factors contributed to what Harrington termed a "feminization of poverty."[24] Unwise gender-related attitudes toward sex, love, parenting, and prestige, for example, contributed to the heavy burden poor, mostly black women now shoul-dered. So did the high concentration of poor working women in a narrow sector of service and retail jobs that paid, on average, 40–60 percent less than comparable, predominantly male jobs. Harrington warned against asking poor women to think and act differently without providing decent food, housing, jobs, and incomes. "If public policy could do so much to make these people what they are," he noted, "it can also unmake the fate it has forced upon them."[25]

The new poverty was thus multifaceted and complex; moreover, the remnants of America's "old" poverty had not disappeared.[26] Rural south-erners, small family farmers, Appalachian coal miners, American Indians, and the elderly all remained on the margins of economic security, with large numbers hopelessly impoverished. These "Other Americans" were once thought to be exceptions to basic social growth trends, minorities living in isolated ghettos who could be saved merely by transferring money from bountiful reserves. Yet even this easily explained kind of poverty couldn't be whipped. Harrington's new poor are not anomalies, but victims of massive structural trends that have transformed the entire society. The very nature of economic growth changed because investment increased the national product without creating enough good jobs: capitalist economic progress had marginalized poor people and corroded the middle class. The awful consequences of automation, internationalization, and job polarization somehow had to be checked, and capitalist structures had failed.

By questioning capitalism, *The New American Poverty* was more sophis-ticated analytically —and more radical—than *The Other America*. But this radical depiction of the deepening economic crisis did not reflect the polit-ical mood of the nation's workers, many of whom were Reaganites, not revolutionaries. Socialists, including Harrington, assumed that widespread impoverishment would drive workers to the left, whereas quite the reverse was taking place. Neither *The New American Poverty* nor *The Other America*, moreover, addressed important questions regarding the nature of social justice in America, or the relative merits of capitalism and socialism.

The New American Poverty, like *The Other America,* depicted the demon poverty that lurked within American capitalism. Harrington's decision to emphasize poverty reflected an Old Left mentality that reduced everything to economics. If in the end, injustice was economic, then capitalism had to change for people to be free, and inevitably unionized workers would effect this change. *The Other America* and *The New American Poverty* subtly communicated this message without inciting red-baiters. Harrington in the 1960s, and later when he focused only on poverty, was a hybrid of Old Leftism: he avoided socialist or even critical rhetoric but accepted socialism's materialist legacy.

Harrington's work on poverty fomented honest concern among many Americans. Its commercial success, however, was deceptive; by hiding its economism, *The Other America* played to a mainstream culture that was individualist but also willing to help others. This sense of community, not nationalizing industry, is really at the core of socialism, but Harrington in the 1960s was still concerned primarily with the nation's economic base. He had not yet discovered that socialism could be popular in America if it were rooted in the public culture, which—at least in good times—celebrated democracy, equality, and community. This public culture, moreover, conditioned working-class behavior more than he realized. Harrington's problem was common among Old Left socialists; it was a holdover from more than a century ago, when U.S. radicals handed the socialist movement to Marxian immigrants who were preoccupied with economics. Even though it didn't work, their materialism was passed down to succeeding generations of socialists and eventually to Harrington, who tactfully disguised it in the 1960s and, as a result, the communalism that makes socialism so attractive also disappeared. As the economy worsened, what people knew best, individualism, turned into selfishness.

Harrington could only surmise that economic crises did not make U.S. workers rebel—Marx's generic proletariat did not exist in the new world. Harrington slowly became more sensitive to the crucial role that uniquely American institutions and values needed to play on the left. This thoroughly empirical insight was driven home by the activists at Port Huron, and a brief look at the history of U.S. socialism reveals its significance.

In the early 1820s, liberal democracy was firmly established in America, external threats to the Republic were dissipated, urbanization and industrialization had begun, and the family farm had become the heart and soul of a thriving economy. With time to spare, America's expanding middle class detected social and economic blemishes. A small number of educated citizens decided to struggle politically to end slavery, enfranchise women, establish state-supported schools, ban alcohol and tobacco, and secure world peace. Within this small group, socialism was born among starry-eyed idealists who decided to build their own settlements.[27] They believed that moral communities of equal citizens, which they called utopias, should be based on ideal values. Unlike reformists, they simply ignored political parties, labor organizations, law, and economics. Here, among the utopians, we discover the first U.S. critique of capitalism. Competitive individualism was condemned as brutalizing and inhuman, and justice was redefined as an organic community of free citizens blissfully living, working, and loving together.

Utopian collectivism influenced several American patriots, including Cornelius Blatchly, Daniel Raymond, Langdon Byllesby, Thomas Skidmore, William Heighton, and William Maclure.[28] These indigenous radicals praised the Declaration of Independence as a noble but unrealized dream. They wanted America to complete its democratic experiment by equalizing property and wealth, and enfranchising the masses.

The first trade unions in America appeared in 1827–28 among workers in the Northeast who fought hard to improve factory conditions, but had little success. In the late 1840s, immigrant German Marxists consolidated the incipient trade union movement and the complexion of union leadership gradually changed, with native radicals losing power to immigrant socialists who were, for the most part, practical and anti-intellectual.[29]

On 7 November 1851, a friend and colleague of Karl Marx named Joseph Weydemeyer landed in America determined to spread scientific socialism among workers. Weydemeyer was a leading Marxian propagandist in the U.S. until his death in 1866, when his associate Friedrich Adolph Sorge, also a German émigré, took over. Both Weydemeyer and Sorge rejected radical utopianism. After the American section of the First International was established in 1869, Sorge, under Marx's direction, purged it of reformists and non-scientific radicals.

When Ferdinand Lassale supporters, who believed the capitalist state would redistribute wealth if pressured politically, arrived in America, they created some turbulence. Lassaleans clashed with orthodox, scientific Marxists, who insisted only unions could change the nation. The former flourished during depressions, when widespread unemployment weakened unions; the latter in full employment, when unions were powerful. Lassaleans believed that trade unionism corrupted the socialist movement by ignoring great numbers of non-unionized citizens. Orthodoxy felt ideological purity would, in the long run, unite American workers. When

Daniel DeLeon took over the Socialist Labor Party (SLP) in 1890, ortho-doxy's victory was assured. Although tactical struggles survived well into the twentieth century, henceforth the organized left unquestioningly accepted materialism and became insulated from native radicals with cul-tural links to U.S. workers.

Some nineteenth-century socialists, known as Fabians, rejected DeLeon and rallied around a new group of utopians led by Laurence Gronlund and Edward Bellamy.[30] Their socialism, like Harrington's, promised a coopera-tive, nationalized economy that equalized wealth and reinforced family-centered, individualist, democratic values. Fabian socialists later split from the SLP and peddled a peaceful, flexible, idealistic socialism aimed primarily at the middle class. Finally, in 1897, Eugene V. Debs, Gronlund's most famous disciple, composed the principles of Social Democracy, which combined socialist idealism and the utopian promise to establish a cooper-ative commmonwealth.

This turn-of-the-century project of joining American ideals to Marxian critique was an anachronism because capitalists shaped cultural and politi-cal values, reinforcing competitive individualism. Even workers with secure jobs were struggling economically, lacked educations, and had little control over public decisions and almost no leisure time. The middle class, on the other hand, was caught up in the American dream of success. Utopian socialists had neither a constituency nor an effective way of communicating their euphoric message. In touch with America's cultural nerve-pulse, they were nonetheless quarantined by economic development.

The utopian left realized that materialism was useless in the U.S., and in this sense was more politically savvy than mainstream Marxists. However these radical utopians ignored the link attaching personal values to public culture. The dislocations caused by America's expanding economy made laborers and the middle class work desperately hard merely to survive. They would choose socialism only if capitalism—boldly reinforced by journals, films, churches, and schools—became obsolete. But this conviction had to follow, not precede, the struggle to improve living conditions. Having aban-doned struggle as indecent and un-American, utopians became irrelevant. Orthodoxy, on the other hand, backed class struggle, but its imported intel-lectual baggage rejected individualism. The indigenous U.S. left was faced with utopian irrelevance and materialist cant, leaving little room to maneu-ver. Like Gronlund, some radicals simply abandoned Marxism altogether. When Debs's reformist workers movement collapsed in 1898, he estab-lished the orthodox Social Democratic Party as a rival to the SLP. Orthodoxy dominated the left because Americans such as Debs had nowhere else to go, but it lost the people and ideas that would be needed in the twentieth century.

Some disillusioned Southerners and Midwesterners established the Populist Party, which aimed to abolish monopolies and special privileges, enfranchise workers and farmers, and nationalize public utilities. Rural Populists and urban Marxists could have fused into a potent anti-corporate coalition.[31] For Marxists, however, Populism's sin was its relevance, what DeLeon called its "petit-bourgeois mentality." Populism stood behind family farms, advocated easy credit, and fought to abolish the gold standard. DeLeon believed that individualism and private property would eventually disappear, and Populism's "curse of gold" theory confused symptom for cause. Instead of blending radical theory and practice, orthodoxy chose to fight a potential ally and remain ideologically pure. It thus moved even further from the mainstream, and Populism wasted a rational foundation for its wrath.

DeLeon's pig-headedness was self-defeating. In 1901, dissatisfied SLP moderates, led by Morris Hillquit and known as "kangaroos," joined with Debs to form the SP, which grew rapidly until 1912. The SP was an open, contentious party that permitted a wide range of tactics, and settled into left and right factions. Leftists favored direct and immediate insurrection, while the right wanted to unionize workers and cooperate with the capitalist state. With DeLeon owning the SLP, and the SP splintered into factions, U.S. Marxism prior to 1919 was preoccupied with tactical questions (economic organizing or political activism, trade unionism or industrial unionism, peaceful or violent action) and riveting personalities (DeLeon, Debs, Hillquit). Materialist to the core,[32] socialists were concerned with getting things done rather than abstract theorizing.

These were the years of socialism's greatest popularity, as the SP cobbled coalitions with farmers, intellectuals, and professionals.[33] But success was short-lived. A widening schism between left and right gradually sapped the SP's internal resolve, as Debs—who had moved left—Boudin, and Fraina ridiculed what they called the social democratic reformism of the Victor Berger and Morris Hillquit–led right. Intellectuals exited the party after 1914 to protest its war policies, and also to support President Wilson. Meanwhile, hundreds of socialists were prosecuted after Espionage Acts were passed in 1917 and 1918, vigilantes harassed socialists and disrupted SP meetings, and rising farm prices and easy credit chased farmers back into mainstream politics. Also, government programs guaranteeing worker safety, the right to organize on the job, and a minimum wage mocked the SP's reformist agenda. And Congressional passage of the Clayton Act and the establishment of the Department of Labor meant that the SP no longer was labor's voice. In brief, inept, factionalized leaders, changing perceptions, and reformist public policies all pricked the SP's ballooning popularity.

SP rolls had declined only fractionally by 1919, but over half of its members were foreigners, compared to 12 percent in 1912.[34] U.S. workers clearly felt excluded from their own party. Fraina, Boudin, and the SP's left wing were expelled in 1919 by the victorious right, and they subsequently helped establish the rigidly orthodox, Moscow-controlled Communist Party (CP) of America.

Decimated by the loss of its left and unable to attract organized labor, the SP became a shadow party, outsmarted and coopted by the CP on the left and the Democratic Party's New Deal on the right. Socialists, meanwhile, jockeyed viciously for control, and Norman Thomas emerged victorious. Thomas's 1940 decision to oppose U.S. war efforts eliminated what little popular support still existed. The SP subsequently spoke out only on specific issues, and emerged after the war as a reformist interest group. Thomas proposed abandoning political activity altogether in 1950, but the motion was defeated by delegates to that year's SP convention. SP factionalism continued sporadically through the 1950s and '60s, and the party dissolved when Harrington exited in 1972. The communist-dominated orthodox left, including its many factions, in 1990 had a total membership of barely 25,000, enough people to fill the end zone of a university arena on a breezy football Saturday in October.

RECOVERING A BURIED PAST

Orthodox Marxism only marginally influenced American history. Even in the 1930s, when the CP was fairly stable and unified, government repression was minimal, the Soviet Union was perceived as a possible anti-fascist ally, and workers experienced economic and social upheaval, orthodoxy was politically impotent everywhere but in scattered immigrant communities and native-born sectors that had special characteristics, such as religious and racial minorities and intellectuals. Although it occasionally influenced the politics and culture of the day, its popular appeal has always been negligible. Harrington needed to get rid of his economistic baggage if the flight to democratic socialism was ever to get off the ground.

Harrington wrote *The Accidental Century* in 1965 to let people know that he was a writer, intellectual, and socialist, not merely a journalist, and he succeeded only too well on all three counts. This sophisticated socialist critique included lengthy essays on Yeats, Mann, Auden, Joyce, Proust, Malraux and Nietzche. It was panned by reviewers expecting something more plebian. In the palace of U.S. public opinion, Harrington's intentions were exposed, and he was permanently dethroned.

During the 1960s some students, intellectuals, and professionals were dropping out of middle-class lifestyles, turning on to drugs and promiscuity, and tuning in to the counterculture. For this large and influential public, mainstream values had vanished but new ones hadn't yet emerged. *The Accidental Century* cited recent economic trends to make the case that Western culture no longer legitimized capitalism. People had become confused and demoralized; their hope had turned into despair, and the future they once eagerly awaited was a nightmare. What made this argument noteworthy was the way Harrington related culture to working-class behavior.

Modern capitalist production, Harrington observed, was automated, centralized, and interdependent. To absorb the enormous productivity of highly efficient enterprises, free markets had to be subsidized by public spending for welfare, investment, and purchases. In short, businesses now raised profits by replacing competition with planning. In classical laissez-faire capitalism entrepreneurs obeyed the market's invisible hand, but today highly visible managers and public officials guided, rather than followed, markets.

Harrington once told the conservative Milton Friedman that "There is no serious big businessman in the world who wants government out of the economy. They want government in the economy on their side." Friedman agreed: "You're absolutely right. The businessmen are almost as bad as you intellectuals."[35] Capitalism, Harrington concluded, had been permanently socialized in an unexpected, anti-social manner. "Four years after Ronald Reagan has taken office as President, our society will be more collectivist than it is now, just as it was after the Nixon-Ford Presidency. There are trends loose in the United States and the world which are much more powerful than political ideologies of the Right or the Left."[36]

This entire process, which Harrington later called "unthinking socialization,"[37] was caused by the need to increase short-term profits. Its long-term consequences, however, radically changed everyday life. No longer was it a question of individualism or collectivism, but who—entrepreneurs or workers—controlled and benefitted most from collectivizing. Nor was it a question of whether or not a global economic order existed, but instead, what kind of economic order it should be. Would it frustrate or fulfill the wishes of nations and people? A revolution had taken place, yet without "conscious revolutionists" to guide it, and Harrington called it an "accidental revolution."[38] Created by greed and technology, it established a new kind of collectivism that centralized and planned from the top down, making businessmen even more powerful than before. Capitalist liberty was torpedoed by capitalist production, and people no longer trusted public rhetoric. The conflict between the free-market image and the collectivist reality embodied the essential dilemma of modern culture.

Marx was correct: capitalism could not keep its productive capacity within the system's basic values. But instead of rebelling, people became more conservative, confusing symptoms such as expanding public bureaucracies with the structural malady. Each dazzling new commodity blurred the larger, darker picture of capitalism, and people hopelessly, compulsively adjusted the anti-social system.[39] Humanity had unthinkingly traded the promise of a better future for some electronic toys. "The West no longer senses either a City of God or of man in the middle or long distance" Harrington mourned. "It has lost its utopia to come rather than its golden age that was . . . . The present decadence is the corruption of a dream rather than of a reality."[40]

Capitalism was polluted by its own economic prowess. As large, automated corporations were privately collectivized for personal profit, oligopoly replaced competition; producers determined prices; federal research programs outspent private businesses; pensions, trusts, and insurance companies invested more than venture capitalists; and bureaucrats replaced risk-taking entrepreneurs. Advertising rationalized and collectivized consumer demand, creating markets to match the most profitable investments. Nonetheless, overproduction made unproductive leisure, once a middle-class sin, an economic necessity. The marketplace was both praised and ignored, and entrepreneurial energy and motivation, which had fueled the system's incredible growth, were guests at their own wake. Corporate collectivism had expropriated capitalism's credo, creating a system that was neither capitalist nor socialist. "In the spiritual name of courageous, inventive, risk-taking individuals," Harrington observed, "bureaucratized corporations, supported and subsidized by governments, were planning in increasing independence of the laws of supply and demand or the judgement of investors."[41]

Harrington then unexpectedly declared that workers were as decadent as capitalists.[42] With their living standards rising, their electoral influence growing, and their proletarian spirit squashed by a brutal Russian dictator, workers simply gave up on utopias, and by mid-century unions had excised all references to class struggle. The postwar democratic left was satisfied with reformism, a mixed economy, and the capitalist welfare state.

Capitalism *and* socialism—in Harrington's words, "faith and antifaith"[43]—decayed as public morality disappeared. People did what they were told and worshipped the status quo, making religion an empty formality and even atheistic humanism an anachronism. Harrington presciently warned that our morally empty culture was now vulnerable to "some fabricated, and fanatic, pseudofaith."[44]

Harrington couldn't explain why materialism had failed. Culture had somehow nullified economics, but he was still not prepared to restate the standard Old Left equation, involving base and superstructure, nor was he certain how to alter working-class behavior or establish socialism other than requesting a proletarian "act of political will."[45] *The Accidental Century* represented the decadence of Harrington's own beliefs. Having lost faith in capitalism and traditional socialism, he no longer had a dream.

The passage from decadence to dialectics brought the sticky problem of inauthenticity. With capitalist production so clearly outdated, why didn't workers rebel, as socialists expected? Harrington came home to America for the answer in the 1960s and early 1970s, examining real-life proletarian experiences to see whether, and why, U.S. workers were anti-socialist.

His suspicion that something unique, or exceptional, in the nation's superstructure hindered proletarianization was not a particularly original insight. Historians had already noted socialism's failure in America, and their "exceptionalism" debate offered several explanations,[46] some of which Harrington dusted off for further development.

Harrington mentioned the sectarianism of leftist parties in the U.S., which were controlled by European émigrés unfamiliar with American culture.[47] They gambled for immediate victory by making the union movement into something it couldn't be: a revolutionary vanguard. When they failed, their bickering destroyed whatever credibility radicalism still had. Harrington also observed a constellation of indigenous traits that inhibited class identification among Americans:[48] the absence of a feudal legacy, the presence of a frontier myth, individualism, the availability of cheap land, class mobility, a relatively high standard of living, immigrant ethnicity, racism, and universal male suffrage. Werner Sombart and Selig Perlman, and others as well,[49] had persuasively argued that U.S. workers had opportunities for personal growth and social identification unmatched anywhere else in the capitalist world. These opportunities worked against class-based appeals.

Facing these cultural barriers, could socialism help to understand American workers? Mainstream historians said no, but Harrington demurred. His socialism was derived from human behavior, rather than imposed from above to rationalize a hidden meaning. Class relations and social development, he implied, could not be judged against some predetermined model, economistic or not.[50] Thus, socialism in the U.S. had to be defined by and for Americans, who lived in unique conditions that Marx could not have foreseen.

U.S. workers clearly had inflated expectations of what hard work alone could accomplish. Cheap land, decentralized electoral politics, and easy mobility all reinforced what Harrington called a "utopian spirit." Whereas working class Europeans often were outcasts, Americans had faith in freedom, trusted themselves, and were challenged by what seemed like unlimited opportunities: capitalism was their salvation *and* their fall from grace. They reached toward the Western frontier, where supposedly everyone could own land and farm independently. In reality, running a farm was expensive, and the economy didn't always support this fantasy. For every worker who became a farmer, twenty farmers became city dwellers. Still, the dream of owning land survived, and even workers trapped in urban poverty were agrarian radicals.

By the mid-nineteenth century these dreams were co-opted by political parties, and in the early 1900s by unions. Utopian working-class radicals were gradually absorbed by a system that couldn't deliver. It was not, said Harrington, that Americans thought socialism was evil, but that Americanism, especially its legal equality, political liberty, and putative classlessness, became a substitute for it. The left-wing character of U.S. society actually hindered the emergence of a consciously left-wing politics—with everyone dreaming they were capitalists, a strange socialist conception of capitalism became part of everyday working life. This is why, for example, in an 1846 quarrel with Herman Kriege, Marx stated flatly that socialism in America would appear first as agrarian anti-socialism.[51] In these exceptional conditions, entrepreneurialism was progressive. To Harrington, working-class radicalism has always existed in the U.S., but it was and is pro-capitalist.

On the one hand, then, America's openness, egalitarianism, and individualism made it, in Harrington's words, "the most radical country in the world."[52] On the other, Harrington noted the lack of a significant socialist movement in the U.S., its penny-pinching welfare system, and its counterrevolutionary foreign policy. He also realized that this same nononsense egalitarianism was often forgotten when it came to minorities and women, and could be rude, anti-intellectual, and violent, especially during crises. In hopeful times people were dignified and united; with fear and pessimism came a more vicious spirit. Although "the larger social context determines which aspect of this [complex and dialectical] . . . personality will come to the fore,"[53] Harrington nonetheless believed that even in bad times a wellspring of idealism could be tapped. After all, Americans were united by a democratic ideal more powerful that the inequalities which, in Europe, had become fixed social hierarchies.

The conditions that made America exceptional also hindered socialism, but the U.S. has never been as exceptional as non-Marxists believed. The complete triumph of American capitalism created the same kind of exploitation and misery experienced by workers everywhere. Werner Sombart himself admitted that "objectively" the U.S. worker was "more exploited by capitalism than in any other country in the world," and nowhere else was he required to "work himself so quickly to death as in America."[54] But, he continued, "subjective" responses mattered, and through "brilliant feats of diplomatic artifice" employers convinced workers they were free.[55] The defection of workers from the socialist movement, Patricia Cayo Sexton has shown, resulted from "hegemonic brainwashing" as well as from unique conditions.[56]

Thus American workers suffered and struggled economically and politically against the system, while corporate power and wealth manipulated the nation's legal, military, and cultural resources to repress unions and progressive political forces. This capital-inspired class war was ongoing, but escalated during business recessions when employers wanted to drive down wages and destroy unions. The combination of exceptional conditions, exceptional repression, and exceptional propaganda affected working-class consciousness, causing workers to rebel in the name of capitalism rather than socialism. American exceptionalism thus hid the class violence that accompanied worker politicization. To the degree that the U.S. was more affluent and egalitarian than other nations, insurgent workers raised their demands and Congress passed primitive, worker-sponsored industrial legislation. "In the course of these developments," noted Harrington, "the class struggle in America was more fierce than in any European country."[57] American employers, far more than those overseas, brutally suppressed strikers and undermined unionization,[58] while proud, independent workers fought their way first into unions and then—via the Democratic Party—into mainstream politics. Despite its democratization of production, labor's rhetoric remained capitalist, and its foreign policy stayed conservative. At least since the New Deal, however, its programs created a socialist definition of capitalism. The labor historian P. K. Edwards commented that this "invisible mass movement," with its "social democratic impulse,"[59] transformed laissez-faire capitalism into a welfare state without ever questioning the system's legitimacy.

Capitalist exploitation was thus real and verifiable, but also mitigated by an exceptional culture. Liberals neglected exploitation, materialists neglected culture, and, to Harrington, they were both mistaken, since economics was always filtered through culture's lens. *The Other America* and *The New American Poverty* had documented objective economic conditions, while *The Accidental Century* portrayed the moral emptiness of advanced capitalism. With this analysis of American exceptionalism, Harrington had underlined the cultural dimensions of socialism. Concluding that what people believed was as important as how they worked, he suggested that socialists reach into public culture in order to touch workers.

America's choice was not capitalist exploitation or socialist justice. Most workers never were, and aren't now, socialists. It was the radical core of mainstream liberalism that Harrington wanted to carry toward socialism. "America," Harrington commented, "will move to the left only when people, acting out of what is best in their liberal commitment and in response to overwhelming events, turn in a radical direction."[60] The U.S., in short, could not be indicted by an imported European ideology. Liberal values were unrealized, not wrong, and Harrington believed that socialism needed to "speak the genuine accents of this country and find a place within its mass left."[61] "I do not want to destroy it [liberalism], I want to 'sublimate' it," he explained. "That is, I want to take all that is good in it, and go beyond it. Liberalism is a profound democratic position, and absolutely critical to any possible good future. But liberalism points beyond itself."[62] Henceforth Harrington used "liberalism," "democracy," and "capitalism" almost interchangeably.

All this led Harrington to what, for radicals, were two rather astonishing positions. First, he disparaged activists who used inflammatory language and shock tactics.[63] He felt that this knee-jerk radicalism, common among New Leftists, angered people without doing anything useful and reinforced the popular stereotype that socialism was a foreign, totalitarian ideology. Radicals at times had to stand up and viciously fight the status quo, but not in contemporary America where workers still dreamt they were free. "What defines the radical possibilities, today as yesterday," Harrington pointed out, "is not a style of thought or an intellectual trend. It is people in movement."[64] Rebels who lacked a sense of community and historical memory became zealots, and, if successful, would destroy the nation's democratic heritage. "They usually claim to be talking in terms of democratic values, and they speak on behalf of the masses," Harrington said as extremists took over SDS, "but it usually is the son or daughter of an upper-middle-class family who is trying to bomb the majority of the American people into taking orders from them."[65]

Second, Harrington concluded that patriotism was the soul of American socialism. Heretofore an important cultural weapon for the status quo, which Old Leftists said would disappear in socialism, patriotism was for Harrington a barometer of one's love for the oppressed and a bond that mobilized and empowered working people. He saluted the dignity of Americans who survived even in hard times and he saw patriotism expressing compassion by unifying victims in shared ideals and a common future. It was a real, powerful emotion that, properly cultivated, could move corporate mountains more easily than any science. "If the Left wants to change this country because it hates it," Harrington wrote in *Fragments of the Century*, "then the people will never listen to the Left and the people will be right. To be a socialist—to be a Marxist—is to make an act of faith, of love even, towards this land. It is to sense the seed beneath the snow; to see, beneath the veneer of corruption and meanness and the commercialization of human relationships, men and women capable of controlling their own destinies. To be radical is, in the best and only decent sense of the word, patriotic."[66]

THE STATE AND POLITICS

IN THE MID-1970S Harrington's ride through radical America was stranded somewhere between the peaks and valleys of days past. No longer the left's rising young star, neither was he the apparatchik that some conservatives once had feared. The project of revitalizing America's left was begun just as the nation's infatuation with liberalism was ending. The U.S. welfare state had joined workers and capitalists in a pact that improved employee living standards and guaranteed employer power. This consensus worked until public agencies ran out of money. Then economic problems returned with a vengeance and the postwar New Deal consensus collapsed. "By 1971," Paul Buhle noted, "the New Left came to a crashing halt,"[1] the middle class ran out of money and compassion, and the nation bent noticeably to the right. Harrington spent his remaining years battling this conservative reaction, and success didn't come easily. What he dreaded most, however, was irrelevance rather than failure.

His most potent weapon, dialectics, proved ineffectual in a land of aspiring entrepreneurs. It could critique capitalism and communism, and create a third, democratic alternative, but it was also too esoteric for the public and too radical for most intellectuals and powerbrokers. Abstract theory alone could not stem the ideological tide. Harrington's cultural critique, in *The Accidental Century* and the idiosyncratic notion of American exceptionalism, were signposts of intellectual growth, but impotent politically. His strong defense of patriotism and incrementalism alienated many young people, and his anti-materialism didn't please the Old Left. In brief, America's shifting political landscape was marginalizing Harrington. He needed a solid core of ideas and tactics for a left offensive: his own reputation as well as the dream of Americanizing Marxism were at stake. At this crucial point in his career, Harrington dusted off and revised some old socialist ideas concerning the capitalist state. The result, a democratic socialist political theory and program, would be his seminal contribution to U.S. leftism.

CAPITALISM'S WELFARE STATE

Critics felt that Harrington, like many of his colleagues, had stepped too far into the liberal mainstream. Real radicalism, they argued, was not accommodating or compassionate, so Harrington couldn't be a radical. In order to dispel this view, and verify his left-wing credentials, Harrington devoted much of the 1970s to critiquing capitalism's welfare state, arguing that it was bound from the beginning to fail.

During the Kennedy and Johnson years the idea that highly developed nations had become "post-industrial" was widely accepted. Public decision-making, many intellectuals claimed, was now controlled by a new elite that impartially solved political disputes. Ideology had become irrelevant as trained technocrats engineered efficient public policies, and politics no longer had to produce winners and losers. Therefore, the post-industrial welfare state, claimed its boosters, was neither capitalist nor socialist. Beginning with *Toward a Democratic Left* (1968), and continuing in articles and books published throughout the next decade, Harrington argued that the modern welfare state remained capitalist: public policy always benefitted some more than others and, as usual, those who controlled the productive apparatus got more than those who didn't. Post-industrialism, which Harrington renamed "socialist capitalism"[2], and today is usually termed "the welfare state" or "social democracy," was actually a new way of protecting the old social order. For as long as the basic relationships of a private market economy survived, they would subvert the popular will.

The genealogy of post-industrialism trails from Bismarck's Germany, when reformers thought they were fundamentally transforming capitalism.[3]

Engels labeled them "state socialists," and others later used the term "state capitalists." They believed that social grievances were remedied by public programs that regulated, but did not alter, existing relations of production. Politics therefore replaced economics as the focus of citizen discontent because political reforms alone could end capitalist inequities, perfecting the system without substantially changing it.

In *The Communist Manifesto* Marx and Engels called this process "conservative, or bourgeois, socialism." Through administrative improvements, politicians reduced the social cost of bourgeois control and lowered public expenditures. Marx and Engels believed this kind of socialism preserved capitalism, "but without the revolutionary, transforming elements."[4] They felt it was a new developmental stage that modified the standard materialist dictum that society evolved from feudal to capitalist to socialist production. Politicians implemented a regulated market with both private and limited public production, public welfare programs, political pluralism, and, where possible, decentralized institutions. This new system was later rationalized by John Stuart Mill, T.H.Green, Leonard Hobhouse, and the Fabian socialists.

As "socialist capitalism" became more popular, especially in Germany and Britain, it threatened to isolate and eventually destroy democratic socialism, handing what remained of the left to Stalinists. Thoughout his life, Karl Kautsky had warned that governments are always either capitalist or socialist: authentic nationalization was administered directly by workers, not by a state bureaucracy, and thus reversed capitalist relationships and terminated the capitalist system. "Socialist capitalists" wisely understood that nations like Germany were not yet fully prepared to nationalize production. But if workers were to support capitalist production, as these same "socialist capitalists" hoped, they would only strengthen the state and postpone socialism.

An unexpected depression caused a reconsideration of the popular Kautskyian theory that capitalism slowly but steadily matured into socialism. Social Democrats throughout Europe gamely called for rebellion, but apart from asking workers to await the inevitable they didn't articulate a practical program to alleviate suffering. Meanwhile, welfare states delivered instant relief without rocking the capitalist boat. In Europe and America they carried the day among unemployed workers, for whom capitalism had won by default because leftists lacked practical alternatives. After the war, the Belgian socialist Henri de Man, in his popular *Plan du Travail*, used "socialist capitalism" to establish a common front of all productive strata, including workers *and* capital, against the power of what he called parasitic money. Capitalism, he implied, should be humanized rather than transformed. Fifteen years later, in the Godesberg Program of Kautsky's

German Social Democratic Party, the democratic left sanctioned its failure by adopting the entire "socialist capitalism" platform. Henceforth, Social Democrats helped plan and administer capitalist economic growth. Absorbed by technical concerns, they eventually forgot socialism's original promise to improve everyday living by altering productive relationships.

"Socialist capitalism" arrived in America in two stages after the depression had already begun. First came scientific, coordinated planning, primarily by business, to alter the market by raising prices and increasing consumption. Administered by the business-dominated National Recovery Administration (NRA), this first stage of the New Deal was eagerly backed by the U.S. Chamber of Commerce, for whom economic planning was a way of preserving private enterprise. By the end of F.D.R.'s initial term in office, however, many unions had deserted the NRA, and the Supreme Court had declared it unconstitutional.

The New Deal's second stage, begun in 1935, shifted decision-making from private to public hands. New Dealers were outwardly hostile to corporations that inhibited competition, and private industry responded in kind, initially opposing most of Roosevelt's key innovations. This opposition proved an overreaction. As John Maynard Keynes wrote to F.D.R., "You have made yourself the trustee for those in every country who seek to mend the evils of our condition by reasoned experiment within the framework of the existing social system."[5] Government would prime the economic pump with fiscal, monetary, and social service programs, and then allow market forces to take over. New Deal ideology was thus an amalgam of Keynes and Adam Smith, which Harrington called "Smith-Keynesianism." Smith-Keynesians defended both the marketplace and government intervention to correct the market's worst inequities. Public money revitalized, humanized, and regulated capitalism, but didn't transform it, leading big business to realize by 1939 that welfare statism both improved the old order and served their interests.

Harrington considered the New Deal an "ambiguous event."[6] It was supported by workers, minorities, and liberals, and signified their political victory over reactionary forces. Laissez-faire myths were shattered as the government promoted full employment and alleviated capitalism's most dismal features. Social security was accepted as a national principle, and many factory workers were unionized and became formidable economic and political players. The political landscape, in brief, had shifted to the left.

But the New Deal could not solve the depression's central problem, mass unemployment. By 1938–39, when Franklin Roosevelt lost control of Congress, unemployment remained at an unacceptably high ten million. World War II and the smaller wars that followed provided some temporary relief, but unemployment, and poverty as well, remained intractable problems, because New Dealers, and "socialist capitalists" generally, presumed that basic corporate structures were sound, and capital should control investment. Thus, employment expanded in profitable industries and declined elsewhere. Worsening unemployment drove wages down and discontent up, but anti-business reforms enraged entrepreneurs, discouraged private investment, and intensified the political crisis. In this context, government subsidies to the impoverished, which had frightened corporate America in 1929, in later years actually resolved the contradictions of free market production by transforming nonproductive ex-workers into consumers. "Once the tumult and social energy of the Great Depression abated," Harrington observed, "the system shaped and coopted the very reforms which most of the corporate rich had abominated."[7]

Beginning in the late 1960s, and continuing through the 1970s, the U.S. experienced new political and economic developments that recreated a crisis atmosphere in some ways resembling the post-depression 1930s. The liberal consensus that had endorsed "socialist capitalism" gradually frayed.

After the Second World War, the victorious U.S., with its economic and industrial strength in tact, asserted supremacy abroad. The quarter century following World War II was characterized by a "Pax Americana:" America's liberal empire replaced European overseas colonial empires, and the worldwide capitalist economy was rebuilt around U.S. industrial and financial strength. At the heart of America's domestic liberal consensus was an agreement on the part of capital to accept trade unions in the economic process and guarantee workers minimum living standards, relatively full employment, and a share of the profits. Labor agreed to accept capitalist control over production, investment, and resource allocation, and to permit capitalist mobility and international trade.[8] This consensus, and the sustained economic growth and political power that accompanied it, seemed to justify America's arrogant self-image as the land of freedom, opportunity, progress, and Manifest Destiny. It also convinced many intellectuals on the right and left that history was fully realized and because classes were cooperating, ideology had ended.

By the mid-1960s, the struggles against poverty and for civil rights and racial equality, and the student anti-war movements flooded the streets of urban America, transfixing the media and frightening the predominantly white middle and upper classes. Also at this time progressive women were forging the struggle against patriarchy and gender discrimination; gays and lesbians were mobilizing rudimentary liberation movements; and "public interest" groups consisting of environmentalists and consumer advocates began protesting against ecologically unsound business practices. As the rise of these so-called new social movements dominated news reports, many U.S. workers also rebelled without fanfare or publicity. "The late sixties saw the most severe strike wave since shortly after World War II," said Democratic Socialists of America (DSA) co-chair Barbara Ehrenreich in a study of American workers, "and by the early '70s the new militancy had swept up automakers, rubber workers, steelworkers, teamsters, city workers, hospital workers, farm workers, tugboat crewmen, grave-diggers, and postal employees."[9] Unsatisfied demands for higher wages, less alienating work, and more input into workplace decision-making caused this labor agitation. As a re-emergent workerism spread across industrial America and as several half-hearted attempts at interclass rapprochement failed, the spector of a broad leftist alliance of workers, students, and intellectuals haunted corporate America.

For as long as the U.S. economy grew and public revenues increased, politicians bought social peace with meliorative programs that mollified subaltern races, classes, and genders. But after 1968, the Great Society came to a thunderous halt because of unforeseen and uncontrollable developments: America was rocked by the assassinations of Martin Luther King Jr. and Robert Kennedy, the ensuing riots in cities and on campuses, the retreat in Vietnam, the dollar devaluation, and the oil embargo of 1973. Moreover, a worldwide capital accumulation crisis, a shift in the global division of labor, and the resulting relative decline of the U.S. economy all generated inflation, unemployment, and regional depressions. As the standard of living declined, new social movements saw the economic pie shrinking and realized they still hadn't received a fair share. The liberal consensus was based on economic prosperity and social peace, both of which were disappearing in the early 1970s.

Large U.S. corporations faced rising salaries and bitter competition from Europe and the third world, where wages were significantly less than in America. Squeezed by escalating costs, increased competition, and decreasing profits, they mobilized against labor in the workplace and political arenas, waging what Patricia Cayo Sexton and others have called "a class war from above."[10] In addition to lowering salaries, breaking unions, raising prices, and increasing workloads, corporations successfully lobbied for public "crisis packages" that cut social spending in order to fight inflation, and left many workers unprotected in an unfavorable job market. The first such package was sponsored by the same party—the Democrats during the Carter administration (1976–80)—that during F.D.R.'s New Deal had established the original liberal consensus. With this consensus now repudiated, and with no replacement on line, Americans became insecure and frightened about the future. This identity crisis—which was intensified by military defeat in Southeast Asia, the Watergate scandal, the fall of Iran's Shah, and the seizure of hostages by fundamentalist followers of the Ayatollah Khomeini—rippled through American society.

With both capitalism and communism apparently failing during the 1970s, the two major post-World War II grand narratives were deconstructed and delegitimized by postmodernists, and replaced by an eclectic, foundationless worldview. Many Americans lost confidence in their leaders, institutions, and politicians, and became cynical about the political process generally. In a 1979 television speech, President Carter discussed the nation's "paralysis and stagnation and drift." America, he said, suffered from "a crisis of confidence . . . that strikes at the very heart and soul and spirit of our national wills." The weary president didn't offer his public new political initiatives or solutions. "Carter," the historian Harvey J. Kaye concluded, "in essence wrote the obit for the liberal consensus."[11] Spreading their proverbial wings in the gathering dusk, intellectuals on the left and right wrote post-mortems. Anthony King discovered "governmental overload" and "ungovernability;" Jürgen Habermas wrote about a "crisis of legitimacy," and Alan Wolfe a "crisis of democracy;" the conservative Daniel Bell analyzed the "cultural contradictions of capitalism," and Samuel Brittan "the economic contradictions of democracy;" Robert Nisbet saw "the twilight of authority," and even the Trilateral Commission noted that America sadly had lost its "residual inheritances of traditional and aristocratic values" and now was threatened by an "excess of democracy."[12]

Harrington's contribution to this literature of discontent, *The Twilight of Capitalism* (1976), reduced America's crisis to the nuts and bolts of capitalist economics: for as long as the system was dominated by private wealth, collectivist measures such as nationalization always favored entrenched interests and hurt Joe six-pack. *The Twilight of Capitalism* examined postwar federal housing, farm, and tax policies to test this assertion.[13] Harrington found that these public programs created enormous benefits for large corporations without substantially improving workers' lives, actually expanding the gap between the wealthy and poor. Public housing, for example, by subsidizing wealthy suburbanites had worsened urban blight and bankrupted the sponsoring agencies. More promising strategies simply didn't make sense within a corporate calculus, so the welfare state was no solution to capitalism's housing problems. Aside from economically punishing the impoverished, failures like this confused a nation that had for so many years unquestionably accepted liberal bromides, feeding its collective insecurity and fanning its discontent.

Harrington also cranked out data to show, first, that as a percentage of GNP, America spent less than any other industrialized nation on social programs.[14] In the twenty years after 1970, U.S. public investments in the non-military domestic economy were 0.3 percent of national output, compared with 1.8 percent in the U.K., 2 percent in France, 2.5 percent in West Germany, and 5.1 percent in Japan. Second, in 1980 American tax receipts were 30.7 percent of gross domestic product, making it one of the least-taxed nations in the Western world, far behind our industrialized European partners. Third, over two-thirds of non-defense, pre-1980 public spending (e.g., medicare, medicaid, social security, and various federal retirement funds) was devoted to the income and medical needs of the aging, most of whom were not poor. Much of the remainder went to wealthy lenders as interest payments on the national debt. Money that did find its way into social programs was allocated according to business priorities, not need. Only about 13 percent of total federal payments to individuals, less than $43 billion, can even remotely be called "welfare." Most of those who complained about welfare cheats were probably recipients of federal funds, approximately 87 percent of which went to the middle and upper classes. Adjusting for inflation and unemployment, and subtracting interest, total federal outlays as a percentage of GNP in 1956 were 17.6 percent, and in 1981 were 18.9 percent. The Great Society's vast increase in welfare hand-outs, in terms of GNP, was a measly 1.3 percent. During this period liberals were responsible for barely a 0.4 percent increase in real federal spending relative to GNP. Truly radical departures, such as legal services for the poor and community organizing, were neither funded nor administered adequately, and quickly died. "Leaders of the '60s talked a bold game, declaring 'unconditional wars' on poverty, proclaiming a 'Great Society,'" Harrington wrote. "But there were neither vast expenditures nor structural changes."[15] He concluded that the Great Society never achieved its promise because it was frugal and conservative. Radical proposals might have worked.

The welfare state, in sum, is a paradox: "It represents," for Harrington, "the reluctant concessions of the ruling class, the increments of reform that function to make basic change unnecessary. But it is also the product of conscience and consciousness, that of socialist workers and middle-class liberals, of militant blacks and students, and of the aging. As such, it has been the instrument of the oppressed as well as the oppressors, a means of partial liberation as well as of partial pacification."[16] Harrington was certain, however, that the welfare state was fundamentally capitalist. Its economy was still privately owned and it maximized corporate profits. Moreover it obeyed capitalist priorities even when expressed in apparently anti-capitalist ways. European social democrats wisely abandoned bankrupt materialist formulas, but didn't create an attractive alternative. Although they humanized capitalism and marginally improved social life, they also sanctioned proletarian misery by reinforcing inherently exploitative relationships. The welfare state, whether or not socialists controlled it, was forced to play by capitalist rules.

Harrington was a "democratic socialist," not a social democrat. Whereas social democracy endorsed the welfare state, democratic socialism expanded proletarian decision-making into every corner of society, including the workplace, thereby reversing capitalist priorities.[17] In America, democratic socialism meant taking the New Deal beyond its first two stages. By empowering workers, a "Third New Deal"[18] would complete the process begun in 1929, when control of key economic investments was passed from unfettered boardrooms to a capitalist-controlled welfare state.

LIBERAL AND MARXIAN LEGACIES

Harrington's critique did not explain how the welfare state actually managed to enact progressive programs. Nor did it say how the transition from welfare-state capitalism to democratic socialism could take place without violence. If the welfare state, as suggested, was still capitalist, why would it permit such fundamental structural changes? Does the welfare state represent more than the dominant class? If so, why does it end up supporting capitalism and capitalists? Who is sovereign? Harrington needed to dress his critique with a richer theory of the state, one that probed capitalist politics and mapped the arena where workers could struggle.

Harrington drew his theory of the state from work done by liberals, Karl Marx, and America's Marxian underground, whose members, largely unnoticed, spiked the left with a dose of common sense. The final product spoke clearly to both liberals *and* radicals in a conciliatory voice, offering pragmatic politics to structurally transform the nation without dividing it into warring camps.

In liberalism, selfish actors live peacefully together by agreeing on a set of natural rights that limit their activities. Within these guidelines, citizens can join with others to compete for available goods and services. Government originated to enforce these guidelines, that is, to protect the self-interest and natural rights of citizens. To eliminate group conflicts that might destroy the guidelines, public decisions became sovereign with respect to all individuals. A government that was too powerful could threaten freedom, so government was weakened by separating its powers into competing institutions, with each capable of checking the others. Thus, public power was divided into legislative, executive, and judicial branches, and the policy-making process became a complicated affair that wound slowly through each branch. Public decisions were made through this institutional tug-of-war, with each branch reflecting the relative strengths of mobilized interest groups. As Harrington summarized the liberal credo, "I am free to do anything that does not interfere with your freedom to do anything that does not interfere with my freedom. Freedom is my right to be independent of the interference of other individuals or the state. Liberalism is conceived as a series of rights possessed by individuals against the limited state."[19]

Liberal government also coordinated and legitimized the struggles between competing individuals and groups. Government decisions, in this view, reflected a general tolerance of diverse interests, and the decision processes also provided an opportunity for all legitimate interests, new or old, to be heard. Fairness, impartiality, and justice were the systemic values to be sought and encouraged, and these were assured by protecting basic rights and procedures, primarily the rights of free speech, press, association, and legal due process. Hence, liberal theory perceived the state as a "neutral" field of conflict. The political system was judged by its ability to achieve equilibrium through the balance of competing interests, and not by the moral content of the participants' demands; regime stability was a value in itself.

Pluralism stressed the advantages to be gained from observing the procedural "rules of the game" and "staying within the system" when resolving conflicts. Protest and demands for change were encouraged only so long as the interested participants were willing to accept conflict resolutions—laws, court decisions, administrative rulings, electoral outcomes—determined by a policy process of bargains and compromises within and between the institutions of government. In sum, once the guidelines were accepted, participants were free to pursue their own interests in society and in government.

Even liberals acknowledged imperfections in their assumptions and in the actual workings of liberal government. The all-important guidelines— the government's promise to protect life, liberty, and (particularly) property—split economics from politics, and blocked public control of private businesses. It also meant that the enormous financial disparity between winners and losers in capitalism became part of its unquestioned rules. Thus, liberalism's belief that the system provided relatively equal access to a multitude of interests was qualified by longstanding evidence that the unequal distribution of resources affected participants' access to decision-makers: poor people could neither influence politicians nor benefit from public policy to the extent that rich people could. Labor activism, for example, was difficult or impossible because liberal institutions blocked the establishment of third parties, empowered special-interest lobbies and pressure groups, exaggerated the influence of money in elections and public policy, and cut into voter participation. "By combining political liberty with indirect economic coercion," Harrington decided, "capitalism uses the legitimacy gained by political democracy to lend legitimacy to economic exploitation. It veils and rationalizes it. One can say that everybody is equal when, in fact, everyone is equal politically but not economically or socially."[20]

During recessions, liberalism's losers—a majority of the population that played a minor role in decision-making—often questioned the game's rules and destabilized the system. Elites then altered the guidelines somewhat by injecting government into the private economy through policies aimed at flattening economic cycles and reducing their painful consequences. To protect liberalism from system-threatening dislocations, what was originally a "laissez-faire" government expanded to become the welfare state.

Welfare states appeased dissenters without altering power relationships. Although a new set of problems emerged, the canons of liberal politics remained the consensual core of what most Americans perceived as their "system of government," and were still the standard for determining whether government action was legitimate. Most people agreed that liberalism resolved conflict through an institutional structure dominated by persuasion, compromise, and accomodation among a multitude of competing interests. For Harrington, the popularity of liberalism was at least as important as its disingenuous claim of "neutrality." His political theory deconstructed the latter and squeezed the last drop of hope from the former.

This project, like so many others on the democratic left, was inspired by orthodox Marxists, who detected liberalism's image in the reality of capitalist exploitation. Constitutional rhetoric hid a central fact of political life: the state protected and reproduced class relations. Wherever workers' labor enriched property owners, the state became an instrument (hence the term "instrumentalism") by which wealthy capitalists maintained power. In *The Communist Manifesto* it was called "the organized power of one class for oppressing another . . . a committee for managing the common affairs of the whole bourgeoisie." Liberalism's complex formula for dividing power and protecting rights merely rationalized concentrated private wealth. Its benefactors then spread the word to others by controlling education and culture. When liberalism failed, as in pre-Nazi Germany or depression-era America, capital redefined its ideology. Orthodoxy insisted that workers destroy liberalism's inherently exploitative state.

Communism simplified what even Marx realized was a very complicated issue. Marx and Engels, in fact, suggested several theories of the state. Harrington thought Marx's ambivalence indicated uncertainty regarding both the bourgeois state's precise nature and the role of working class politics. Capital's welfare state, for Harrington, provided an unexpected opportunity for meaningful political activity. Liberal government was certainly a mechanism of social control, but it had become labyrinthine and was no longer in capital's pocket. In the U.S., where workers trusted government at least as much as unions, the left no longer could rely on orthodoxy's dogmatic anti-statism.

In letters to Lassalle (22 February 1858) and Engels (2 April 1858), Marx promised a systematic theory of the state,[21] but he never delivered. Nonetheless, his scathing critique of bourgeois politics, particularly in *The Communist Manifesto*, unfortunately reinforced instrumentalism. Yet Marx also suggested that the state is occasionally independent of—and even superior to—all social classes, becoming, in effect, the dominant social force rather than the instrument of the dominant class. In *The Eighteenth Brumaire of Louis Bonaparte*, for example, the Bonapartist state "represented" a disorganized peasantry and petite bourgeoisie that were incapable of governing. It was also autonomous and absolute: independent of any specific class and superior to all of them. Marx implied that a politically independent state could protect an economically and socially dominant class without becoming its instrument.

"Independent" meant that the capitalist state was separate from ruling-class institutions (e.g., employers associations, chambers of commerce, etc.) and class-oriented political parties. Although public officials often governed on behalf of capitalists, they didn't hold office simply by virtue of being capitalists. The public, or common interest of the capitalist state somehow transcended the narrow private interests of the capitalist class. Capitalism was unique in that its state represented the entire community, even though public programs benefitted some more than others.

Winners and losers were determined by who actually defined what the "public interest" was. Marx knew that society's most powerful class, the bourgeoisie, defined the public interest in light of its private interests, but this did not automatically turn the state into capital's instrument for dominating society. Capitalist states, in fact, often enforced policies that favored workers.[22] The extent to which a state was dominated by capitalists was based on the relative strength of contending classes. If classes were relatively equal in strength, neutralizing each other politically, the state was free to operate independently, defining the public interest as it saw fit. This structural independence legitimized the state, allowing it to "objectively," "neutrally" enforce laws that empowered a small class of property owners.

Marx thus distinguished state power—that is, the political power of a dominant class, based on the balance of class forces in society, to protect its private interests—from the structural nature of the state, i.e. its independence from the economy. The latter assured that accumulated private wealth remained outside the public realm, and capital maintained a dominant position in the class struggle. State power therefore could be won by mobilized workers lobbying for political reforms such as enfranchisement and free mandatory public education. In order to alter the way in which public power was used, Marx actively supported and campaigned for the entire range of worker-supported reforms.[23] But even these couldn't affect the nature of the state, which remained structurally independent of the economy. Only proletarian rebellion could change the state's structure. When organized workers gained sufficient political power, they would smash the bourgeois state, reattach politics and economics, and establish, in

Marx's words, "a community of free individuals, carrying on their work with the means of production in common."[24] In a famous letter to J. Weydemeyer in March, 1852, Marx called the ensuing social formation a "dictatorship of the proletariat," but never actually described what type of state this short term dictatorship would be.

Marx didn't anticipate the state expanding into the economy, or the stunning increase of public employees whose livelihoods depended on the state. Harrington believed these events structurally transformed the state by linking government policy to the careers, health, and well-being of millions of workers, as well as to private wealth. Political power was now legitimately employed to regulate the economy and the struggle among classes for state power could be transformed into a struggle for socialism.

Harrington wanted to tap an enormous, potentially active working class constituency. With state power up for grabs and public policy, since 1929, legitimately regulating private businesses, a progressive electoral majority could spotlight the state's contradictions and significantly alter the system. This new political tactic could turn Marx's enigmatic "dictatorship of the proletariat" into a majoritarian, popularly elected workers' state.

Harrington was not the first to mine this political vein. Even Engels realized that it made good political sense in the U.S. to electorally contest the bourgeoisie. Campaigns mobilized workers, popularized socialism, and stimulated needed reforms, for which socialists then took credit. The state remained a capitalist tool, but political activism was a tactic that could destroy bourgeois politics. In the years from 1890 until 1920, political activism, once an economistic tactic, became an integral component of socialist political theory. Harrington's politics thus grew from, and resolved, a contradiction between theory and practice that fractured the orthodox movement.

Central to this process was the Socialist Party (SP)'s right faction, led by Morris Hillquit, John Spargo, and Victor Berger, which stumbled into a Marxian theory of the state that was richer and more useful than anything communists could visualize.[25] Harrington's debt was direct and obvious.

The SP right believed that U.S. socialism first appeared as publicly financed and regulated police, post office, and transportation systems, as well as legislated restrictions on the dividends of public service corporations. This so-called "police-department socialism" transformed the state from capital's weapon into a potential ally of workers. The sole missing link was proletarian political power—that is, having socialists in public office. By electorally conquering the state, workers would stretch government intervention into heretofore unregulated economic and social activities. Each new public program would strengthen socialism, until the bourgeois state was entirely transformed into a workers' state. When large trusts were peacefully nationalized, workers, through duly elected representatives, would become the dominant class.

Seventy years before the term became popular, SP rightists detected the "relative autonomy" of the capitalist state, its transformation from being merely a tool of capital into an institution that reflected and influenced the relative power of competing classes. Hillquit, Spargo, and Berger also agreed that the transition from capitalism to socialism would be slow and complicated, and characterized by reforms that financed working-class programs by gradually divesting capitalists of their excess wealth. In this way social relations would also be slowly transformed, class divisions abolished, and exploitation ended. The rebellions that socialists were expecting arrived, in Spargo's words, "with as little friction and pain as possible."[26] Even without orthodoxy's "stupid phrases and senseless catchwords"[27] and bolshevism's violence, however, America's "revolutionary evolution" verified historical materialism. SP Marxism, then, overthrew capitalism, not the state, and remained stubbornly materialist.

This theory of the state re-established the ebb and flow of political economy and the authenticity of U.S. liberalism, which bolsheviks had consigned to history's rubble. The message was sorely needed by a left buried in a blizzard of disputes that neglected the central problem of instrumentalism's irrelevance. SP electoral successes during the years preceding World War I, when its right faction ruled, turned socialism from a dream into a real possibility.

These modest electoral victories were sweet, particularly after all those bitter SP quarrels. Furthermore, they troubled the bourgeoisie and strengthened reformists. Public programs gradually raised salaries, improved conditions, and legitimized bourgeois politics. The cycle of political activism stimulating economic growth and security, which encouraged more political activism, turned the SP and its leaders toward the concerns of growing numbers of politically sophisticated, affluent workers and professionals. Unable to dialectically measure short-term gains, each increment of political power begat the dream of more power. Hillquit, Spargo, and Berger eventually sanctified politics in place of economics, duplicating the reductionism that had inspired their own innovative state theory. From being only one of many arenas where workers contested bourgeois power, the state became the sole dispenser of justice, and reformism the only appropriate tactic. Worker exploitation was reduced entirely to insufficient representation in government.

Norman Thomas purged SP ideology of whatever residual radicalism had survived the 1920s. Widely regarded as "the conscience of America," the humanitarian Thomas nonetheless outsmarted his opponents (e.g., the conservative Old Guard, ultra-radicals, Trotskyists, and anti-pacifists) and directed most of the party's resources into unsuccessful electoral campaigns. Political activism had become both means and end. Since the New Deal had already co-opted its reformist agenda in the 1930s, the SP soon owned neither a cause nor a constituency.

A THEORY OF THE STATE

Like the SP's right faction, Harrington at first rhetorically backed materialism while hacking it to death with practical criticisms. In *The Other America* he itemized the suffering of America's forgotten poor and urged all classes to support anti-poverty legislation. By emphasizing suffering rather than inequality, class cooperation rather than conflict, reform rather than structural change, Harrington indicated that politics alone could eliminate capitalism.

With the crisis of legitimacy as a backdrop in the 1970s, however, Harrington decided to strike out on his own by synthesizing the entire spectrum of state theories. His version of the capitalist state formulated and administered public policy by juggling the interests of significant groups in order to serve the public and maintain power. Liberalism, then, was partially correct. But the state didn't control social production, so its ability to act effectively, its very survival, was in the private sector's hands. In Harrington's words, "If capital goes on strike—as it did during the Popular Front in France in the '30s, during the second Wilson Government in Britain, and in Allende's Chile in the '70s—it can bring a government down or, which is almost the same thing, force a government to abandon its program . . . . Therefore, because private management is given an essentially social function in our system, the elected authorities must adopt their priorities to those of the board room. This is not the result of a conspiracy; it is, rather, the inherent logic of our system of economic and social power."[28]

By withholding investment or terminating production, capitalists could wreak economic havoc on large segments of the public. "The state's interest in perpetuating its own rule is thus, in economic fact, identified with the health of the capitalist economy."[29] The capitalist state also intervened in the economy with countercyclical policies that prioritized corporate interests. Communists were correct in spotlighting the political power of capital.

The state was neither capitalist nor an unthinking tool of capitalists, but depended on capitalists to survive. It could legislate impartially, but for as long as investment was privately controlled, the public's interest was best served by the state appeasing capitalists. "The most honest and incorruptible of public servants," Harrington felt, "wants and works for the maximum happiness of General Motors and Ford."[30] Public officials "want" and "work for" corporate happiness because it warms the economy and enlarges their campaign war-chests. They do not just mechanically reproduce capitalism. The state, then, was conditioned by capitalist structures and also had a life of its own. Even when it reinforced capital it articulated a unified national interest that somehow transcended everyday business transactions and the ability of specific capitalists to control events. Why else could the state occasionally enact pro-worker legislation?

Neither fully autonomous nor determined, the state is what Harrington called "co-determined:"[31] it initiated action within a constellation of defining forces. The state passively crystallized its environment and also actively sculpted it. It was both determined and determining, depending on what one chose to examine.

Harrington thus agreed that the welfare state was the "executive committee" of the bourgeoisie, defending capital's long-range interests, but not always the immediate interests of specific capitalists.[32] New Dealism, for example, temporarily empowered workers but eventually reinforced capitalism. The state and its wealthy benefactors emerged from the New Deal stronger than ever, despite some short-term sacrifices.

Millions of workers, however, were also more economically secure than ever before. Their political influence was greater than they ever dreamed it could be, and their multiplying opportunities for educational and cultural enrichment improved their lives. Reformism had transformed the state from an instrument of capital into an agent of profound change. By empowering the poor politically, introducing minimal economic security, and establishing mass cultural education, reformism had raised proletarian expectations beyond the system's capacities. Reformism, in short, had become subversive.[33]

The state thus exists in a capitalist system, never fully satisfying proletarian needs, but the dynamic flow of social events means that government activity, for example, can incrementally transform the system. Norman Thomas was partially correct: who governs really does matter, at least as much as what children learn in school or the economic demands of unionized workers. When the totality changes, so will everything in it, and activism changes the totality. The many-faceted, agitated, incessant fusing and splintering of the whole with its parts—the social dialectic—legitimated left political activism even in an undemocratic system.

So Harrington agreed with both orthodoxy *and* liberalism—and with neither.[34] Capital now ran the state, but popular forces could win valuable practical victories. These eventually strengthened the wealthy because the state was structurally tilted toward capital. Hence, even in the best short-term scenario, workers could expect only to increase absolute living standards, not eliminate systemic inequities. Political struggle, however, also mobilized coalitions of unhappy voters. As reformist victories mounted, and the coalition was empowered, social "normalcy" drifted left-ward. Democratic socialists therefore could push the state to the brink of systemic change, and then let progressive voters abolish profits, transform capital accumulation, and alter productive relationships. The state could not legislate socialism, however, until the rest of society, conditioned by years of reformist state policies, became socialist.

Harrington's political agenda thus lay, in his own words, "midway between immediate feasibility and ultimate utopia."[35] While socialism was clearly democratic, in an everyday world where even poor people were anti-socialist "it will never come to pass in its ideal form."[36] Socialists had to create enlightened attitudes without shrinking the nation's economic capac-ity or trashing public culture; they had to be progressive and practical, not dogmatic. The transition to socialism would be slower, more intricate, and much less dramatic than the founders of socialism had believed. A third New Deal, extending political reforms originally enacted by F.D.R. and the Kennedy-Johnson team, would nest safely inside of U.S. political culture, but also be as radical today as were, in their days, the first and second New Deals. "The next step," for Harrington, "will not be revolution or even a sudden and dramatic lurch to the socialist Left. It will be the emergence of a revived liberalism—taking that term to mean the reform of the system within the system—which will, of necessity, be much more socialistic even though it will not, in all probability, be socialist."[37]

As a loyal SP official Harrington emphasized economic and govern-mental reforms during the 1960s and early '70s. In the late 1970s and '80s, as political parties dealigned, he accented the cultural dimensions of change. The two strategies were complementary, even though one angered New Leftists and the other traditional socialists.

A POLITICAL PROGRAM, PART ONE

Harrington's initial political program incubated in his theory of the state, but hatched in a historical setting that was lurching to the right. The rise of the New Right Coalition (NRC) during the crisis-plagued 1970s brief-ly calmed the nation's troubles and redesigned its political landscape. It also jolted Harrington into delivering the political goods before it was too late.

The election of Ronald Reagan as President in 1980 symbolized the tri-umph of U.S. conservatism, but the process of refashioning liberalism's postwar labor-capitalist accord had actually begun much earlier. Business leaders believed the crisis of the 1970s was a real threat to capitalism that was sponsored by leftists and that portended redistributive legislation. Squeezed from below by labor troubles and from above by international competition and stagflation; subject to new government controls protecting the environment, consumers, and workers; and tormented by political and corporate scandals, the 1973–74 energy crisis, a deepening recession, and a nationwide anti-business hostility, capitalists felt besieged. In a 1975 survey of almost 2000 readers by the *Harvard Business Review*, for example, almost 75 percent doubted that laissez-faire capitalism would last into the 1990s. Over one-third of Fortune 500 CEO's told *Fortune* in 1976 that government regulations had become a serious problem for business. And a large consensus of executives at a meeting sponsored by the Conference Board in 1974 felt that rising entitlements and taxes would restrict capital formation and eventually bury free enterprise.[38]

Capitalists responded carefully and decisively on several different fronts. Anti-union campaigns were initiated across the nation in specific factories to drive down wages and "zap" labor's growing militancy.[39] The Business Roundtable was founded in 1972 to politicize U.S. business and mobilize the resources of its largest corporations. It negotiated business alliances, established corporate political action committees, and created "advocacy advertising" campaigns to market the business slant on current events.[40] The Trilateral Commission was formed in 1973 by banker David Rockefeller to develop consensus and cooperation among the economic and governmental elites of Western Europe, Japan, and the U.S. It accomplished on a worldwide scale what organizations like the Business Roundtable did domestically, that is, create a favorable environment for pro-business initiatives. By the late 1970s, all this effort paid off. Business managed to defeat major legislation sponsored by organized labor and consumers, and to neutralize environmental legislation. It also succeeded in turning the nation's attention from fighting poverty and unemployment to combatting inflation, ripping apart labor's social safety net that had grown piece by hard-earned piece since 1929.

Where the Trilateral Commission and Business Roundtable represented wealthy business interests, the NRC hoped to establish a new grassroots conservative culture to replace the postwar liberal consensus. The NRC was generously funded by wealthy corporations and intellectuals, and easily captured the mass media. By 1980, it helped restructure political discourse in America to be anti-labor and pro-capitalist.

The NRC was actually a fragile alliance between libertarian neo-liberals and secular and religious neo-conservatives.[41] The latter stressed order, hierarchy, authority, nation, and traditional family values, but was divided into Christian fundamentalists led by Jerry Falwell and Pat Robertson, and secular activists many of whom were Jewish and former leftists. Secular neo-conservatives—including Irving Kristol, Daniel Bell, Robert Nisbet, Daniel Patrick Moynihan, Michael Novak, Peter Berger, Seymour Martin Lipset, Nathan Glazer, Norman Podhoretz, Midge Dector, and Jean Kirkpatrick—

congregated in the American Enterprise Institute (AEI) in Washington D.C., which originally was established in 1943 to promote free enterprise. Financed by Fortune 500 companies, AEI became a major social science and policy think-tank that produced neo-conservative research, publications, and educational activities. Neo-liberals, on the other hand, favored the anti-statist, free-market, monetarist ideas of Frederick Von Hayek and Milton Friedman, and formulated the "supply-side" economic program that Ronald Reagan used to win the presidency in 1980. They helped sponsor the Conservative Caucus, the National Conservative Political Action Committee, the Committee for the Survival of a Free Congress, and the Heritage Foundation, another leading conservative think-tank.

The NRC was most effective when it concentrated on "single-interest" issues such as abortion, pornography, lawlessness, communism, unions, feminism, or gun-control, confirming George Gilder's thesis in his influential *Wealth and Poverty* (1981) that free-market capitalism and Christian morality were allies. President Reagan galvanized the alliance with charisma and electability. After 1988, however, it became clear that a long-term struggle between Christian fundamentalists, libertarians, and secular conservatives to control the Republican Party and shape the meaning of conservatism had begun. The issue was still unresolved in the early 1990s.

This many-sided corporate response to the crisis of the 1970s neutralized Great Society social programs and re-tooled political discourse to reflect the needs of business. It was well under way in the mid-1970s when Harrington articulated his own alternative to the conservative juggernaut. With the nation moving right, and the hapless Democratic Party insecure and fearful, Harrington wanted to attract the vast electoral center, turn it around with attractive programs, and then let democracy take over.

Harrington built on New Deal reforms that had humanized capitalism for so many workers. He advocated expanding public works and services initiatives, federalizing and then expanding welfare benefits, progressively taxing income and inheritance, nationalizing health care, making decent low-cost public housing a basic right for all Americans, raising the minimum wage, guaranteeing free and open access to upgraded public education programs, and rewarding socially responsible corporate investment with tax incentives.[42] These proposals maintained or improved living conditions, and were also popular with workers, minorities, and professionals in the Democratic Party, who in the conservative 1970s had nowhere else to turn.

Capitalist reforms, like charity, help poor people but don't eliminate poverty. The centerpiece of Harrington's long-term program, what he called the "precondition of all social progress,"[43] was full employment. Full employment would flow through the nation, first creating ripples and later tidal waves of change, eventually improving the social standing and motivation of the unemployed, and also reducing crime and violence, which thrive on hopelessness. Full employment raised salaries, resolved racial tensions, pacified cities, motivated students, and created compassionate citizens— even businesses prospered because new consumers increased private production and profits. In short, good economic news for the impoverished helped everyone. "If America accepts an official rate of 6 to 7 percent unemployment as necessary for the system," Harrington pointed out, "the problems of misery and social breakdown will increase in 'good times' and become epidemic in 'bad times'."[44] Full employment, said Harrington, was the precondition for solving every significant social problem.

With politicians overwhelmed by corporate lobbying, Harrington realized that full-employment programs were not very popular on Capital Hill, even to reformists. His other long-term proposals—democratic planning, socializing some investment, and redefining property ownership—were designed to gradually empower workers and to change the pro-business configuration of U.S. politics. They reallocated resources to create decent jobs for the un- or underemployed and also altered capitalist structures without destroying everyday values or creating panic on Wall Street. The issue for Harrington was not whether economic planning was appropriate—history had already answered "yes"—but instead *who* will plan, *how* will it be done, and for *what* purposes.[45]

In most developed democracies since World War II, unions have cooperated with government officials and employers in creating policy on a broad range of issues, including investment, collective bargaining, wages, occupational safety, and equal opportunity. Unions also have won seats on governing boards of corporations and pension funds.[46] With this in mind, Harrington suggested that a team consisting of elected officials, worker and community activists, and entrepreneurs could replace the corporate elite that now controlled U.S. economic planning. Public servants and capitalists in each industry could then sit down together and decide economic priorities, with their relative power based on the nature of production and the expertise and technology each brought to the table. To prevent bureaucratic or corporate abuse, which Harrington called "command planning," community groups were encouraged to "counterplan,"[47] and would be given public funds, computers, and expertise. Workers and other interested consumers would become watchdogs, scrutinizing major private or public planning decisions and requesting accessible explanations for questionable policies. Perhaps a portion of profits, in the form of equity capital, might be deposited into a fund that financed this kind of worker activity.[48] The president could channel information to local groups by reporting periodically to the nation on basic economic choices and their consequences.[49] Congress then would debate the options and select one as the nation's "Democratic Plan."

Harrington didn't clarify when and how the federal government, through its Democratic Plan, overruled anti-social corporate decisions, but he believed that the threat of lost government contracts, tax subsidies and shelters, and guaranteed loans would probably solve the problem. The financial and symbolic costs of corporate haggling with consumers, workers, and public officials likely would exceed the benefits.

This proposal to democratize planning centralized a process that was now splintered and haphazard. Centralization, however, was a precondition for decentralizing policy decisions into local communities and factories, where people whose jobs and income were finally secure participated in local decision-making. Harrington felt that their input into the planning process would create a need to control planning entirely. New structures of neighborhood, metropolitan, and regional government reflecting the actual locations of empowered communities then replaced traditional state and local units.[50]

Although Democratic Plans carry moral weight, and tax subsidies can stimulate responsible corporate investment, Harrington pointed out that the private sector was still free to invest wherever it maximized its return, regardless of social consequences. When resources are mostly privately owned, as in the U.S., government planning alone cannot end unemployment. Moreover, government is left to clean up the economic and social mess often created by private investment. American democracy was always subject to the economic veto of a wealthy minority.

The nation finally had to democratize corporate investment without upsetting the capitalist cart at least initially because "under our present institutional arrangements," Harrington realized, "it is necessary for the political foes of profit to treat profit more gently than any other sector of the economy."[51] Harrington suggested that employee and public representatives be placed on the boards of major industrial and financial corporations, including the Federal Reserve Bank, to publicize key investment decisions related to pricing, plant location, technology, wages, and personnel.[52] "All of the corporate books must be opened;" he counseled, "all of the major investment decisions must be subjected to scrutiny."[53] When necessary, corporations had to defend these policies publicly.

Pension funds, insurance companies, and retained corporate profits now provided most investment capital. If workers could take control of their pensions away from corporate managers and trustees they would also take control of steadily increasing amounts of investment wealth.[54] Then their role in corporate investment decisions expanded with their share of the profits. If workers also received company stock from profit-sharing arrangements, democratic investment grew even more rapidly.

Harrington assumed that workers would rationally defer consumption in favor of increased investment, and balance corporate profitability with the public's welfare. As they earned larger shares of corporate wealth, and became powerful actors, Harrington also assumed they would want even more, and eventually socialist production relationships would be commonplace. In the short-term, however, corporate profits remained the major single source of new investment funds. Harrington's investment reform program placed workers on an activist track but didn't challenge capitalist structures. By trying to reduce private profits, Harrington warned that workers "would cause the entire economy to malfunction."[55]

Capitalism separated economics and politics, and created a wealthy, powerful elite. When and how should they be reattached? Harrington warned that nationalization could substitute one elite for another, transferring power from corporate boardrooms to bloated public bureaucracies, and guaranteeing elitism and inefficiency.[56] Since corporations now controlled the state, this kind of public ownership was actually reactionary. Americans during the 1970s, moreover, were in a dark mood. Vietnam, Watergate, the energy shortage, the crisis of values, and later the nation's public humiliation at the hands of Iran and third world terrorists, had all drained its trust and confidence in public leaders. Initially this disillusion spilled into anger, and often fell on corporations. Some editorials appeared in local and regional dailies suggesting that nationalization, especially of oil companies, wasn't such a bad idea. After capital's mid-1970s counter-offensive, however, business became the good guy and middle class whites attacked "welfare cheats," minorities, and "special interests." Harrington would not be swept up by momentary shifts in public opinion. Americans had to cook many small reforms before they tasted real economic freedom. The millions of on-line producers first had to be prepared and motivated to make key economic decisions, and this followed rather than preceded pertinent reforms. Real socialism was democratic: neither law nor charter, it crowned the long process by which people learned to govern themselves. An economy could be nationalized overnight, but the light of freedom might never arise.

Thus, most large industries had to remain privately owned, at least for the forseeable future, but the absolute freedom now enjoyed by business executives had to be reduced. Sometime after Harrington's program was enacted, people might actually take over corporate decision-making. Although the title to private property would remain undisturbed, its functions would have been socialized—without rocking the nation's democratic heritage.

When are industries ready to be socialized? Harrington knew that by taking over failing, mismanaged factories, workers merely socialized capitalism's losses. These experiments invariably failed and reinforced the feeling that socialism doesn't work. Entire industries, not just unprofitable factories, had to be socialized if socialism was to ever to be fairly tested.

Given the nation's legal traditions and untrained workforce, expropriating private property was out of the question, but if a large corporation or bank pleaded for help Harrington advised that "the government should consider nationalizing it."[57] Properly managed, these businesses could become models for other experiments in public ownership, and also yardsticks for measuring how similar private enterprises were performing.

Harrington also wanted to negotiate a federal takeover of the troubled U.S. railroad system, establish a federal gas and oil corporation (with "privileged rights to develop new energy technology in the public interest and for public purposes"[58]), create a national bank with enough resources to issue credit, require banks that are beneficiaries of federal services to give a percentage of their loans to socially useful investments, and charter major private corporations to mandate public and employee representation on their executive boards as a condition for participating in interstate commerce. These small examples of public ownership and regulation would help people live better, and also create a favorable climate for other democratic experiments.

Socialized property is a public authority responsible to the nation's elected representatives. To avoid the inefficiencies of centralized management each enterprise must pay its own way and return a surplus for depreciation, new investment, and the social dividend. Profitable public tractor factories, for example, maintain high employment, satisfy real needs, and still have enough left over to invest in socially useful industries that might produce non-polluting pesticides or fertilizers. Unless society decides to subsidize unprofitable but socially useful activities (e.g., rural postal and rail routes) from the profits of the system as a whole, these failing enterprises are terminated. "There are obviously limits to such [inefficient] practices," Harrington observed, "There must be a surplus in each year's annual production."[59] Unprofitable subsidies bankrupt the system and infuriate taxpayers, and soon hurt the same people they meant to help. Decisions to subsidize are therefore justifiable only when they are also affordable, and public firms that release workers must do so only after consulting with the public and retraining and relocating displaced employees.

Within the guidelines of a national full-employment plan, public enterprises could be run efficiently and profitably. Harrington realized that worker representatives could not veto national directives, and the public could not ignore local producers and consumers. The process required a system of political checks and balances attuned to the relative intensities of local and national opinions.[60] Even then, however, workers might lose interest, and public agencies might become intrusive. To prevent apathy and absolutism Harrington wanted to establish structural safeguards such as mandated employee and public input into decision-making, public funds for counter-plans, keeping wages and working conditions on the bargaining table, legislating a National Bureaucratic Relations Act to establish and protect the legal rights of "whistle blowers," and protecting worker privacy with legislative initiatives ranging from soundproofing urban buildings to maintaining public spaces for quiet leisure activities. On the other hand, Harrington knew that "there also must be provision made for the representatives of the society as a whole to have a say in . . . decisions. A democratically-managed steel plant could not on its own determine the steel policy for an entire region or for the whole country. Therefore, there must be national political representation—and ultimately international political representation—even where one has a system of worker self-management."[61]

Socialists, in short, had to balance efficiency and democracy, and also thoughtfully evaluate the social consequences of economic decisions. They often tried to do too much, and achieved nothing. When they endorsed new public enterprises, for example, power was usually conferred on an economic and cultural network that remained capitalist. Prematurely nationalized enterprises such as the Tennessee Valley Authority behaved like private corporations. "There is a tendency," said Harrington, "for islands of social property in a bourgeois sea to sink beneath the waves."[62] Harrington's step-by-step approach wasn't glamorous, but it wasn't dangerous either and it finally got the socialist ball rolling.

In addition to large private and public enterprises, and small privately owned consumer businesses that functioned largely outside national planning, Harrington also saw a need for cooperatives, that is, locally controlled, face-to-face enterprises where community spirit outweighed class interests.[63] These business enterprises overlapped tight community associations, and their employees were neighbors as well as workers—what Marx once approvingly called "associated producers." Workers owned as well as managed their enterprises, and this personal commitment stimulated innovation and imagination. The same decision-making structures and public subsidies that existed elsewhere in the economy also existed here, but mutual affection and trust maximized production and minimized discord. Harrington felt that cooperatives represented the highest level of democratic production, something workers everywhere could aim for.

Wages in Harrington's three-tier, post-capitalist system were tied to the enterprise. In private corporations, for example, employee compensation was based on collective bargaining that linked salary differentials and job performance. Workers in socialized industries de-emphasized differentials in order to equally redistribute income, wealth, and work. And in cooperatives income was paid mostly in "free" goods and services such as health care, education, transportation and leisure activities. "So a part of the wage," Harrington noted, "would be received collectively, as a social dividend from heightened productivity."[64] Wages in socialized and cooperative enterprises were negotiated by workers, consumers, public officials, and concerned citizens, so that total salary packages compared favorably with salaries received by workers in private industry. Harrington expected the wage structure, like public opinion and the economy, to gradually slide leftward.

Post-capitalism's social product was distributed in two ways. Free goods and services—e.g., health care, education, welfare, and transportation—were allocated based on need, and were publicly financed. The distribution and price of everything else was determined by the market. Harrington did not fully define the market's social role until the late 1980s, when conservative intellectuals had sold the nation a cult of free-market economics. He realized even in the 1970s, however, that unregulated markets were effective only under special conditions:[65] when income and wealth were equalized, consumers were accurately informed, and monopolies were abolished. Harrington suggested in the 1970s only that markets must operate within the broad limits of a democratic plan, and alongside the free sector, and he intimated that progressive reforms drove the distributive mechanism toward need rather than demand.

The costs of Harrington's political program were paid from several sources.[66] Private corporations remained the largest single source of investment revenue, and pension funds also provided an enormous pool of capital for all three sectors. Progressive income and inheritance laws would increase public revenues and also convince qualified professionals to serve others instead of just getting rich. Savings would dramatically increase with simple innovations such as resurrecting the post office savings system, factoring depreciation and new investment costs into the market price of consumer goods, and regulating advertising costs. A peace dividend created by reasonable cuts in the military budget would also raise needed revenue. Finally, profits from public enterprises could create new jobs and programs. Harrington was certain that "it would . . . be possible in a socialist transition to plan democratically, to effectuate that plan realistically, and to finance the entire process."[67]

America's future was thus neither capitalist nor socialist, "but something in between," Harrington wrote, "with elements of both."[68] As reforms kicked in, and life improved, people would start noting the gap between image and reality, between the nation's promises and its commitments: poor people would become angry, the middle class no longer would chase a receding rainbow, and an electoral majority would realize that by pulling together politically it could achieve more than ever before. These were Harrington's practical goals. Afterward, a mobilized polity, without blueprints, might establish socialism.

5

CRISIS

SOCIALIST POLITICAL THEORY IN AMERICA, one pundit remarked, raised human suffering from a fate to a tragedy. Orthodoxy reported that capitalism's "neutral" state was inherently evil, and political activism was unjustifiable. The Socialist Party (SP)'s right faction pointed out that the state was actually a bourgeois instrument *and* a means of raising proletarian living standards. Socialists had to control rather than destroy it in order to legislatively complete the transition to socialism. Electoral conquests and a powerful middle class soon turned SP reformism from a tactic into the party's sole project. Like orthodoxy, it became reductionist.

Harrington blended orthodox radicalism and SP realism, but didn't reduce life to economics or politics. Socialism, he claimed, ended the social division of labor and democratized decision-making, hence reversing capitalist priorities. It also respected the capitalist state's ability to help people and the mass appeal of reformism. Harrington believed that socialists finally should enter the mainstream and debate their nation's future. But what could they contribute? For two hundred years capitalism—poverty and all—had survived remarkably well. Why should Americans even discuss socialism? What events lifted the nation off the dead center?

With resources dwindling, needs growing, expectations stabilized at a high peak, and conservatives taking power, the U.S. in the late 1970s was in trouble. Economics were at the root of the problem, but economics was linked to politics and culture. It was a systemic crisis, and although the system wasn't yet collapsing, traditional bromides no longer worked. Harrington felt it was the beginning of the end. Capitalism no longer delivered on its political, cultural, and international promises, and the safety-valves were locked shut. With the election of Ronald Reagan in 1980, the U.S. was entering a period like no other in its history. Although the nation would soon celebrate a Cold War victory, Harrington suggested that perhaps its fate was tied to the sinking communist enemy.

The Crisis of the Welfare State

The growth years from 1946 to 1969, the so-called Second New Deal, were a boon to everyone.[1] Businesses expanded, profits and public revenues increased, and ordinary Americans lived better than ever before. One-quarter of the nation's citizens, who otherwise would have fallen into poverty, were rescued by public transfer payments. For the aging there were stunning increases in federal spending for social security, medicare, and medicaid. Real wages increased in every year but two, even though the relative distribution of wealth remained constant. There was also a steady annual increase in consumer buying power. New social programs helped minorities and women, a ten-fold increase in funds for public higher education filled universities, environmental protection laws were passed, funds for libraries, museums, and cultural events grew, and, in general, life for most in the U.S.—even the impoverished—was better than it was in 1945.

During these years traditional Keynesian policies flattened economic cycles and kept the economy on a steady growth course. An expanding workforce, with money to spend, stimulated new production and industrial competition, fueling an inflation-free economic explosion.

This expansion ran out of steam in the 1970s, when factories re-tooled for computerized production. The workforce changed from blue to white collar, unemployment shot up, poverty increased, and salaries declined for non-skilled workers. Farms and factories had overproduced, leaving unsold inventories and the prospect of severe recession. Foreclosures and bad bank loans reduced the pot of investment capital, driving up mortgage rates and shoving marginal enterprises into bankruptcy. Public safety-net programs became more costly just when public revenues were declining, clogging urban streets with the homeless. This painful recession punctured the nation's inflated dreams of neverending affluence.

During other recessions, standard Keynesian remedies corrected such imbalances. Easy money and expanded public programs had always inflated the economy, while tight money and reduced spending cooled it. What made this new crisis so vexing was that these mechanisms no longer worked: by reducing inflation the government also worsened unemployment and poverty. Economic stimulants drove inflation, already dangerously high, through the roof. This situation—particularly after the national debt skyrocketed during the 1980s—was unacceptable to key policymakers. Capitalism's manual controls could regulate recession *or* inflation, but not both simultaneously.

Inflation was the chief culprit. Economists agreed that a modest dose of inflation promoted economic growth, but when inflation became uncontrollable, as in the 1970s, it upset the entire international monetary system and threatened to bankrupt government agencies. The causes of inflation were well-known: the OPEC oil embargo, concentrated industrial production, and a solid core of well-paid workers had all combined to keep wages and prices high even when the economy was plummeting. The nation, many felt, had to break the oil cartel, eliminate federal regulations and taxes, lower wages, and drastically cut public programs. Jimmy Carter's administration was restrained by the Democratic Party's traditional ties to organized labor. But with the landslide Republican victory in the 1980 presidential election, these restraints dissolved. President Reagan's anti-labor agenda did lower the rate of inflation somewhat—to an annual rate that previously had been considered unacceptable—yet also widened the income gap, increased impoverishment, corroded the middle class, and frayed the public safety net.

The welfare state was in trouble. If public assistance were cut, millions of voters who depended on it for basic services that were otherwise unavailable would be punished. If public assistance were not cut, inflation and deficit spending would keep rising. Globalization, moreover, meant that key economic decisions no longer were made by national governments. In the new world economy U.S. corporations, for example, traded in national currencies and found ingenious techniques for creating new money. The power of national banks to control monetary policy was thus undermined by transnational corporations that could defy governmental constraints with impunity. "Tight" and "easy" monetary policies no longer had much effect, and the government could not regulate imbalances such as stagflation. The system was self-destructing and the fail-safe mechanisms weren't working. What had gone wrong? Harrington pored over the left for an answer.

For orthodox Marxists, the crisis began in the economy, where accumulation was threatened by a falling rate of profit, and cycles of economic growth and decay became a chronic problem. The constant battering experienced by workers and small entrepreneurs gradually eroded the system, as liberal institutions, especially universal suffrage, translated economic misery into political crisis.

Keynesianism prevented these small crises from becoming mass rebellions. As the state regulated the economy it also shouldered a large share of production costs, expanded its bureaucratic structures in complex and expensive ways, and found new sources of public revenue. The state's enlarged economic role meant that crises emerged from intersecting state forms, potent new interest groups and parties, economic changes, and international events. The number of variables exploded, and the state soon decided how, when, and where the substructure was altered.

Rational-choice Marxists, who were also called analytical Marxists because of their Anglo-American philosophy, devised a new crisis theory that accounted for capitalism's recent configurations. Led by G. A. Cohen, John Roemer, Jon Elster, and other self-styled "analytically sophisticated" Marxists, this group began publishing in the mid-1970s, and used state-of-the-art methods in logic, mathematics, and model-building to clarify the valid core of Marxism that was trapped within orthodoxy's mystical shell. Their brew of methodological individualism, empiricism, and critical theory immediately impacted academic leftists, many of whom had to publish or perish in hyperempirical disciplines. Rational-choice Marxism soon became arguably the most popular leftist theory on U.S. campuses, in part at least because non-Marxists also took it seriously. "To the extent that Marxist categories could be crystallized into 'testable hypotheses," Eric Olin Wright noted in 1978, "non-Marxists were willing (sometimes) to take these ideas seriously; to the extent that debate raged simply at the level of theory, non-Marxists found it relatively easy to dismiss our challenge."[2]

Welfare-state capitalism, rational-choice Marxists argued, exhibited a structural conflict between capitalists, state managers, and workers, with each rationally maximizing its material interests. Faced with grassroots political demands, for example, rational state managers acquired mass support by expanding public services, which then threatened capitalists whose interests were nullified by public regulations. In normal times, for state managers the consequences of angering capitalists—e.g., divestment, blocked access to commercial media, and punitive collective bargaining—are rationally unjustifiable. So state managers reproduced capitalism because, as the German Claus Offe also noted, their legitimacy depended on a healthy capitalist economy.

State power, then, was not reduceable to class power, but the exercise of state power occured within class configurations that limited its form and content. Production relations shaped the class structure, which conditioned how state power was exercised, and then state policies affected the class structure. The rationality of the capitalist state, in Fred Block's words, "emerges largely behind the backs of the social actors involved,"[3] in the economic structure and the actual conjuncture of class forces. States, however, also have what Theda Skocpol and Ellen Kay Trimberger called "an underlying integrity and a logic of their own"[4] that is keyed to international, geopolitical, and personal factors. State autonomy, neither fixed nor impossible, is thus linked to internal and external institutions that are always changing.

Empirical research has shown that capitalism defined what "rationality" meant to rational public officials. Evidence also suggested that state managers reacted to worker complaints by redistributing resources only to an extent that did not destroy business confidence. Socialists therefore needed to make the consequences of capitalist-state manager cooperation intolerable to rational state managers by intensifying the class struggle and persuading state officials to switch sides.[5] The most important crisis was that between the dominant economic class and the state.

Harrington and other socialists were uncomfortable with rational-choice Marxism. For as long as "rationality" was linked to productive relations, the interests and behavior of classes and state managers were tied to capitalist structures. The state's autonomy was then relative rather than absolute, just as Harrington and the SP right already had noted. Rational-choice Marxists, however, were predisposed toward contextual definition, or analysis, that unpacked linguistic complexes into more comprehensible, testable units. This accent on rigorous definition and empirical inquiry muted their radicalism, and eventually silenced it entirely. If rationality was conditioned only or primarily by a state manager's perceived self-interest, and the state was absolutely free, then as Nicos Poulantzas and others have observed, we are dealing with a pluralist, not a Marxist, theory of the state. From Harrington's point of view, rational-choice Marxists purchased their empirical credentials by cashing in their dialectical method.

Orthodoxy worshiped economics, and rational-choice Marxism, individuals. Neither satisfied Harrington. Marxian state theorists in Europe, especially Louis Althusser, tapped into a rich structuralist tradition, but the practical Harrington didn't like abstractions: he wanted a dialectical crisis theory that also was empirically verifiable and cogent. Surprisingly, he was aided by two old-line materialists.

Instrumentalists had a difficult time explaining reformist policies that penalized substantial segments of the dominant class. The American Paul Sweezy, and Ernest Mandel, a Belgian national and a leader of Trotsky's Fourth International, reconceptualized orthodoxy's theory of the state with the help of neoclassical (Marshallian and Keynesian) economics.

The distinctive problem in advanced capitalism was not falling rates of profit, said Sweezy, but absorbing surplus.[6] Large U.S. corporations were producing more than could profitably be consumed, and were thus promoting overconsumption, built-in obsolescence, burgeoning sales and advertising expenditures, and militarization. The rapid growth of monopolies merely slowed economic growth and modernization without significantly reducing output.

Mandel added that modern capitalism also increased capital-intensive—at the expense of labor-intensive—investment, thereby reducing the total hours of productive labor and limiting real wages.[7] Workers, however, still wanted higher wages, and capitalists still sought wider markets. Mandel thought the contradiction between the material interests of capitalists and workers was unsolvable. Automation thus manifested the best and worst of capitalist production: it portended enormous affluence, and also insecurity, anxiety, unemployment, and demoralization.

Sweezy and Mandel defined state activities within the context of these structural problems. The welfare state eased surplus absorption by preventing actual or anticipated recessions and boosting demand. Its activities briefly hurt some capitalists in order to enhance capitalism's long-term survival prospects. The state was thus relatively free from the immediate interests of particular capitalists, except insofar as these conflicted with the state's purpose of acting for the class as a whole. It was a tool of capitalists *and* of capitalism's internal contradictions. Empirical inquiry needed to isolate instances of state activism and determine, in each case, the relative significance of each factor.

Whether directly or indirectly controlled by millionaires, state activities for Sweezy and Mandel reflected the contradictions of an economic system that produced too much. Nicos Poulantzas, Claus Offe, and Jürgen Habermas were also investigating the capitalist state, and they found that it both organized capitalist class interests and represented all its citizens, including workers. The state's crisis was therefore only indirectly linked to economics because its multifaceted role as defender of capitalism and democracy created a unique set of problems that evolved on its own. State activities might even displace the class struggle from the base onto the superstructure. The fusion of economics and politics thus altered the form, content, and locations of class struggle, in effect legitimizing state theorizing as a means of understanding the dilemma faced by today's welfare states. In brief, the work of Sweezy, Mandel, and the Europeans intimated the kind of non-reductionist crisis theory Harrington was looking for, but James O'Connor, not Michael Harrington, saw it first.

O'Connor noticed that as modern technology improved and production became more specialized and efficient, many small industries were taken over by large, wealthy firms. This expanding segment of monopoly capital required skilled workers, and also very expensive physical overhead capital such as transportation and communication facilities, research and development programs, worker education programs, and energy supplies. Organized workers sought improved wages, health and retirement benefits, factory and living conditions, and recreational facilities. Entrepreneurs lacked the ready cash needed for capital investment and the confidence that with so much overproduction profits would actually improve. When management perceived employee demands as exorbitant, workers were layed off, fired, or forced into inferior jobs. Monopoly capitalism thus discouraged economic growth and created poor, unemployed, angry workers.

Except in rare cases, the state couldn't get directly involved in production. It had to manage things without alienating capitalists, whose economic interests it represented, or workers, for whom it impartially mediated social conflicts. The state, in effect, kicked class conflict upstairs, into the public bureaucracy, by regulating both interclass conflict and intraclass conflict. All this increased state activity was enormously expensive. The costs of the state's efforts to rescue capitalism produced what O'Connor called "the fiscal crisis of the state."

The state fulfilled two basic and often contradictory functions: sustaining or creating the conditions for profitable capital accumulation, and sustaining or creating the conditions for social harmony. O'Connor called the first state function "accumulation," and the second "legitimation." State expenditures have a two-fold character corresponding to these two functions.

"Social capital" expenditures, O'Connor wrote, include investments in "projects and services that increase the productivity of a given amount of labor power and, other things being equal, increase the rate of profit"[8] (e.g., physical items like roads, airports, and railroads; and human services like education, administration, and job training). They also include social consumption expenses for "projects and services that lower the reproduction costs of labor and, other factors being equal, increase the rate of profit"[9] (e.g., goods and services—such as urban renewal, hospitals, child care, and development programs—consumed collectively by workers; and social insurance programs—retirement, unemployment, health, and medical—which increase worker efficiency and lower labor costs). These social capital expenditures lower costs and increase productivity, provide incentives for higher capital investment, and alleviate capital's accumulation crisis.

"Social expenses," O'Connor also claimed, are the "projects and services which are required to maintain social harmony—to fulfill the state's 'legitimation' function. They are not even indirectly productive."[10] Social expenses include all the components of what O'Connor called the "warfare-welfare state": social-welfare benefits, the military, and foreign-aid programs. Social expenses keep workers happy and create favorable environments for profitable investment and trade.

Social capital outlays increase productive capacity and aggregate consumer demand; social expense outlays expand demand but do not affect production. By adjusting capital and expense allocations the state manipulates economic growth through the budgetary process. This function has become indispensable to private industry, which in an unregulated market wouldn't have access to such investment resources. As the state sector grows it also stabilizes monopoly capital and becomes irreplaceable.

The state socializes production costs, but private corporations earn the profits. This situation has created a fiscal crisis, or "structural gap," between public expenditures and revenues. "The result," O'Connor decided, "is a tendency for state expenditures to increase more rapidly than the means of financing them."[11] The state cannot issue debt and borrow against future tax revenues, or raise taxes, because the former creates inflation and deficit spending, and the latter either penalizes successful workers or drives out corporate investment capital. State activity that reproduces capitalism thus also reproduces capitalism's economic problems, but the state has a life and logic of its own. It is linked to the base but not its instrument, and its activities are freely chosen yet also conditioned by the economy.

O'Connor noted the importance of class struggle in production. By organizing workers and demanding higher pay and improved conditions, socialists strain accumulation and propel the state further into the economy. O'Connor also wanted alliances between state employees and state dependents to maximize public programs, and state workers and private-sector workers to oppose regressive taxes, because militant demands can either undermine the state's legitimacy or hurt capitalists. Eventually, he felt, everyone will see that costs *and* profits must be socialized.

Harrington disagreed with O'Connor on one fundamental issue: the rapport between big business and big labor.[12] Large corporations and the unions representing their workers both wanted more social investments, social consumption, and defense outlays. By cooperating, workers and corporations shifted their conflicts onto small capitalists and into the state sectors. Some workers, said O'Connor, were therefore thoroughly integrated into capitalism. O'Connor did not think that auto workers, steel workers, and coal miners, for example, would play socialist politics. Harrington believed that these workers were the heart and soul of America's working class, and thus indispensable.

Harrington, however, conceded O'Connor's point that unions and big business often converge to oppose legislation dealing, for example, with environmental restrictions. O'Connor also acknowledged that big unions often support direct government production of goods and services even when their employers don't. In brief, Harrington emphasized the shared interests—even the most shortsighted—of all workers in order to frame a coordinated electoral assault, while O'Connor tabulated verifiable splits among workers in order to be taken seriously by social scientists. Their dispute was not based on principle.

Harrington's rhetoric in the 1970s depicting the crisis of modern capitalism is empty without O'Connor's nuts-and-bolts diagnosis. What Harrington called the "social costs" of capitalist expansion (e.g., pollution, urban decay, the need for new public services, highways, hospitals, etc.) are O'Connor's social capital and social consumption expenses. Harrington's analysis of inflation presupposes O'Connor's theory of the structural gap between public expenses and revenues. Harrington observed that compassionate state policies were "double edged," and hence crisis-prone, because "they were vitiated and subverted by the capitalist context in which they were undertaken."[13] This anomaly was based on the contradiction that O'Connor discovered in the state's legitimation and accumulation functions. The cornerstone of Harrington's crisis theory, the inefficacy of Keynesianism, was built on the dialectic of growth and decay that O'Connor traced directly to the depletion of accumulation capital. And all the data that Harrington marshalled in his debate with conservatism on the merits of the welfare state merely verified the logic of O'Connor's crisis theory. Harrington's discussion of a doomed welfare state being "wrecked by its own booms,"[14] is merely icing on O'Connor's cake.

The welfare state rescued the economy, and became the locus of new contradictions. Harrington's prognosis was mixed. America had shifted its economic problems onto the state, but didn't abolish them: capitalism's fate was postponed rather than altered. "The successor to capitalism," Harrington pointed out, "will be collectivist, of course. That has already been settled . . . . But there are many possibilities within this tendency, the totalitarian, the authoritarian, and the democratic-socialist among them."[15] Recent events in the U.S. were only moments in what Harrington called "a complex process of decline and fall that will certainly go on for some time to come and just as certainly will end with the collapse of the bourgeois order."[16] Politicians were pulled in opposite directions by workers and capitalists. They juggled and danced during electoral campaigns and then cured structural maladies with band-aids. They stuffed the gap separating image and reality with patriotism, religion, fear, bigotry, war, sports, and anything else that could muzzle discontent. Still, inflation stubbornly persisted, deficits increased, unemployment rose, cities deteriorated, social services withered, impoverishment grew, the nation's infrastructure decayed, public education shriveled, wealth and income distributions widened, state and local governments went bankrupt, and the quality of life declined. New Deal liberalism saved lives, and also worsened inflation and discouraged investment. It was an anachronism.

In what Harrington termed a "triumph of illusion over reality,"[17] Americans solved these problems with variations of the corporate ideology that caused them. The welfare state undermined popular principles of individualism, competition, and weak government, but angry voters nonetheless demanded that life be politicized. The state became a savior and an enemy because it provided needed goods and services that markets no longer delivered, but an expanding bureaucracy also threatened individual freedom, and an exploding debt made the state unreliable. People didn't know what or who to believe.

This ideological crisis actually predated the depression. The system's core values have been culturally sustained so thoroughly through the years that we now take them for granted. In fact, capitalists have always wanted the state to protect individual freedoms, especially the right to own property, and workers have always depended on the state to enforce democracy. For many years prosperity concealed the contradiction. As the economy turned sour in the 1970s, the state, pressured by the New Right Coalition and other corporate-sponsored institutions, reproduced capitalism at the expense of democracy. In Samuel P. Huntington's words from a 1975 Report on the Governability of Democracies prepared for and issued by the Trilateral Commission, "some of the problems of governance in the U.S. today stem from an 'excess of democracy' . . . . The effective operation of a democratic political system usually requires some measure of apathy and noninvolvement on the part of some individuals and groups."[18] Huntington then cited the new social movements and what he called "white collar unionism" as immediate threats to the American way of life. The system then redirected working class anger onto issues that didn't threaten its survival or disrupt the corporate hierarchy. People wounded each other for emotional crumbs, and the struggle for social decency was called indecent. Harrington eventually noticed these cultural safety-valves in the 1980s, when he added more historical flesh and blood to his theory. Without legitimate solutions to America's political crisis, however, he felt that some kind of anti-system outburst was likely. He wanted to funnel this critical energy into creating democracy and socialism.

CULTURAL CRISIS

In *The Politics at God's Funeral* (1983), a journey through the history of Western theology, Harrington stated that religion, like politics, was mired in a profound crisis that was also linked to economics. It was his first major publication since *The Accidental Century* that was written with a sophisticated, highly educated audience in mind.

With the triumphs of Thatcher (1979) and Reagan (1980), and with Europe's left deconstructed by postmodernists, third world leftists turned to God for help. A decade-old religious movement known as liberation theology spread rapidly, especially in Latin America, among those looking for Christian answers to pressing social problems.[19] Christian faith, it argued, held the possibility of social *and* spiritual emancipation. Believers accepted the gospel and then acted *in* history to achieve salvation on earth as well as in heaven. Marxism was liberation theology's tool for explaining and destroying the sins of everyday life because it had tied together economic colonialism, liberation, and revolutionary organization.

Predominantly Catholic, rural, and third world-oriented, liberation theology was initially unprepared to struggle in the U.S. During the 1970s, James H. Cone, soon joined by his young colleague Cornel West, remodelled liberation theology along North American lines. Building on the traditions of Walter Rauschenbusch and the Social Gospel, as well as on the black-power project and its religious analogue, black theology, Cone translated the periphery's theology of emancipation into a familiar vernacular and style, particularly for African Americans.[20]

U.S. conservatives were then beginning a counterattack against labor. They realized that leftists no longer reduced the "woman question" and the "negro question" to economics, and hence the left had belatedly taken two giant steps toward relevance. But the inscrutable fact of working-class religiosity remained. More time, money, and effort, by far, were spent by common people on church-related activities in America than on gender and race combined. And religion, in general, had reinforced conservatism. If, as usual, the line was drawn with Marxists on one side and God on the other, then conservatives knew leftist rhetoric would bounce endlessly between empty barricades. The atheistic, soulless left needed religion badly, or it risked eternal marginality. But at a time, the 1970s, of diminishing trust in U.S. institutions—including mainline religions—religious leaders also knew they needed to capture the political energy raging through the unhappy nation. When Catholic, Protestant, and Jewish religious publications reached tentatively toward leftists, and when radical intellectuals, smitten by third world anti-imperialism and liberation theology, reached back, conservatives anxiously noticed. If U.S. religion went critical, so would its mostly working-class believers.

With the approval of conservatives, Daniel Bell accused America in *The Cultural Contradictions of Capitalism* (1976) of "substituting utopia for religion—utopia not as a transcendental ideal, but one to be realized through history (progress, rationality, science) with the nutrients of technology and the midwifery of revolution." The U.S., Bell warned, faced a spiritual crisis. "Lacking a past or a future, there is only a void,"[21] which was filled with hedonism, "a denial of any limits or boundaries to experience."[22] Bell, and the right generally, argued that religion was based on transcendence (a "new rite of incorporation," Bell explained, "signifying membership in a community that has links with the past as well as the future"[23]), which required a sense of the sacred. Americans needed to reexamine conventional religions because their salvation was, in Bell's own words, "through the resurrection of traditional faith."[24] This rebirth of traditional religion would forge a new, transcendent public philosophy to mediate private conflicts, and stop the fall into nihilism. Bell's transcendent principles predictably rejected bourgeois hedonism and endorsed political liberalism. We had to reaffirm our liberal, capitalist past, Bell wrote, and also regulate private property only to an extent that didn't discourage reinvestment and provided even for the least fortunate a "sense of fairness and inclusion in the society."[25]

In the early 1980s, Harrington found Marxian rhetoric on the religious left and warmed-over capitalism in the mainstream. He also recalled the profound and practical spirituality that Dorothy Day had created for Catholic Workers. Day's theology of liberation was realized in peaceful activities that improved everyday life. Her religion was critical rather than other-worldly, inspired by divine truth but covered in Bowery grime and the foul odors of big-city political machines. With the beloved Day in mind, Harrington endorsed the religious left's radicalism and the center's respect for tradition. Instead of choosing sides he synthesized.

"God," Harrington announced, "one of the most important political figures in Western history, is dying."[26] The question was not the existence of God itself, which was too intensely personal to debate publicly, but whether God existed socially and politically. Religion had justified the status quo by providing moral standards for acceptable lifestyles. God was then alive in the nation's character and in its popular institutions. Now religion was "relocating" from society to the inner self, becoming, in effect, a spiritual lifejacket on a sinking ship of state and appealing to believers for whom social life had long since disappeared.

Harrington believed that religious fundamentalism, whose popularity was spreading, was a quick spiritual punch that jolted people emotionally as the community sank into despair. It was a pillar of faith buried beneath shattered hopes and a fragmented civil society. Fundamentalism could not ethically rebuild society because it lived in and for lonely individuals, and became fashionable only because people had already lost faith in public life. It "may well be profound and even holy," Harrington admitted, "but [fundamentalism] is not the organizing principle of a civilization. That is what Judeo-Christianity was for several millenia. That is why it is so sorely missed now."[27]

As the transcendent symbol of shared consciousness, religion once was an ethical beacon, and now it was in crisis. Harrington wasn't surprised, because society broadly defines the limits of religion, and religion also evolves through its own structures, thinkers, and believers—when religion exists in a troubled society, it too will be troubled. "The spiritual crisis of the late twentieth century is, in this reading, not simply derivative, a projection, of the contradictions of late capitalism, but it cannot be understood apart from those contradictions."[28] Harrington examined 300 years of Western religious history as a path marked by great thinkers, watershed events, frequent contradictions, and structural continuity. The turmoil around religion today was not reduced to an evil force or misguided individual, but emerged gradually as religious structures changed in history and mingled with capitalism.

After thousands of years when religion imparted sacredness and sanctified everyday morality, the Enlightenment—and the rise of capitalism—put humanity, not God, at the center of an amoral universe, and asked science to replace faith. Although rationalism did not disprove God's existence, it fenced God in. As modern technology ate large bites of public space, religion quietly receded further into the background, and society became relativist and mechanized. Men and women played with their fabulous machines, but without a transcendent ethic, toys eventually became idols, technique replaced morality, and laser pulses zapped commitment. "In a relativist, technical society," Harrington asked, "where is there a social ethic that can save us from our own brilliance?"[29]

Rationalism became acquisitive and soon created yuppies, religious zealots, and even fascists. Once a crime, selfishness became a cult, and the god of our grandparents no longer protected us from demonic shopping malls and videos. Old-time religion conceded to science, and science to consumerism. Bell and the right had correctly cited modernity's moral emptiness. The social foundation of their traditional religion, however, was gone forever. If religion were to morally inspire again, it needed to transcend technology rather than, as before, ignoring it.

Socialists also were children of the Enlightenment, but they believed that reason and science could benefit everyone rather than just rich people, and progress could be humane not exploitative. They were atheists, at least until scientific socialists in Russia made them look foolish. History, they finally realized, had become unreasonable, and science had defiled the planet. Thus, religion—albeit a theology of liberation—reappeared even among socialists after World War II. While the broad middle languished in an electronic utopia, leftists and rightists went to a dry spiritual well one last time. "That strange symmetry testifies to the fact that both traditional faith and Enlightenment rationalism are in trouble," Harrington observed, "that at God's funeral there is a crisis of the legitimacy of both 'is' and 'ought,' of the status quo and its opposition as well."[30] Lacking a trancendent morality that could put things in order the way traditional religion once did, modern science and religion became problematic.

When God died intellectuals created false gods like nationalism and materialism, but none revived a universally sanctioned social ethic.[31] Harrington was especially interested in what he called the "Cult of No God .... The first proletarian church of No God" that was established by orthodox Marxists, and became a bogus religion for millions in Europe and the third world.[32] Despite a shameful legacy, something about orthodoxy for a time fascinated thoughtful people. Harrington went back to Marx to find out what it was.

Marx always was hostile to religious beliefs, practices, and institutions. First he compared religion to the drug-like stupor of opium addicts,[33] and later he depicted religion, like ideology, as false consciousness. Religions, Marx said, were tied to economic systems, rationalized extant class relationships, and thus sanctified the dominant class. The "superiority" of modern Protestantism was based on its popular theological defense of capitalism.

Marx realized that religion also was the language of suffering people seeking consolation. Born in social misery, religion was, for Marx, "the expression of real suffering and the protest against real suffering. Religion is the sigh of the oppressed creature, the heart of a heartless world, and the soul of soulless conditions."[34] Religion certainly created what Marx called "illusory happiness," but it also enriched empty lives and thus emotionally sustained most of humanity. Therefore, Marx didn't want to forcibly destroy religion. Conventional religions would disappear only when the inhuman conditions that caused them did, but even in socialism "everyone should be able to attend to his religious as well as his bodily needs," Marx wrote, "without the police sticking their noses in."[35]

Orthodoxy noted only the economic component of religion, and defined spirituality, in Marx's words, as a "reflex of the real world."[36] Socialist "faith" in proletarian science cracked after World War I. "In the ruins of those hopes, however, there came a second 'Marxist' religion, utterly unlike the first," said Harrington, "the compulsory state church of totalitarian Communist countries."[37] Instead of demolishing its *sources*, Leninists directly challenged religion rather than waiting for it to self-destruct. Leninism banned religions altogether and propagandised for atheism, the new divinity. Under Stalin, the totalitarian state religion of atheism replaced God, and the Communist Party ruled with divine sanction, at least until Khrushchev's 1956 speech denouncing Stalinism, when it was largely ignored by a restive congregation. When communism finally collapsed the phony gods of nationalism, consumerism, racism, and anti-semitism reappeared.

The atheist Marx emphasized critique rather than faith and his follow-ers surmised that religion would die with capitalism. Instead, God died, capitalism didn't, and socialists created a new divinity; even when life improved, mortal people apparently needed the solace only religion pro-vided. "The very fact that people begin to die," Harrington noted, "not because they were born poor, or born in a pre-scientific age which lacked the serum to fight plagues, but because they were born, because humanity is finite even at the very height of its development, could provide the basis for loneliness and alienation and religion."[38] Socialism did not cause God's death, and God's death did not create a rational, humane world—perhaps socialists could even be religious.

Traditional religion was hopelessly outdated, and modern society had binged on amorality. Fundamentalism made individuals feel good, but lacked transcendent norms to redefine the community. Harrington wanted an alliance of believers and atheists around transcendentals that were nei-ther supernatural in the traditional religious sense nor profane. This kind of "social religion" anchored spirituality in real human needs rather than dogma. It grew from the shared experiences of citizens painfully coming to terms with life during a crisis, and thus was accessible to religious and non-religious traditions. By moralizing social life, it might convince selfish people to cooperate with each other for the common good. Its critical, emancipatory spirit was thus imminent in humanity *and* society, and could spark a widespread social renewal—some people might call it God.

Four principles activated Harrington's social religion.[39] Since legitimacy today arises from the claim that people need to govern themselves, trans-cendent principles, first of all, are binding only when society democratically formulates and endorses them. These directives, moreover, encompass com-mon, not individual, experiences and emanate from a unified people rather than some new spiritual or political messiah. And the new consensus is to be truly universal, because in today's global economy all are neighbors. Harrington's social religion thus sanctifies common actions of a bonded community following its best interests, not some abstract, uncontrollable spiritual force.

Although spiritual values are not economically determined, religion and economics are linked, and hence, Harrington pointed out, "it is useless to talk about that spiritual crisis and its possible resolution without suggesting, not simply a politics, but a politics which confronts social and economic structures."[40] Harrington's religious consciousness arises amidst the strug-gle for democratic socialism, and socialism arises in the struggle for a new religion. Capitalism's crises are linked, and so are their resolutions.

Nations today are electronically linked in a global community: the actions of one impact directly on others and cultures intermingle. When goods, services, and communication flow cross-nationally, class is defined not only by one's position in national relations of production, but also by that nation's position in global production. This worldwide system isn't controlled by one state. When only capitalist options are available to nations, domestic class formations become capitalist. Although it lacks legal standing or the power to legitimately sanction deviant behavior, the capitalist global system accomplishes internationally what the state does domestically: it reproduces capitalist relations of production. Rebel nations are informally punished for anti-system activities, limiting a state's room to maneuver politically. Domestic activities are thus linked to the world system, which regulates who controls resources, how development is apportioned among national actors, and when the balance of world power is reordered. The global system conditions our most intimate personal experiences.

Marx once argued that colonialism was an acceptable means of setting Asia on the same economic track as Europe, but later he acknowledged that British colonialism actually hindered India's development by siphoning resources into Europe. He quickly detected how cheap Irish labor and agricultural exports nourished British industry and drained Ireland of needed capital resources. Irish independence, he concluded, preceded Irish economic development.

Lenin examined how capitalism squeezed production into large industrial monopolies, and money into powerful banking monopolies that controlled investment capital. These industrial and bank interests were what Hilferding called "finance capital," that is, capital controlled by banks and used by industrialists. Faced with surplus domestic capital, banks exported capital abroad into cheap resources and export markets, linking domestic and world markets. A financial oligarchy forged an international capitalist order and assigned roles to each national actor. Imperialism, said Lenin, was now the highest stage of capitalist development.

Harry Magdoff, since 1969 the editor of *Monthly Review*, believed that Lenin correctly linked monopoly capitalism and imperialism, but mistakenly blamed finance capital.[41] Magdoff discovered that, since World War II, multinational corporations, not finance capital, determined international capital investment by marshalling enormous funds and national power for their global adventures. The contemporary world order was thus designed by multinationals reacting to domestic variables (e.g., economic, political, military, even religious) that determined where, when, and how capitalism expanded.

Orthodoxy outlined the needs and problems of industrial capitalists and urban workers, and interpreted capitalism as a troubled but dynamic global system that eventually encompassed the entire underdeveloped world. Paul A. Baran, a Stanford University professor, held that capitalism programmed third world nations into perpetual economic backwardness by disrupting native internal markets, uprooting potentially competitive native industries, and creating a local comprador class—that is, a native group employed by, or executing duties for foreign interests.[42] These activities assured western imperialists cheap resources and labor, and an export market that boosted domestic prices. Development and underdevelopment were not accidental. Underdevelopment was created by unfavorable universal economic constraints that evolved historically and were reinforced by Western capitalists.

With Andre Gunder Frank and the Brazilian Ruy Mauro Marini, Baran formulated Dependency Theory. In order to fuel Western development, they argued, capitalists extracted from underdeveloped nations raw materials and light consumer items that were no longer profitably manufactured in Western factories. Wages in underdeveloped areas were kept low, internal markets aborted, and accumulation severly deformed. Dependent nations had to import expensive manufactured goods from the West, and these unequal exchanges strengthened the system as a whole even as they impoverished some national actors. The surplus produced in underdeveloped lands—whom Frank labelled "satellites"—was appropriated by and at the centers of capitalist production, the so-called metropoles. This surplus was profit for Western capitalists and improved wages and living standards for their workers. By modulating import quotas and prices of exported manufactured items, and coopting feudal and comprador allies, capitalists forced underdeveloped nations to conform.

Industrialized nations, then, created the global division of labor and accumulated capital from it. As their technology matured they assigned new tasks to underdeveloped nations. Because third world states were dependent on foreign monopoly capital, they became its tool, reproducing at home the international division of labor. As Western capital's accumulation crisis deepened, and domestic pressures rose for even more capital extraction and accumulation in the third world, dependent states subjugated their populations. Low-paying manufacturing jobs moved further south, worsening unemployment and poverty in developed nations. The dependent state was thus conditioned by the same universal process of underdevelopment that shaped the dependent economy.

The transition in America from Dependency to World-System Theory involved a subtle shift in perspective. World-System theorists assumed that the globe, not developed or underdeveloped perceptions of the globe, was the starting point for understanding regions and nations.[43] It had to be studied on its own terms in order to understand the behavior of nations. A state's mode of production thus had worldwide boundaries—that is, its internal class and political struggles were shaped by its place and function in the world economy. Global exploitation conditioned national exploitation. Urban workers in the West, for example, were coopted with extracted third world surpluses, and rural workers in impoverished regions were coopted into multi-class anti-Western alliances. The system survived by muting internal national class struggles and defusing working-class consciousness. Regional economic development originated in the historical process of global accumulation, with each region assigned a mode of production corresponding to its role in the system. "National economies" simply didn't exist.

Most of this theoretical work had already appeared by the mid-1970s, when U.S. capital was inflating its class war from above against labor. As part of this business counteroffensive, neo-conservatives, writing in journals like *Commentary*, were "moving" public opinion beyond the extreme caution that had characterized U.S. foreign policy since 1972, the so-called Vietnam syndrome. Two campaigns of historical revisionism were begun in *Commentary* during the 1970s. First, neo-conservatives rewrote the record of failed military interventionism during 1950–75 in order to build support for what they hoped would be new interventions in the 1980s. Second, they resurrected the 1950s McCarthyite accusation that Stalin simply outsmarted FDR at Yalta, and, in effect, stole Eastern Europe. The U.S., in short, had failed to stop communist postwar aggressions because spineless, naive, misinformed liberals were in power.[44]

Under attack from the right, Harrington aggressively defended the legacy of progressive historiography that began in 1959, when William Appleman Williams described how expansionist corporations worked with a military-industrial state to mold U.S. foreign policy.[45] Williams shocked intellectuals, who had bought the original 1950s version of neo-conservatism, into critically examining Cold War rhetoric. Harrington realized that U.S. wealth and power could wreak havoc on the impoverished third world, worsening an already terrible situation for a majority of the world's people. His own slow conversion from Vietnam hawk to dove remained an embarrassing memory and now he wanted Americans to feel what life on the periphery was like before they again endorsed capricious military interventions. *The Vast Majority* (1977) consists primarily of journals that Harrington kept while travelling in the third world, with pertinent commentary.[46] It frames the global crisis and the fateful choices America will face in the future.

Harrington wrote *The Vast Majority* with *The Other America* in mind, "that is to say . . . addressed to the general reader . . . and interpolating reportage and economic and social analysis."[47] He reiterated basic principles of Dependency and World-System Theories,[48] and used anecdotal evidence to convince readers that capitalism had sentenced a vast majority of people to poverty and powerlessness. "It seems to me," Harrington noted, "that something like the invisibility of poverty which distorted our vision in the 1950s is now taking place on a world scale."[49] Capitalism had also ignored potentially rich consumer markets in the third world, and siphoned factory work from the North to the South at a time of economic crisis. It was in America's and the third world's rational self-interest to reorder the world system, and Harrington hoped—vainly as it turned out—that *The Vast Majority* would galvanize public opinion the way *The Other America* once did.

Harrington had travelled extensively accumulating evidence for his book for a lengthy period preceding its publication. These years in the mid-1970s were not easy for him. Factionalism had destroyed his beloved Socialist Party in 1972. He then struggled to make a go of it in the Democratic Socialist Organizing Committee (DSOC), began a new career at Queens College, slowly and painfully recovered from a breakdown, maintained a hectic speaking schedule, insulated himself and his family from hostile critics, and wrote prolifically. Harrington also worked hard to get DSOC into the Socialist International (SI), and in so-doing befriended Willy Brandt and Olaf Palme—European socialists who closely followed third world issues—as well as many third world leaders. The journeys, and later the book, pleased his distinguished new friends (Harrington dedicated *The Vast Majority* to "Julius K. Nyerere of the South and Willy Brandt of the North"); enhanced DSOC's reputation overseas among SI leaders (who finally accepted DSOC's application in 1978); and furnished time and space for Harrington to relax, silently reflect, reread the classics, and mingle anonymously with ordinary people. They also put a human face on all those frigid academic theories, and let Harrington plainly tell the U.S. what a democratic socialist foreign policy looks like.

How, Harrington asked, can human actors alter a worldwide system that evolved over centuries? In this nationalist age how do we get from capitalist to socialist world-systems? Whenever anti-system states have appeared they found the immediate costs of withdrawing from the world-system greater than they could politically sustain. They operated, instead, state-level "catching-up" strategies by competing economically with core states. Each participant in the capitalist world-system, regardless of ideology, acted like a capitalist. Communist states therefore became what Immanuel Wallerstein called "collectivist capitalist firms,"[50] extracting surpluses and accumulating capital. They had to accept the rules of the world-system, which only strengthened that system in its struggle to survive.

Andre Gunder Frank took a fatalist's view, dismissing proletarian activism. Socialists, he felt, had to wait patiently for the global system, in its own time and through its own mechanisms, to self-destruct. Harrington disagreed because the current world division of labor assigned menial positions primarily to nonwhites, and this inequity created an explosive racial caste system where a "racial accident of birth" became, in Harrington's opinion, a "permanent social and economic fate."[51] For Harrington, Frank's fatalism was outrageously provocative. He foresaw bloody wars of redistribution led by outlaw nationalities and races armed, perhaps, with nuclear weapons.

Samir Amin, on the other hand, felt that regional liberation movements could alter the global division of labor. Amin's research indicated that regions—i.e. combinations of peripheral states with common bonds—could break, or delink, from the capitalist world-system and create new social and economic formations. Each successful regional struggle made it more difficult for core states to accumulate wealth in the periphery, and worsened their domestic crises. Eventually core states and the capitalist world-system would collapse. Fernando H. Cardoso and Enzo Faletto found that domestic markets in dependent economies that are linked to internal wages do expand, albeit slowly. Moreover, local entrepreneurs who are linked to, but not controlled by, core capitalists also become more independent.[52] These two findings flatly contradicted Frank's conclusions, and meant that unrelenting domestic class struggles in dependent nations could lead to meaningful reforms for workers, even within the capitalist world-system. As proletarian political victories in the third world increased, the political outcome of global crises were skewed leftward.

Even Marx, said Harrington, finally realized that unique conditions offered unexpected options in underdeveloped lands. But socialism, for Marx, could not survive in poverty.[53] It became feasible when workers were a majority, were concentrated in large numbers and forced to organize economically, and were familiar with modern workplace technology. Socialism thus survived only in highly developed, exploitative conditions. Perhaps, Marx suggested, it could precede capitalism in the third world, but only with massive economic aid from sympathetic European nations that already were socialist.

Wealthy core nations today are neither socialist nor willing to subsidize the third world. To Harrington, the idea that non-Western socialist movements could delink nations and regions from the world-system was nonsense. Without an educated, self-governing working class, and modern technology capable of large-scale production, the preconditions for socialism that Marx envisioned were absent in most of Africa, Asia, and Latin America.

Capitalism was also impractical in the third world because poor nations lacked domestic investment capital, and government or foreign corporations would have to take up the slack. Corporations, however, invest only in factories that reinforce the international division of labor and also are profitable. Government finances public investment from taxation and credit, and then subsidizes the poor to create a domestic market. These efforts are often torpedoed by foreign corporations that slash profits in order to maintain markets. Neither scenario creates the preconditions for socialism.

With classical capitalism and democratic socialism ruled out, third world intellectuals had little room to maneuver, but were nonetheless pressured to act. They wanted to modernize without creating capitalism's maldistribution of wealth and urban chaos, and they were already predisposed to reject everything associated with imperialism, including capitalism. Many succumbed to what Harrington called the "Stalinist temptation," the dream of modernizing from the top down because a mass movement didn't exist.[54] Substitute workers such as peasants, dispossessed city dwellers, military officers, or educated elites were marshalled to replace nonexistent workers, and they forcibly extracted huge surpluses. Elitist party-states created command economies and became self-styled Marxists. Third world socialism intimidated people with "progressive" tyrannies that even the pitiless imperialists would have endorsed. Then these same nations quietly resumed their duties in the world economic system, transferring resources and wealth to Moscow, Western Europe, and the U.S. Revolutionary activism had merely sanctioned the world-system.

Thus, third world socialists were trapped between two unacceptable alternatives: by doing nothing they endorsed de facto state capitalist regimes run by and for compradors; by seizing power they became Stalinists. Neither significantly altered the world-system, and both were exploitative.

Harrington suggested that a non-capitalist and non-communist strategy might affect global injustice in the same way his domestic program affected U.S. capitalism.[55] Democratic socialists needed to support modest changes in the way nations did business that would help poor people live better. This was a humane and worthy objective, and also a first step in establishing the preconditions for third world socialism. The cumulative effects of such reforms, the empowerment of poor nations and people—now about 3/4 of the world's population, with 1/6 of the world's wealth—would democratize the world-system. Reformism immediately reduced exploitation and started the ball rolling toward the erosion of international capitalism.

Harrington realized that third world nations often lacked democratic traditions, and that democratic socialism originated in the industrialized West, where many problems experienced by third world nonwhites didn't exist. He still insisted that authoritarianism was immoral and inefficient wherever it appeared, even among the victims of global capitalism.[56] In the past, communism had mobilized resources and created impressive short term economic growth, but only by institutionalizing inequality and annihilating creativity, ambition, and self-respect. And even radical regimes that once had squeezed a surplus from their parched workers had recently drowned in inefficiency. Third world communism at best lifted people to a raised level of inhumanity; at worst, as in Cambodia, it sank beneath comprehension.

America was economically prepared for socialism, but was underdeveloped politically. Third world socialism, on the other hand, crashed into economic underdevelopment. Harrington's program for the U.S. counselled enlightened reformism, and so did his third world agenda.[57] Newly independent states were cautioned to steer a middle course between free-market capitalism and communism. Private and foreign investment capital was desperately needed to fund development projects, but since affordable housing, roads, education, and public utilities weren't usually profitable investments, public capital also was required. Governments therefore needed to integrate private, foreign, and public investments into a developmental plan based on helping people rather than maximizing profits. This meant abolishing corporate-sponsored agriculture and subsidizing voluntary cooperatives or middle-sized, publicly regulated private farms. Harrington also supported a policy of "selective engagement," whereby developing nations protected some of their budding industries at a cost but also participated in the world market to pay for industrial losses and inefficiencies. A mixed third world economy, with some state regulation, nudged society to the left without endangering democracy.

Harrington did not stipulate how, when, and where developing nations finally established socialism, and he did not know how to co-opt stubborn elites. He sympathized with armed revolutionaries fighting conservative dictators, but admonished those who incited wars of national liberation or indiscriminately backed guerrillas. Post-colonial governments had to abolish archaic practices and guide development, but not suppress dissent or dissenters. Since impoverished regions have unique problems, no master plan for development existed. Harrington's advice, finally, was patience and humility. Even though international capitalism sentenced innocent people to impoverishment, socialism still could not be built on poverty. Therefore, socialists had to take into account distinctive histories and structures. A public-spirited mixed economy, the details of which varied from nation to nation, had to suffice until the system itself was transformed.

Harrington never was comfortable telling others how to live. He also agreed with Marx that industrialized nations could help democratize the global system and, with his friends Willy Brandt and Olaf Palme, that what Brandt later called a "new international order"[58] first and foremost required changes in the behavior of developed capitalist nations. Beginning in December 1977, Brandt headed the Independent Commission on International Development Issues, which issued its first report, *North-South: A Programme for Survival*, in 1980, and its second, *Common Crisis North-South: Cooperation for World Recovery*, in 1983. Olaf Palme chaired the Independent Commission on Disarmament and Security Issues in the early 1980s. Its report, *Common Security*, was published in 1982. Brandt's and Palme's findings are remarkably similar to Harrington's in *The Vast Majority*: third world development depends on modifying the international behavior of capitalist nations at least as much as on the internal policies of developing nations. Three years before the first Brandt Commission report suggested it, Harrington decided to emphasize the role America could play in revamping the world-system.

The priorities of capitalist economics reinforced third world poverty. Rational U.S. foreign-policy makers thus sustained injustice merely by doing their jobs. Even "charitable" foreign policies such as financial aid, loans, or reconstruction programs made money for America while impoverishing recipient nations. "This monstrous subsidy from the miserable to the fat," Harrington concluded, "is, after all, quite logical."[59]

Capitalists responded by endorsing "fairness" in international trade. If nations exchanged with each other on a reciprocal basis—that is, if advanced nations lowered duties on raw materials and poor nations did likewise on industrial imports—all nations gained a larger market for their exports and each specialized in what it did best. Since a benevolent free market enriched every nation, rational, fair behavior corresponded to the free and equal treatment of all nations according to classical free-market principles.

The problem was that the free and equal treatment of non-equals reinforced inequality. "Fair" trading stopped non-Western nations from protecting new industries during the crucial first phase of development, whereas industrialized nations merely reduced duties on a few raw materials, the cost of which was easily absorbed by producers or consumers. The payoff of free-market economics widened the gap between wealthy and poor nations, and strengthened the world-system by encouraging multi-national corporations (MNCs) to move freely around the globe, maximizing profits by pitting Southern and Northern workers against each other.

Harrington felt that this cycle had to stop, and the U.S. was uniquely qualified to stop it. An unregulated free market sometimes hurt many more people than it helped, and in these instances regulating the market was a decent thing to do; "In order to compensate for the tremendous disadvantages that have been imposed on the poor lands for well over a hundred years, they must," warned Harrington, "in strictest equity, now be given special advantages."[60] America once sought such relief in the New Deal, and the welfare state represented a significant new opportunity for U.S. social-ists. Now the Southern hemisphere awaited an international New Deal, a "welfare world" in which third world socialists could also operate. The Declaration of Principles of the Socialist International, which Harrington wrote, put it this way: "Socialist struggles in the original capitalist nations made gains in welfare and solidarity, which in turn made the extension of democracy possible in individual countries. Likewise the work of abolish-ing international inequality will be a crucial step forward on the road to a democratic world society."[61]

Harrington suggested a modest foreign policy agenda that left America's economy and the world-system intact.[62] It included a national commit-ment to abolish "absolute poverty" throughout the globe, increase and stabilize prices of third world commodities, increase the nation's develop-mental aid to .7 percent of Gross Domestic Product (GDP), renegotiate the third world's debt burden, and transfer technology and some industries to the third world in order to speed industrialization.

Having witnessed first-hand the squalor of life in the periphery, Harrington was clearly embarrassed by his restraint,[63] but he maintained that even these modest changes were better than inflated rhetoric. By leav-ing the world order "impeccably capitalist," and by letting U.S. business make money from the moderate increase in social justice, Harrington believed this program stood a reasonable chance of being implemented sometime soon. If the U.S. took that first step toward a more equitable future, the seeds of more dramatic changes would be planted.

These seeds, in time, would reap an impressive harvest.[64] International economic planning, perhaps administered by the U.N. and funded by pro-gressive national taxes, eventually would allocate massive resources to nations on the basis of needs and capacities. This new Marshall Plan for the South could lessen poverty and create additional markets for the North. A new Economics Security Council, consisting of Northern and Southern nations, might someday supervise world economic development. Foreign aid then would be a right, like social security, rather than a charity. Rights imply duties, in this case for recipient nations. The U.N. or regional agen-cies need to target funds primarily toward efficient, democratically planned projects, with a central fund compensating any nation whose export income dropped. MNCs then would be restricted from siphoning cash from poor nations or profiteering from anti-social investments. Finally, industrial, agricultural, and population control research undertaken in the West has to be shared with developing nations. All these proposals would slow the rate of American economic growth, not reverse it. They would also reverse a U.S. trade policy that now discouraged economic development where it was most needed, and strengthen worldwide institutions through which reforms were initiated and administered. "I believe that some kind of world government is absolutely necessary," Harrington confessed, "but at present there is little reason to hope for one."[65]

Harrington was optimistic about a U.S. foreign policy reassessment.[66] For one thing, the nation's democratic legacy was at odds with its international policies. Events like the 1985 Live-Aid concert convinced Harrington that when Americans know others are suffering they "want to be decent."[67] This didn't mean that U.S. workers had to lower their own living standards. Harrington wanted to protect American workers from the disastrous effects of free markets,[68] but protectionism was a temporary device to facilitate global changes that would make protectionism unnecessary. It did mean, in Harrington's own words, that "the economic relevance of a global recovery should be stated in moral terms, as part of a commitment to the essential oneness of humanity."[69] Economic *and* moral arguments might build an electoral majority to alter U.S. foreign policy.

Except for the oil industry, Harrington maintained, U.S. corporations no longer needed to exploit the third world.[70] High-tech synthetics were already replacing third world natural resources, and profitable American investments in Europe and Asia had made third world investment less attractive. Harrington felt that U.S. capitalism easily could absorb a humane trade policy because now prosperity depended on maintaining high mass consumption at home and in other industrialized nations, not on exploiting hungry peasants.

Finally, Harrington claimed that the end of the Cold War freed military funds to be invested in domestic social programs and third world development projects.[71] Surplus public cash could magically transform hard-boiled politicians into compassionate leaders.

American prosperity, in short, did not depend on exploiting the third world, so U.S. support for an unjust international system was not economically necessary. The crucial factor in transforming an imperialist legacy was thus political, not economic. Harrington suggested that a hopeful, enlightened public would agree to increase U.S. support to the third world.

Democratic socialists had to inform wealthy liberals that social justice actually expanded markets and increased profits. The "growing gap between an international economy and inadequate international political structures," wrote Harrington, "has been a contributary factor to the poverty and underdevelopment of the South, as well as to mass unemployment and new forms of poverty in many areas of the North."[72] Harrington's foreign-policy proposals would thus enrich capitalists and solve a worldwide crisis. As always, he believed socialism was sweetened when it delivered real benefits, and poisoned by unrealistic promises; unchastened socialist pride couldn't feed the hungry, whereas a new agenda of legitimate options outperformed hordes of militants. Harrington's proposals, he admitted, were unfair to the impoverished, but certainly were better than the status quo. And a healthy, self-governing periphery could spearhead auspicious international changes.

Global economic and political development created the preconditions for third world socialism. It also shifted the balance of international power toward the world's population centers in the Southern hemisphere, created new third world markets for high-tech commodities, and drove U.S. businesses back home by raising wages. By doing the right thing abroad, America also increased jobs, consumer demand, and confidence at home. Democratic planning among nations set Harrington's domestic agenda squarely in the political mainstream.

THE NEW CLASS AND REALIGNMENT

HARRINGTON BECAME MORE SENSITIVE to racial, gender, and religious loyalties during the 1980s, but he still realized that jobs and incomes, not self-image, allocated goods and services in the general population. Social structures condition what we want and how we live, so different kinds of societies provide different economic opportunities. These structures also determine the relative social importance of race, gender, religion, ethnicity, region, and age, especially in the U.S., where a pluralist tradition inflates their significance. The non-economic traits of subordinate classes, however, are rarely considered social assets, while those of dominant classes are usually valued. At any particular economic level a package of attributes reinforces the pertinent lifestyle.

Class, then, is not an objective category, because it is economic, social, political, and cultural from the very beginning. Attitudes toward sports, leisure, child-rearing, food, marriage, and politics are all part of a coherent way of life whose most basic trait is the work we do. A worker thus has many attributes, each of which occasionally predominates. During certain periods of history the economic interest asserts itself, bonding workers into a mobilized force. In the 1930s, for example, workers created a welfare state in a nation that otherwise was individualist. Popular expectations were permanently radicalized, even though most Americans still declared themselves capitalists.[1] Harrington believed that worsening crises, a practical strategy, and socialist agitation could reawaken an economically self-conscious working class.

THE MEANINGS OF CLASS

Class—perhaps the central concept of Marxism—was never adequately defined. The last section in the final chapter of *Capital*, entitled "Classes," unexpectedly stops after only one page, following Marx's admonition "The first question to be answered is this: What constitutes a class?" Engels later commented, "Here the manuscript breaks off."[2] Marx's work nonetheless repeatedly refers to class, and introduces two contradictory ways of conceptualizing this key term.

The first, adopted by Engels and the orthodox movement, defines class objectively in terms of one's relation to the means of production. In capitalism, people naturally split into two major classes: those who own labor power and those who own capital. The former are workers; the latter, capitalists. As production matures, class relations become antagonistic, until they explode into violent conflict. Objective classes summon people to their fates.

Primarily in the historical works, however, Marx acknowledged the contingency of class formation—that is, the importance of subjective factors such as shared struggle, perceived interests, common lifestyles, and political organization. Each stage of history, in this view, needs to be studied empirically to see whether the conjuncture of objective and subjective factors leads to authentic class formation.

Especially in *The Class Struggles in France, 1848-50* and *The 18th Brumaire of Louis Bonaparte*, Marx detected a gap between the objective and subjective factors of class formation that distorted class behavior. Instead of polarizing working and capitalist classes, Marx concluded, in *Capital*, that "middle and intermediate strata . . . obliterate [objective] lines of demarcation everywhere," and create an "infinite fragmentation of interest and rank" among both workers and capitalists.[3] Those who own capital, for example, are fragmented into industrial, financial, landed, social, and political subgroups, and each of these is subdivided yet again based on net worth. Those who own labor power are split into workers (urban or rural, large or small industry, manual or intellectual, unionized or non-unionized, well or poorly paid), peasants, and lumpenproletariat.

The intra- and inter-class lines fade and sometimes disappear entirely, but Marx assumed, perhaps naively, that as capitalism matured, only industrial workers and capitalists would survive. Disregarding for the moment contrary evidence, there remains a theoretical problem involving the relationship of existing historical classes to structural classes: do "objective" workers who live, think, and behave like capitalists actually become capitalists? Do classes, in other words, automatically evolve in a structurally determined history, or are they created by people struggling collectively to be free? Marx's perfunctory class theory is inconclusive.

Not surprisingly, some Marxists have used factual evidence to support Marx's structural definition of class.[4] Capitalist society, they observed, really is polarized into workers and capitalists. Deep internal divisions create intra-class frictions, but do not alter productive relationships, hence leaving the basic class structure untouched. Workers especially have been split into several subgroups, each with distinct traits. Some subgroups are based on ethnicity (religious, linguistic, racial, and cultural differences), and others on social, economic, and educational factors (blue and white collar, intellectuals, professionals, and managers). However, all workers, regardless of living standards or values, remain workers because of their location in social production—that is, because they sell their labor power. Inauthentic behavior by privileged workers occurs within the capitalist class structure and complicates mobilization. Socialists needed to show the so-called middle classes that they were really workers, and then organize the workplace.

Other Marxists have claimed that struggle actually creates classes, and thus no valid structural theory of class exists. In E. P. Thompson's words, "class is defined by men as they live their own history, and, in the end, this is its only definition."[5] These struggles are conditioned by the totality of economic, social, political, and cultural factors that influence class formation or disintegration. Socialist movements thus take place in capitalist social relations, but are not determined by capitalist relations of production. Classes are formed when collective actors decide to organize around their position in production. The politics of class formation, therefore, precedes economic struggles between classes. Politics and ideology, not economics, create struggles during which classes organize, disorganize, and reorganize. The "middle classes"—laborers who sell intellectual rather than manual labor power often for surprisingly high wages—are fair game to any political movement, including socialists. Thus the configuration of the U.S. class map depends on how well socialist ideology attracts wage earners.

A third perspective on class, in America associated mainly with C. Wright Mills, Alvin Gouldner, and Eric Olin Wright, revises Marx's structural argument: classes *are* determined by objective relations of production, but, as Marx described in the *Grundrisse*, three rather than two classes exist.

In addition to capitalists and workers, capitalism now requires a new class of intellectuals who control cultural capital that produces saleable utilities bringing in sizable incomes. Like old capitalists, they derive incomes from capital, but their capital takes the form of knowledge and ideas about how to manage productive capacity. Those who control this new capital often have attitudes that resemble those of traditional workers more than those of old capitalists. This new class's ideology, in other words, rationalizes the special material interests of a cultural bourgeoisie. These include upgrading the professional quality of its work, using its own sophisticated skills to control work activities and environments, raising its income, and gaining political power. Highly educated new-class members use what Gouldner, in *The Future of Intellectuals and the Rise of the New Class*, called a culture of critical discourse to justify their interests. This rhetoric negates excessive profit, rent, and interest, advocates self-govern-ment, and seeks higher salaries, goals which are thoroughly proletarian. On the other hand, the new class also occupies what Wright called "con-tradictory locations within exploitation relations."[6] In relation to some productive assets (e.g., capital) it is exploited; in relation to others (e.g., organization and skill) it exploits. Thus, the new class has some material and political interests that are fundamentally different from, and opposed to, those of workers *and* capitalists.

What the new class, particularly technicians, lacks is a broad historical perspective to thwart its innate elitism and articulate its interests. Socialists can provide it, thereby cobbling a worker/new-class alliance that transforms a middle-class buffer into a socialist vanguard.

THE MEANINGS OF CLASS STRUGGLE

Harrington's definition of class was theory and fact driven. It drew from an ambiguous Marxian legacy and interpretive studies by social scientists, as well as the existing situation of U.S. workers. Therefore, leftists' descriptions of the class struggle influenced Harrington as much as their theories of class.

A large and impressive body of evidence, for example, supported Marx's original structural argument that society was polarizing into objective working and capitalist classes. It showed that the distance between those who own labor power and those who own capital was steadily widening, establishing a nation of rich and poor, capitalists and workers, and also pri-oritizing workplace struggles.[7]

This data indicated that wealth in the 1980s and early '90s was now more concentrated than ever before, with the top 1/2 of 1 percent of U.S. families owning 44 percent of the nation's wealth and business assets (up from 31 percent in 1963) and averaging $8.8 billion of wealth per household (up 147 percent from 1963). The bottom 61 percent of Americans owned 7 percent of net wealth; the bottom 45 percent, less than 2 percent. The richest 20 percent in the U.S. had more than 9 times the income of the poorest 20 percent, and this number was rising as rich families bagged higher proportions of income during the 1980s. Families in the bottom 40 percent had actual declines in income, with the lowest quintile losing 9 percent. In families with children headed by young adults under 30 years old, adjusted incomes dropped an astonishing 32 percent since 1973, from $27,765 to $18,844 in 1988. About half of all U.S. children are born into such families. Incomes in female-headed households fell by 27 percent, to $7,256. The top tax rate on personal income was cut to 31 percent during Reagan's tenure, from more than 90 percent during the Kennedy years, and then rose marginally under Clinton. And, while their tax payments amounted to a somewhat larger share of the total federal tax bills than in 1977—because their incomes grew so much—families in the top 1 percent paid less than 27 percent of their income in taxes in 1989, compared with more than 35 percent in 1977. Although income of the poorest Americans declined about 9 percent since 1980, and their personal taxes were cut, their total tax bill in 1992—including social security, medicare, and state and local taxes—increased almost 28 percent. If the top 1 percent of American families were taxed at 100 percent, no one else would have to be taxed.

Since 1973, real wages—that is, income per employed person rather than income per capita—declined to the point where the bottom 5/6 of the income distribution not only fared worse in relation to the top 1/6 but also saw its net income in adjusted dollars actually fall. One reason for this was the loss of good manufacturing jobs to the third world and their replacement in the last ten years by minimum-wage jobs in the service sector. Low incomes and high unemployment increased the number of families living below the official poverty line by 36 percent since 1970. In 1992, almost 15 percent of Americans—roughly 37 million people (up from 24.7 million in 1977)—lived below the poverty line, 69 percent of whom were white (up 3 percent since 1979). Millions more could barely make ends meet, despite incomes that exceeded the official minimum standards of impoverishment. Skyrocketing prices for private services like health care and school tuition outpaced the inflation rate and trivialized gains in disposable income for those marginally above the poverty line. More than 14 million children under 18 were poor in 1990, about 40 percent of all those in poverty. In the same year, 22.5 percent of U.S. children under 6 years were impoverished, compared to 16.6 percent in 1967. A shocking 40 percent of New York City's children lived in poverty. But contrary to common misconceptions, a study by Northeastern University's Center for Labor Market Studies concluded that most poor children were white, lived in small cities, suburbs, or rural areas, and came from working families; nearly half of them lived in families in which the father was present.

The Children's Defense Fund estimated in 1989 that the incomes of every poor family with children could have been lifted above the federal poverty line for $28 billion. The Reagan and Bush administrations spent $30 billion to bail out the failing savings-and-loans, the Pentagon exhausted $26 billion in two years just in inflation adjustments, and the richest 1 percent of America's tax payers received in 1990 some $39 billion in tax breaks approved by the White House and Congress during the 1980s, yet the federal coffers turned up empty when poor children cried for help.

At stake here is the glue that fastens millions of working Americans to their economic system: the promise of access to middle class lifestyles and incomes. The "middle class" is usually defined by academics as households headed by people with high-school diplomas and sometimes some college, incomes between $20,000 and $60,000, and in recent years a home, two vehicles, and one or two full-time workers. By these standards, about 60 percent of Americans are middle class, with most clustered around the lower income figure. According to data from the Survey Research Center at the University of Michigan, however, as the gap separating rich and poor widened, a shrinking proportion of Americans were classified as middle class, and a growing percentage were becoming either wealthy or, more frequently, impoverished.

To average workers, the material and psychological costs were devastating. For the first time since World War II most men who became 40 in 1973 saw their earnings decline by an average of 14 percent by the time they reached 50. Middle-class children, as individual wage earners, were unlikely to reach the adjusted salary levels of their parents. A young man, for example, who left home in 1973 was now earning about 20 percent less than his father earned in the early 1970s; when the young man's father had left his home in the early 1950s, he could expect to earn 15 percent more than his father. Education, moreover, was not the great equalizer it once was. A 1992 economic report from the Economic Policy Institute discovered that from 1973 to 1990 incomes fell 15 percent for young families headed by a college-educated parent. This trend was likely to worsen as white-collar lay-offs increased.

Nor, for most Americans, would things soon improve. Conservatives like to emphasize America's economic fluidity, the constant ebb and flow of fortunes made and then lost, of average people becoming millionaires through hard work. Rags-to-riches, however, remained the economic exception. Census Bureau data, and studies published in 1992 by the National Bureau of Economic Research, the Levy Institute, and numerous economists, suggested that true economic mobility in the U.S., for most people, was a myth. The nation was polarizing into very rich and very poor, and the best indicator of how well one would do was still how well one's parents had done.

Two-income families were laborers' only sure ticket into the middle class. Yet in 1990, even with the enormous increase of such families (over 2/3 of young families now rely on two earners), average family income only reached $35,353. When the 1970 average family income of $9867 was adjusted for inflation, it was the equivalent of $33,238. The effective increase over 20 years was actually less than 10 percent. Most of this small increase in purchasing power came because two wage-earners were present; individual average wages fell about 14 percent in real terms during this period. Put differently, median household income in 1990 was $29,943, or $1000 *less*, after adjusting for inflation, than it was in 1973. The Congressional Budget Office calculated that middle-income families with children had lower inflation-adjusted after-tax incomes in 1992 ($29,500) than they had in 1980 ($30,900). As "acceptable" rates of unemployment rose, even in the once prosperous suburbs, and inflation stubbornly persisted, the trademark optimism that had always belonged to ambitious U.S. workers was replaced by anxiety. Businesses brazenly raided pension funds, terminated pension plans, reduced benefits, lengthened hours, and shortened vacations. Blue- and white-collar workers could no longer count on raised income, wealth, and status as routine rewards for hard work. The vanishing middle class cast a giant shadow on America's future.

Proletarianization, moreover, was apparently progressing in the U.S. despite the growth of relatively nonproletarian service industries.[8] Of the large wage-earning population, approximately 25 percent were educated professionals, with the remainder performing traditional, routinized activities. The objective U.S. class structure, with its terribly unequal distribution of productive assets, was thus empirically verifiable.

All this data fused into a powerful case for orthodoxy's structural class theory. Other evidence existed, however, that the effects of class were mediated by politics, and thus classes were not objective structures impersonally evolving in history. While economic structures set the environment, this less accessible evidence indicated that political activism actually defined the process of class formation.

Sweden and America, for example, were both economically developed capitalist societies, but proletarian class-consciousness in Sweden—i.e., shared working class perceptions of a common relationship to productive assets—was more widespread and intense than in the U.S. Pro-labor Swedish state policies initiated by powerful proletarian interests had reinforced working-class identity. While U.S. classes were polarizing and workers as a group were suffering more than ever, union membership nonetheless declined from 36 percent in 1954 to 15 percent in 1991, the lowest percentage of any developed democracy except France. By comparison, 95 percent of the laborers in Sweden and Denmark were in unions; 85 percent in Finland; 60 percent in Norway and Austria; 50 percent in Australia, Ireland, and the U.K.; and 40 percent in Germany and Italy.[9] Survey research implied that anti-union attitudes had actually declined during the same years that U.S. union membership had declined.[10] Apparently employers found it necessary to restrict unions, and, since at least the mid-1970s, government officials cooperated. This combined activity diluted proletarian class-consciousness and convinced many otherwise sympathetic U.S. workers to forego unionization.

The use of the political and legal systems to obstruct American labor has a long and ugly history. There was virtually no federal protection of unionism until well into the twentieth century. Conservative courts narrowly defined labor's rights, court injunctions coralled most union activity, the Supreme Court routinely found pro-labor legislation unconstitutional, and most state and federal courts were openly anti-union.

The National Labor Relations Board, which administers the Wagner Act—labor's major legislative achievement—was taken over by conservatives and in the 1980s largely ignored corporate anti-unionism.[11] No longer was it an instrument for aiding union growth or redressing grievances. Its Reagan-appointed chairman accused organized labor of causing the "decline and fall of our healthy industries," and called strikes "concerted efforts emphasizing violence, intimidation and political intervention to prevent people who want to work from working."[12] AFL-CIO President Lane Kirkland in 1984 asked Congress to repeal the National Labor Relations Act. A year later the House Subcommittee on Labor-Management Relations concluded that "labor law has failed . . . the evidence is clear that the law does not encourage collective bargaining . . . perhaps the most striking evidence of the law's failure is that . . . unions, which exist to engage in collective bargaining, are calling for repeal of the law that is intended to encourage that process."[13]

Federal legislation regulating the use of replacement workers and protecting strikers was also regularly defeated on Capitol Hill. Strikes, traditionally unions' most powerful weapon, became ineffective. Wealthy corporate-sponsored political action committees, moreover, could virtually veto pro-labor legislation, even with Democrats in power. "In the context of weakened unions, reduced political influence, the use of replacement workers, and employer threats to close plants," Patricia Cayo Sexton concluded, "the success rates of strikes and other union tactics have plunged."[14] And so did working-class consciousness and the percentage of unionized American workers.

Relatively independent institutions such as law and politics, then, have influenced the way objective class structures turn into collective actors with specific ideologies. Class theorists cannot agree on which factor to emphasize: economic structures or proletarian values. After years of equivocating, Harrington finally sided with the third, neo-structuralist version of Marxian class theory. The prospects for a viable U.S. socialist movement, he concluded, depended on the capacity of working-class organizations to create favorable political and ideological conditions. Class, moreover, was determined by one's objective position in production.

HARRINGTON'S CLASS THEORY

Harrington initially believed that organized, disciplined, blue-collar workers were the heart and soul of socialist politics, and this bedrock faith in organized labor remained with him forever. In the 1960s it made him unconditionally support even right-wing unions as the only alternative to capital. "It was a point of pride with us that we did not look to the working class as it should be, but as it actually was," Harrington later admitted. "In doing so, we risked our socialist souls, but then taking risks is a normal hazard for any serious leftist."[15]

Several factors, however, made him reconsider orthodox Marxian class theory: at Port Huron he saw the political limits of economism; he noted that U.S. intervention in Vietnam had turned many large unions even further to the right and the automating, internationalizing economy was wreaking havoc on traditional workers; and he was affected by the power struggle in the Socialist Party (SP) between Max Shachtman's conservatives, who were rigidly pro-union, and those like himself who courted liberal intellectuals and professionals.

Harrington thus formally abandoned orthodox class theory during the late 1960s, too late to salvage his reputation among New Leftists but soon enough to appreciate the revisionist monographs that were showing up in Europe and the U.S.[16] His revised class theory rationalized the politics of a disillusioned SP leader preparing to bolt the party. Whether Harrington's tentative comments on the subject of class were due to his unbudgeable faith in unions, his pragmatism, or his respect for Shachtman is difficult to determine. The fact is, however, that Harrington's signal contributions are in the area of tactics rather than theory.

Harrington finally had realized that organized labor, Marx notwithstanding, was not—and on its own likely wouldn't become—revolutionary. Yet, it remained "the most powerful single force for social change within capitalist society,"[17] with a vested interest in democracy. Concentrated in industrialized urban centers, packed tightly on the production line, disciplined by Taylorism, factory workers were clearly more cohesive than other so-called middle-class employees. They would always be the backbone of a socialist majority, but the combination of improved living standards and technically advanced production had altered class formation even among workers. Although more blue-collar workers were on the scene than ever before, they had become a shrinking proportion of the nation's labor force and their middle-class lifestyles cooled the progressive impulse that once spearheaded New Deal and civil rights reforms. Self-interest replaced the larger vision that had redefined capitalism in the 1930s and 1960s. Marx had intimated that intra-proletarian divisions complicated the process of social change. Harrington now identified two classes in addition to capitalists and blue-collar laborers: a "new" class of non-traditional workers, and a class composed of the young, educated, and mostly unemployed.

The latter consisted primarily of students, anti-war activists, and bohemians, and was Harrington's sop to New Leftists. These individuals lived mostly outside the economy, surviving on funds wired by middle class parents, and their issue-oriented views were based on converging social, political, and personal factors rather than a common economic function. They were certainly fair game for organizers, and many performed courageously in progressive causes, but as the economy contracted, the Vietnam War ended, social altruism faded, and young activists left college, their Aquarian alliance crumbled.

Real classes, for Harrington, were defined by shared interests based on their members' common function in the economy.[18] The economic bond endured for as long as class members remained in a capitalist system, even if, as in the U.S., they were unaware of it. Angry young people had finally entered the workforce in the 1970s as either capitalists or workers; the former laughed away their youthful escapades, and many of the latter tried to forget them. The next generation of young, educated, not-yet-employed people, in different social and political circumstances, was conservative instead of radical. Harrington realized this in the early 1970s,[19] and never again referred to this group as a class. He subsequently unpacked non-capitalists into two major categories: blue- and white-collar employees, the so-called "old" and "new" working classes. Students and unemployed intellectuals were appended onto the new class.

The old working class had become a smaller percentage of the general population with an expanding share of non-voters, so its political clout had diminished. The social forces that hurt blue-collar workers, however, also begat the new class. Harrington believed that an old-new class alliance would countenance a powerful new constituency.

Capitalism's inability to cope in a traditional way with its internal problems upset the nation's class structure. Capitalist states now stabilized markets, stimulated production, and passified workers. Important economic decisions were made by public officials, and a new breed of bureaucrat arose to plan and manage production as well as administer public services. Salaries for these public bureaucrats, as well as for workers in high-tech manufacturing, rose. So did the need for more knowledge to efficiently manage the burgeoning bureaucracies. Marginal, labor-intensive industries found cheap labor in the third world. Unskilled blue-collar workers, most of whom were unorganized and insecure, were disempowered just as the wealth and status of managers, bureaucrats, and intellectuals were peaking.

Everywhere capitalism was collectivizing in this manner. Harrington surveyed the confusing debate surrounding the meaning and significance of the new class, and admitted that he couldn't solve anything: "the very concept of the new class is about as solid as jello."[20] Was the new class truly a class? Or, as orthodoxy held, was it merely part of the proletariat? Was it, as Schumpeter and Bazelon argued, part of the "new middle class" of employed, educated people (as compared to the "old middle class" of doctors, lawyers, and medium-sized property owners)? Was it composed of bureaucrats (Djilas and Shachtman), managers (Burnham, Galbraith, the Ehrenreichs), engineers and hard scientists (Veblen and Bell), or a new kind of worker (Gorz, Mallet, and Touraine)? Would its members consolidate capitalism (Pareto, Bell, Moynihan, Gorz), reform it (Veblen, Galbraith, Kristol), help overthrow it (Kautsky, Boudin, Mills, Touraine, Gorz [again], Mallet, Garaudy, Carillo), or bureaucratize it (The Frankfurt School, Shachtman, Djilas, Laurat, the Ehrenreichs). Theorizing about the new class had become an intellectual hall of mirrors.

Harrington actually began reforming orthodoxy's class theory in 1962. In *The Retail Clerks*, a study of the Retail Clerks International Association that was published in that year, he agreed with C. Wright Mills that automation was creating a new kind of worker, one located mid-way between white- and blue-collar stereotypes.[21] As mechanized systems of supply, production, and distribution became common, the non-routinized, informal, customer-oriented duties of white-collar workers disappeared. Harrington speculated that this trend eroded the white-collar psychology of public and private service employees. He felt that dehumanized workers who were neither white nor blue collar would respond to organizing efforts that emphasized the theme of alienation. By automating larger sectors of production, service, and management, capitalists thus hastened unionization.

Harrington discovered in the late 1960s that office and sales workers were a diminishing fraction of the workforce. Educators, healthcare workers, scientists, technicians, and computer specialists had become the fastest growing segments of white-collar labor. Highly-educated, these workers were not yet automated and they often worked alone, at their own pace, for large salaries, and thus couldn't easily be unionized. Although they were paid employees, their lifestyles did not resemble those of traditional workers. Nor were they like the traditional middle class, who often owned property and in place of knowledge were addicted to tiny bits of old-world dignity. Harrington didn't know what to do with these class hybrids. Welfare-state capitalism, however, needed them in ever greater numbers and their impact on U.S. politics was growing. "If the speculations about them are true," he noted, "then contemporary technology is giving rise to politically and socially unprecedented types of human beings."[22]

Harrington decided in 1979 that these people were actually a new class, or at least a new stratum of the traditional middle class. Making no claims to a "rigorous and finished analysis,"[23] he nonetheless held that the key to this new class/stratum was what he felt were the expanding educational opportunities in industrializing capitalist societies. College graduates often went into prestigious occupations in the burgeoning information, service, and management sectors of the economy. They fell naturally into four kinds of professions: those directly engaged in developing technology, such as scientists, technicians, engineers, and computer specialists; educational workers in the service sector, including professors, school teachers, and nurses; students, artists, and communication workers such as journalists and writers; and the traditional practices of medicine and the law. Harrington simply combined into one category all the traits identified by other new-class theorists. These new workers had incomes, educational levels, and occupations not normally found among the old working class and the poor, but weren't nearly as wealthy or as powerful as their employers.

Harrington subsequently re-evaluated traditional middle class professionals such as doctors and lawyers, who were created by turn-of-the-century monopoly capitalism and were always a small fraction of the total workforce that favored laissez-faire capitalism.[24] They became small-scale entrepreneurs or wealth- and leisure-seeking professionals, not workers. Today's personnel managers were also part of this conservative middle-class legacy. Educated, salaried, and creatively occupied, personnel managers—like doctors and lawyers—nonetheless were excluded from Harrington's new class because their material and political interests overlapped those of the wealthy.[25] The dominant purpose of personnel management is to cut costs, adjust workers to their jobs, and dampen unrest. Like their traditional middle class predecessors, they often supported the free-market policies of the Republican Party.

The new class, wrote Harrington, emerged from a more developed phase of capitalism, when the cooperation of government and private enterprise was taken for granted. The New Deal was part of its heritage, and this new class supplied the knowledge needed to manage public and private sectors of the economy. The very existence of a new class legitimized social planning as opposed to an unregulated market. Granted, the new class was ambiguously positioned between workers and capitalists; incomes and working conditions fluctuated dramatically among its members, so they were fractious. Highly educated, busy professionals often didn't even care about politics, and, unlike unions or businesses, the new class was not homogeneous, disciplined, or self-conscious enough to establish ongoing organizations committed to one program. Still, the new class had backed progressive Democratic Party platforms; almost doubling in size during the years from 1950 to 1970, it was a powerful force in favor of civil rights, feminist, anti-war, and environmental reforms. Its continued growth, particularly in dynamic professional and technical sectors, assured the new class an even more decisive political role in the future.

Harrington was uncertain what this role would be because the new class was inherently neither progressive nor reactionary. As employees and subordinates, new class members had material interests opposed to corporate power and hierarchy, but as privileged professionals they also benefitted from maintaining workers in subordinate positions. At different times in history the new class exhibited tendencies toward both elitism and democracy. Harrington felt that the question of which tendency would prevail could not be settled theoretically—it all boiled down to politics, and the new class was up for grabs.

With their enormous wealth as bait, capitalists in the 1980s captured new-class loyalty. Entrepreneurs purchased knowledge and organizational skills to keep their businesses profitable and their workers busy. Corporate wealth and power were maintained, and effective control of research, communication, and workplace decision-making passed quietly to professionals. This arrangement enriched the new class without empowering it: the new class possessed and sold knowledge, but controlled neither the means of production nor the labor process, and its status depended on income, not power or property. New class fidelity to corporate values, therefore, was conditional, and could rapidly evaporate in unfavorable conditions.

This, in a nutshell, is what Harrington expected.[26] As the number of good jobs dwindled, and the crippled economy became dependent on unskilled and semi-skilled labor, it would soon cost more to educate people than society received from their productivity. College and professional degrees would then be devalued, and late-capitalist social limits would slam into new class aspirations. Capitalism, in this scenario, no longer would be able to deliver on its promises.

The new class could then differentiate its own economic needs from those of capital. Already predisposed toward planning, it could decide to plan for itself and for other workers, severing its allegiance to capitalism from its own material interests. Most members of the new class did not own large amounts of property and were employed in the public and semi-public sectors, depending on federal policies for their economic well-being. Educated, wealthy workers, moreover, were more sensitive to ethical questions in politics than were laborers struggling to make ends meet.[27] These factors increased the chances that—as the French sociologists André Gorz, Alain Touraine, and Serge Mallet had already suggested—the new class might choose collectivism to satisfy its own frustrated dreams. Harrington believed that the journey from new class dissatisfaction to class-centered planning to advocating democratic public reforms would be direct and short.

But not inevitable. The new class had to choose its fate, and the issue was still far from settled. Wars, economic growth, inflated salaries financed by welfare cuts, and reactionary politicians could all incite new class elitism or even authoritarianism. Socialists had to use the system's internal crises to promote democracy.

The demographics of modern leftism, Harrington concluded, had changed. The old class of small-property owners and entrepreneurs, Marx's *bêtes noires*, was shrinking when compared to the growth of new class scientists, technicians, teachers, and public-sector professionals. In the 1980s a higher percentage of the labor force was engaged in professional and technical occupations than in factories. Trade unionists, the poor, and minorities shared an objective interest in reform but weren't an electoral majority, whereas the new class was a growing cluster of potentially progressive voters. These two constituencies, traditional workers (including the unemployed, underemployed, and impoverished minorities) and the new class, needed to merge into what Harrington called a "conscience constituency,"[28] an electoral alliance that could challenge and transform corporate power. In *The Next Left* (1986),[29] Harrington expanded this constituency to include feminists, environmentalists, peace activists, and anti-nuclear groups. They were not classes but their decisions to challenge the status quo joined them to the left's democratic class alliance. U.S. capitalism was self-destructing at home as it consolidated world power. With the system ripe for change, Harrington hoped for an alliance of the old and new working classes to support his political program.

THE POLITICS OF NEW CLASS THEORY

Many class theorists had fantasized such an alliance, but few dared cross into the everyday world. New class theories rose like helium balloons in a suburban sky, tickling clouds instead of rocking politicians.

Since that rainy day in St. Louis when his Ivy League training dissolved in the stench of urban poverty, Harrington's socialism was always pragmatic. He eagerly attacked the difficult question of how new class theory could be operationalized in the U.S. Party realignment, he concluded, was the answer, because it could mobilize a multi-class coalition that stood a reasonable chance of succeeding. Harrington argued this case so forcefully and for so many years that tactics were gradually disengaged from theory, and many unsuspecting Americans lost sight of his socialist agenda. Socialism was anathema, but realignment was debated on television and in national journals. Harrington was probably better known as an advocate of Democratic Party reform than of democratically transforming a capitalist party.

Realignment originally referred to the socialist strategy of using the Democratic Party to gain power. The idea that Marxists should cooperate with capitalists to achieve long-term socialist gains goes back to Marx himself, who often joined liberals in fighting for democracy. During the 1848 Revolution, for example, Marx and Engels de-emphasized proletarianism in their journal, *Neue Rheinische Zeitung*, in order to support an alliance with left-wing liberals, and in the 1860s they cooperated with liberals in the People's Party. German Marxists eventually altered these coalition tactics to deal with the exceptional situation in their own nation, where Bismarck and the Junkers controlled a powerless Parliament. They concluded that Lasallians, who wanted to reform capitalism with the help of liberals, had actually strengthened rather than weakened German capitalism. Since these same Germans dictated orthodoxy's canon, Marxists henceforth rejected coalition politics as a revolutionary tactic.

Marx's flexibility reappeared in America's Shachtmanite tendency. For most of his life Max Shachtman had denounced the capitalist Democratic Party and urged workers and minorities to form their own movement. Eventually, however, he realized that rank-and-file U.S. workers were organizing as Democrats and as long as labor was allied with the Democratic Party, socialists had no choice but to work from within the party system. He persuaded the SP, which he joined in 1957, to sanction realignment as a means of creating a mass labor movement, establishing a welfare state, destroying Democratic-controlled city machines, and disempowering Southern racists. Realignment theory maintained that labor, minorities, and middle-class progressives would coalesce into a new Democratic Party, with labor at its center.

As a "fierce socialist sectarian" and an aspiring early 1950s bohemian, Harrington would "have nothing to do with a bourgeois institution like the Democratic Party."[30] He enrolled instead in New York City's Liberal Party, which emerged from a split in the American Labor Party, an old sanctuary for trade unionists, communists, and socialists who supported F.D.R. but didn't want to join the Democrats. When the inevitable feud arose between communists and non-communists, the union-oriented Liberal Party was established. Its working class flavor appealed to Harrington, but the Liberal Party was virtually invisible in the brassy, hustling world of New York politics. Harrington joined the Village Independent Democrats, a reform movement inside the Democratic Party that the *New York Daily Mirror* said consisted of "Village Commies, lefties, eggheads, and beatniks," when he realized it was, in his own words, "the only game in town."[31]

Harrington spent 1958 roaming the nation representing the YPSL and demarcating his own position in the third party realignment debate. Influenced by Max Shachtman, the pragmatic Harrington decided America's two major parties were not alike.[32] SP intellectuals had talked a good game by informally cooperating with liberals to support civil liberties and racial reforms. By refusing to vote for liberal candidates, however, they fractured these reform movements and became irrelevant politically. In the meantime, unions, minorities, and even the poor were fighting against "right-to-work" laws from inside the Democratic Party, accomplishing more for workers than millions of SP pamphlets ever could. The debate itself was misconceived, and Shachtman, claimed Harrington, was simply thinking too much. Workers had *already* established a labor party inside the Democratic Party.

This ad hoc proletarian association sponsored the nation's most progressive legislation, but was always swimming upstream against a vigorous corporate current. Eventually it ran out of steam. Class, however, remained decisive in shaping proletarian political attitudes, particularly during the Reagan years when workers finally understood their disproportionate tax burden. Unfortunately, they reacted against public services rather than the financing of public services. Harrington explained this reaction later in the 1980s. His point, however, even during the 1970s, was that socialists needed to redirect this collective anger away from public programs and toward corporations.

This redirection would be impossible for as long as the two major U.S. parties were controlled by corporations. Wealthy Republicans in the 1970s exploited rampant fears—of minorities, crime, communists, foreigners—to win over traditional economic enemies among workers. Frightened Democrats demurred, or shamefully joined the rout. An irrational, self-defeating working class cultural conservatism thus replaced New Deal liberalism. As Democrats strayed from bread-and-butter economic issues such as full employment and higher wages, their power ebbed. Realignment would chase wealthy conservatives to their natural home in the Republican Party, while providing workers and professionals—a majority of whom already were Democrats—a place to debate legitimate grievances and transport economic complaints into the political arena.

Harrington felt that the alternative for socialists, establishing a radical third party, would prove futile. America's two-party system penalized third parties by making it virtually impossible for them to win congressional and presidential elections. The last inchoate party to buck this pattern was the G.O.P. in the mid-nineteenth century, when many powerful interest groups wanted to break old party alignments. Abolitionists were concerned with the moral issue of slavery, businessmen wanted high tariffs, and western farmers and eastern workers wanted free land and feared competing against Southern slave labor. This kind of broad coalition could immediately win elections and hence maintain a national constituency. The Republican Party was thus born as a fully developed national political player.

At the turn of the century, on the other hand, a small but growing fraction of voters, including unhappy middle class professionals, small-scale entrepreneurs, and skilled workers, coalesced within the Republican Party rather than create a new third party. By realigning the existing two-party system they were able to use the enormous power of wealthy Republican industrialists, who shared their general outlook, to satisfy their own material interests. The coalition also guaranteed Republican electoral dominance for the next three decades. Similarly, disgruntled workers during the depression joined the Democrats instead of building a new party because they realized that exhortations alone could not feed their hungry children. The new majority Democratic coalition of industrial workers, blacks, educated professionals, and progressive industrialists created the welfare state, and finally pointed government toward satisfying the material demands of working Americans. Democratic Party dominance lasted until the 1970s. As a small, marginalized third party, workers during these years would likely have swaggered more and eaten less.

Unless a socialist third party today immediately attracted a voting majority—like the nineteenth-century Republicans did—it would siphon votes from the Democrats, in effect defeating liberals and electing conservatives. The difficulty of establishing a successful third party was in part intended to block labor from becoming a significant political force. The new socialist party would be forced into a coalition with the Democrats, which is where Harrington felt it should always have been.

It is unlikely that a socialist third party could garner an electoral majority. While the percentage of U.S. workers who call themselves Democrats has recently declined, at nearly one-half it still constitutes a formidable, loyal core of voters. The rest are either Republicans, Independents, or nonvoters. Only a tiny fraction of Independent and nonvoting workers could reasonably be expected to vote socialist. Even if the nation's customarily activist professionals, liberal Republicans, and minority groups were recruited en masse into the new socialist party, it still would lack an electoral majority. Of course, minorities have traditionally supported Democrats, liberal Republicans aren't radical, and the new class could swing left or right. It was inconceivable that a socialist third party would be anything but a small, eccentric player on the national scene. "What the nation needs is not just a new party of conscience and ideas, but a new party that can win as well," Harrington scolded socialists. "Programs are easy enough to write, but national majorities are hard to organize."[33]

Thus, the Democratic Party offered socialists the best and perhaps the only opportunity to be a meaningful political force. It encompassed reformers and a large bloc of workers, but it also sheltered wealthy industrialists and their outspoken defenders. Realignment would elucidate the murky principles that were submerged in partisan bickering. Parties would become program-oriented, principled associations held together by shared ideology rather than shallow promises. Republicans would represent big business, and Democrats would speak for a progressive coalition of workers, professionals, minorities, women, and the poor.

The newly realigned Democratic Party, Harrington acknowledged, wouldn't be "socialist." But this was an advantage in a nation where the socialist label was falsely associated with communism, bureaucratic planning, atheism, and wickedness,[34] and at a time—the mid-1970s—when conservatives were attacking. The socialist Harrington, moreover, wanted the federal government to redistribute wealth, intervene on behalf of workers and the poor, and expand public ownership. So did many liberals. In the past, anti-socialists unscrupulously blocked such reforms by red-baiting. Liberals thus had a real interest in making rational discussion of socialism possible in mainstream America. "We are not a conspiracy 'boring from within' the Democratic Party," Harrington insisted in 1973. "We are an open and democratic organization seeking to make a contribution in the mainstream of American political life."[35] Many liberals also might discover that they were socialists without really knowing it; that a shared belief in equality and racial justice outweighed their loyalty to capitalism. The Democratic coalition, in short, might initially campaign for socialism without ever invoking the idea of socialism. Socialists subsequently would emphasize that "an idea of socialism should animate and radicalize all those socialist ideas."[36]

Party realignment was the precondition for legislating Harrington's political program during the 1970s. In practical terms, it was a necessary first step on the path to socialism, "the only place where a beginning can be made."[37] It also was ethically defensible. The idea that an enlightened few enacted socialism for everyone was, like capitalism and communism, elitist. Therefore, an independent democratic socialist third party was neither democratic nor socialist: it lacked voters *and* labor power. A powerful moral concept became, in practice, immoral.

Harrington's commitment to realignment was, from the beginning, remorseful and conditional. He always saw it as, in his words, an "undramatic, and even tedious strategy,"[38] which he gladly would have abandoned were it not for America's exceptional history. "I would prefer it if Gene Debs had fulfilled his dream and led the Socialists from the founding convention in 1901, through the great campaign of 1912, onward and upward to become a mass labor party of the democratic left."[39] He endorsed the Presidential campaigns of Lyndon Johnson and Jimmy Carter on what he called "lesser evil grounds": voting for radicals was self-defeating given the hopelessness of third-party candidacies. Nonetheless, he was bothered that reality had sanctioned this marriage of convenience when leftists whose beliefs he shared grew restive. "I assume," he remarked after championing the Democrat L.B.J. over Independent Eugene McCarthy, "that the foregoing is as depressing to read as it was to write."[40]

For as long as workers, professionals, and blacks remained mostly Democratic, the left could not start a party of its own. "There is in America," Harrington pointed out, "a political class struggle taking place at the ballot box. And I suggest that from my point of view, I'm going to go where that workers' movement is and where that corporate movement is not."[41] Realignment became problematic only if and when a mass defection from the Democratic Party took place, allowing a new party to attract a significant number of voters. Realignment was thus a regrettable means of achieving socialism, not a moral priority. It was the radical edge of a jejune world.

No such exodus occurred in the 1960s and '70s, although Harrington remarked presciently in 1968 that "it could happen in the next twenty years."[42] Almost two decades later the complexion of both parties changed, but Harrington was shocked and saddened by what he saw: a conservative offensive had succeeded in redefining political discourse in the U.S. Republicans baited frightened workers with patriotic slogans and racial innuendo, inflaming the nation's conscience as its economy cooled. Large sectors of organized labor, the solid core of the Democratic Party, were also disengaged from factory unions and released into a deregulated workplace. The internal balance of power in the Democratic Party leaned toward "moderates" who often re-packaged and marketed Reaganism. Lacking a solid institutional home, and uncertain of the future, voters became easy prey for media jackals who now sold politicians instead of soap. America experienced a decline in party loyalty and identification, and the party system became "dealigned," not realigned.[43] This electoral anarchy empowered image-makers and their wealthy clients, who shrewdly manipulated campaigns by selling phony heroes and false issues to vulnerable people. Organizations became less significant than thirty-second television spots, and commercial polling replaced the wise judgements of candidates and parties. U.S. individualism was trumped.

Harrington's realignment strategy promoted what he called a "quasirational party system,"[44] that is, cohesive, doctrinal parties representing distinctive classes and viewpoints. Socialists then could operate in the political mainstream by becoming Democrats. The Democratic Socialist Organizing Committee (DSOC), established after Harrington exited the SP in 1972, tried to organize the warring constituencies of the "three Georges" —middle-class, anti-war McGovernites; blue-collar supporters of George Meany; and George Wallace's mostly working-class, racist audience—into a progressive coalition inside the Democratic Party.[45] It endorsed Democratic platforms and candidates in 1976 and 1980, and worked with congressional Democrats to pass reformist legislation.

DSOC achieved a measure of success: the 1984 Democratic Presidential ticket included two liberals and one woman, and was endorsed by the influential African American Jesse Jackson, the technocrat Gary Hart, and by organized labor and feminists; convention rhetoric celebrated working people and minorities, women and immigrants, and the poor; the worst of the Dixiecrats became Republicans, and some liberal Republicans were sounding like Democrats. Yet despite uniting all the social and economic forces Harrington deemed essential for realigning the parties, the Mondale campaign still lost pitifully. Working voters had chosen image rather than substance. A Democratic platform trumpeting their shared economic interests fell ignominiously to the Great Communicator, and a script that made the nation feel good despite its afflictions. The Democratic Party was cashiered by its own army of workers, who opted for patriotism and a glassy smile. There was nothing left to realign.

In DSOC, insiders had detected problems even before the Reagan years. Despite a three-fold increase in the Committee's membership during the 1970s, its "left caucus" questioned whether the payoff of realignment was worth the price, whether the means had become an end. Harrington and his DSOC colleagues were lobbying Democratic Party politicians but socialism seemed no closer in 1979 than it had six years earlier. Designed to realign the nation's parties, DSOC had instead become a fixture on the Capitol Hill working-lunch circuit. Harrington had fallen into the same reductionist rut that once derailed Norman Thomas and the SP. Bogdan Denitch, a DSOC national board member and Harrington's friend, said what many were thinking: "We have tended to blur the distinction between mass work and creating a socialist presence."[46]

Pressured by left caucus critics, DSOC resolved in 1975 to re-emphasize grassroots educational and organizing campaigns, and to support socialists in serious Democratic Party primaries. Its national board concluded that DSOC had to be "more explicitly socialist in its politics, more aggressive in its approach, and should develop more issues."[47] Harrington agreed to merge with the New American Movement (NAM), which one of its leaders, Harry Boyte, called "a kind of adult successor to SDS [Students for a Democratic Society]."[48]

NAM, founded in 1971—two years after SDS collapsed—was established as a national organization that reflected the actual needs of U.S. workers. Not long after its initial convention in Davenport, Iowa in November 1971, however, NAM decided to get its own act together before organizing nationally. For 5 years NAM supported its independent local chapters, which were often mobilizing neighborhood anti-nuclear campaigns. By the late 1970s, NAM officially committed its resources to strengthening community-action programs sponsored by local chapters. Unlike the New Left, NAM was explicitly socialist and feminist, but it was also invisible nationally, refusing to intervene on the side of workers during the anti-left conservative offensive in the 1970s. It never enrolled more than 1500 members.

NAM rejected Soviet-style communism, sympathized with third world revolutionaries, and supported direct-action initiatives, mass anti-corporate organizing among trade unionists, and militant opposition to U.S. intervention abroad. DSOC was committed to organizing nationally, with a well-defined chain of command, and establishing links to the electronic and print media. Both organizations held generally similar views on other issues.

Contact between the two organizations began in 1974,[49] but was stymied by radicals in NAM who felt that DSOC was too reformist, and conservatives in DSOC who argued that NAM rejected realignment and was too radical. Although more than 100 DSOC members, including Irving Howe and Michael Walzer, went on record in 1980 as members of a "committee against the NAM merger," in 1982 negotiations were concluded successfully. NAM needed DSOC's organization and national leadership, and DSOC needed NAM's energetic activism. The Democratic Socialists of America combined DSOC's realignment tactic with NAM's more urgent struggle for community action and cultural change.

A chastened Harrington experienced first-hand the real meaning of dialectics. Realignment was merely one small part of a broader strategy that needed to touch people personally, economically, socially, and culturally.

Dealignment had diminished political parties. DSOC had devoted too much time to the politics of realignment, and not nearly enough to affecting everyday life.

Harrington continued to pursue realignment, even after the Mondale debacle, but he used it more sparingly and with less confidence than before.[50] It became an ace-in-the-hole that socialists could whip out after an economic "shock," perhaps a severe recession or a Wall Street "meltdown," finally jolted U.S. politics into a semblance of rationality. This kind of crisis would propel the Democratic Party back into its New Deal legacy, representing the economic interests of workers. In the meantime, Harrington wanted democratic socialists to remain alert, to be ready on a moment's notice to jump into a reborn political arena. Admittedly a hopeless task as party loyalty ebbed, strategic realignment nonetheless kept socialists inside the electoral system, from where, in a crisis, they could act decisively.

Harrington's realignment tactic presumed that the economic majority in America was impeded only by an an irrational party structure. Parties became dealigned during the 1980s, smashing the expectation of achieving meaningful party reform in the near future. Harrington confessed that new, noneconomic cleavages based on gender, race, age, region, lifestyle, and outlook had ripped his coalition apart. Progressive Democrats had simply added new demands to the party's platform whenever an emergent force coalesced into a significant interest group, turning it rapidly into a patchwork of special interests. The Democratic Party, and the left generally, lacked a broad vision that clarified workers' common economic concerns. Where once Harrington chose realignment, now he realized that democratic socialism, like Reaganism, thrived only by touching Americans' everyday experiences. The newly dealigned parties were too weak to reach that far. Harrington decided to formulate a social ethic that dealt with the putative concerns of workers, the new class, minorities, women, and other issue groups, and also reattached these concerns to their economic roots.

Cultural and moral factors have always played an important role in U.S. politics, where class is rarely mentioned. Republicans had already succeeded in the politics of symbolic identification by linking traditional values to a conservative, elitist program, attracting precisely those groups who stood to lose the most. People, of course, don't live by bread alone—either economics is translated into familiar cultural idioms or it is ignored. By focusing almost exclusively on politics, Harrington had lost touch with people who took their own cultural and moral heritage at least as seriously as their economic security or their loyalty to the Democratic Party. His decade-long journey to political reductionism ended; Harrington was turning back home.

During the 1980s, Harrington seldom preached realignment. Instead, he tackled the Gramscian project of spiking traditional values with a dose of radical critique. This was his last and in some ways most ambitious venture.

SOCIALISM REBORN

INVALIDS ARE OFTEN BUMPED INGLORIOUSLY into drowsy pastures, while downtown their final passage is duly noted only in the daily obits. Harrington's last decade, however, was fraught with the same wicked paradoxes he had wrestled for almost fifty years. He refused to exit quietly because the cause was just, conditions were intolerable, and his ingenuity had outlasted a cancerous body. As his life ebbed, he decided that a retooled socialist campaign would usher in a new, more hopeful century.

After two fleeting moments during the 1930s and '60s at the precipice of meaningful change, America had fallen back into the past, and Harrington's reputation went with it. Having put all his chips on a political tactic, realignment, that failed miserably, he now had to address why this tactic—and the left with it—collapsed.

The power of America's big business to manipulate workers and set the cultural agenda was far greater than that of other industrialized democracies. In a serious crisis workers could not defend themselves, in part at least because they didn't know what socialism was, whereas corporate platitudes were outdated but still warm and comfortable. As workers were battered, bruised, and confused by business and the state, their innocence was understandable. Harrington was less sanguine about socialists because, incredibly, they didn't know what socialism was either. The left mistakenly believed that workers would automatically embrace socialism even if it was not clearly defined, and leftist strategies presupposed broad proletarian consensus on a fuzzy futuristic egalitarianism. Socialism was lost somewhere in left field while capitalists circled the bases.

Socialism had failed because almost no one—even on the left—knew what socialists were saying. Harrington shouldered some of the blame. He once remarked that Americans were institutionally conservative and operationally liberal: they were laissez-faire capitalists who nonetheless endorsed needed public programs. He tailored his strategy to liberalism, but it never caught the public's imagination. Workers were still individualists, and reformism was received as a worthwhile end rather than a means of fundamentally changing everyday life. A competition for the nation's soul was at hand, with the utility of mainstream tactics at stake. If socialists squeezed the egalitarian consequences from liberalism and marketed them, Harrington's nontraditional radicalism was still salvageable. Ideas were important, even for pragmatists like Harrington; if people believed, then small victories, instead of vanishing, cascaded into larger ones. Harrington proposed to rescue and revitalize socialism by attaching its rediscovered ethics onto U.S. public culture.

THE DEATH OF SOCIALISM

Confronting the certainty of his own death from cancer as well as the sick state of socialism, Harrington wondered in 1989 why a theory that explained capitalism so well was such a failure.[1] His response clarified why a lifetime project of explaining democratic socialism had fizzled.

First, socialists were terribly imprecise about what "socializing" the economy actually meant, and how it was to be accomplished. Communism's theory of centralized management became by default the left's designated alternative to business-as-usual.

Second, U.S. workers had decomposed into competing sectors based on skill, gender, religion, race, and region, each with a bureaucracy and a vested interest in staying independent. Workers once had united into what Harrington considered the most important mass movement in Western history, but in 1989 proletarian unity was a distant memory. "The united, revolutionary working class which would act as History's right arm for the creation of socialism," Harrington sadly noted, "did not, and does not, exist."[2] This fact helped destroy the identity and appeal of socialism.

Third, socialists never explained what path lies between capitalism and socialism. What were revolutionaries to do with capitalist structures? Capitalism no longer was just mass production in private factories. Corporations now specialized in a variety of complex functions, including investment, technological innovation, pricing, and distribution, as well as manufacturing. Salaried managers had replaced owners as key decision-makers, and industrial production was often so dependent on government policies that the line between public and private was blurred. How could workers just "take over?" They were not prepared or willing to suddenly seize power. What would replace capitalism's free market? Socialists in the past had chosen to reform rather than transform capitalism, unexpectedly strengthening the system. "How," asked Harrington, "does a political movement make basic change gradually when at the same time it must observe the constraints of the system it seeks to transform?"[3]

Finally, socialists were completely unprepared for the post-World War II internationalization of politics and economics. After finally mobilizing against colonialism, they discovered the old enemy very much alive in the worldwide free market. This neocolonialism was a conundrum for socialists, who wanted to end the exploitation of poor lands but were too confused and afraid to act. Already searching for an identity and an agenda inside of their own nations, socialists could not design a program for the entire world, particularly since this would have demanded sacrifices from powerful domestic players and a temporary dip in workers' living standards. Socialist governments were thus handcuffed by the unfair rules of a capitalist world system.

These rules affected politics at home as well as abroad. Socialism required a growing economy, but capitalist investment was impossible without the cooperation of international financiers and traders who blocked demand-side, deficit-producing domestic programs. When the French socialist François Mitterand had to choose between axing his expensive reforms or losing needed imports, investment capital, and markets, he decided that France would do better economically without socialism.[4] Even left-wing workers were hard pressed to disagree.

Harrington didn't reiterate old statist programs and strategies, which hadn't worked anyway. Socialism instead had to renew what Harrington considered its diversity and complexity, "the various and conflicting ways that the movement tried to give specific meaning to its profound and imprecise demand for democratic socialization."[5] Old forms of socialism, reconsidered, might provide insights into socialism's new dilemmas, and also generate a moral consensus to stoke the fading embers of proletarian idealism. Harrington's last works depicted how one version of socialism, now discredited, triumphed over others. Since capitalism had changed, forgotten socialist theories were again fashionable; perhaps yesterday's placebo was today's panacea.

Harrington's pilgrimage into socialist history began with the nineteenth-century utopians Saint-Simon, Fourier, Owen, and Blanc, who had substituted an ethical community for the liberal state, and transformed raw competition into a harmonious union of equal citizens.[6] Utopian socialism was clearly communitarian, moral, feminist, and activist, but it also presumed that morality determined behavior, that ethical decisions alone could move capitalist mountains. It simply ignored the class struggle and proletarian politics. Marx's and Engels's scathing critiques immediately transformed utopian socialism into a noble mistake, and its communalism, the ethical harmony that must precede democratic socialism, was unceremoniously dumped.

Marx subsequently buried ethical socialism by democratizing the idea of utopia.[7] Where utopians depended on artisans, intellectuals, and policymakers to initiate and administer socialism, Marx's socialism rose like steam from the boiling anger of workers. The revolutionary process, moreover, wasn't necessarily violent. Marx and Engels suggested that reformism, at least in liberal democracies, was a powerful weapon.[8] As workers formed unions, and unions became working-class parties, the masses became an unbeatable electoral force that transformed the state, in Marx's famous words, into "the proletariat organized as a ruling class." In short, there was a democratic route to utopianism. The nascent working class and trade union movements could turn utopian idealism into political power, redesigning socialism for its passage into modernity. Legally and nonviolently, workers would seize and centralize power before establishing the decentralized, stateless communities that all socialists—scientific and utopian—coveted.

Marx had mistakenly suggested that centralized tactics could create decentralized communities. Harrington nonetheless argued that in key respects Marx remained a utopian because he wanted to transform society, not merely abolish the state. Marx also envisioned a "kingdom of freedom" where redundant work disappeared and creativity flourished, where goods were distributed based on need, not profit or performance. In the third volume of *Capital*, Marx equated "socialized man" with "associated producers," the phrase French utopians applied to worker-managed enterprises. Harrington concluded that Marx personally supported utopian socialist morality, even though his critique did quite the opposite.

Marx hedged on several important issues: How could a parliamentary system whose genius was incrementalism and consensus-building legislate utopian programs? Which measures transformed the state into an instrument of socialization, and which were absorbed into the system? What role did race, gender, age, and religion play if socialism was defined only in class terms? And how was socialism an objective science as well as an ethical theory? Marx refused to engage this last issue philosophically. When Kautsky and Lenin decided that Marx was primarily a scientist, all the other questions magically disappeared, and Marxism became messianic. Proletarian scientists became communist prophets who decreed that socialization meant state ownership of industry. Marxism was transformed into a Party dictatorship that was neither socialist nor capitalist, and was committed only to staying in power and pumping the economy. "It was not just that the utopian vision was lost in the process," Harrington remarked, "so was Marx's lifelong stress on utopian values such as decentralism, cooperation, and above all, women and men creating the new society as an act of human freedom."[9]

Germany's Social Democrats adopted Kautsky's "either/or" formula: either capitalism or, when history had run its course, socialism. Harrington called them "passive revolutionaries,"[10] timidly awaiting capitalism's inevitable collapse while conservatives filled the political void. In power after the First World War, Social Democrats formulated Keynesian transitional programs that used parliamentary reforms to humanize capitalism, and became legitimate players in Germany's capitalist system. When German capitalism nearly expired during the depression, however, they had no remedies and no real idea what socialism meant or how, other than waiting, to create it. Social Democracy had unwittingly civilized capitalism in the name of a doctrine it didn't even understand.

At the end of World War II socialism was a two-pronged scam. On the left was Lenin's vanguard party running a factory society with capitalist technology and rules. Third world socialists imitated this model to rationalize the brutalities of postcolonialist industrialization.[11] On the right, Social Democrats, lacking a transitional strategy, complacently awaited a socialism that lay somewhere to the left of reality. The ethical principles of genuine socialism, as well as the political savvy to get past capitalism, were buried with Marx and the utopians. Frustrated Social Democrats decided to play a liberal democratic game that workers couldn't win. Harrington called this "pragmatic utopianism," that is, socialists actually believing that "a democratic political order could dominate an undemocratic economic order."[12] Failing to either dislodge Western capitalism or establish real socialism in the third world, the decentered left became its own worst enemy.

THE IMPENDING DEATH OF CAPITALISM

Conservatives blamed Social Democracy and its welfare state for capitalism's recent economic troubles.[13] Harrington agreed that the welfare state had outlived its usefulness, but also maintained that it had not caused the current crisis. He challenged conservatives by reformulating the crisis of modern capitalism.[14]

Until the 1880s, he argued, laissez-faire capitalism suffered from periodic economic crises—over- and under-production, recessions, depressions, panics, and inflations. Production was small-scale, flexible, and governed by market forces. More efficient and productive forms of factory technology and corporate organization were introduced by the turn of the century, when large concentrations of workers used huge machines that made standardized products. The dramatic production increases which followed aggravated the economic cycles, making them harsher and more draining.

This mass production also required mass consumption. Henry Ford responded by modifying the free market without altering productive relationships. He raised workers' salaries, financed their new automobiles, and gave them a small role in factory decision-making. In return, workers had to obey a moral code that prohibited gambling, drinking, atheism, and other examples of what Ford considered self-indulgence. Antonio Gramsci later commented that Ford's programmed capitalism formed a new epoch in history, using high wages and different cultural and consumption patterns to regulate the market.

As consumption rose so did production and worker morale, and Ford accomplished all this without union or government interference. When the depression hit in 1929, the New Deal, with union support, nationalized Fordism by starting public programs that created jobs and stimulated consumption. In Europe, these same reforms convinced economists like John Maynard Keynes to revise capitalist theory. The new social structure of accumulation used public benefits and high union wages to create a market for mass production. Proletarian living conditions improved dramatically, and the rise in corporate profits was far greater than the growth in welfare spending. This wave of prosperity crested after World War II, lasting until the early 1970s. Social democracy and the welfare state had rescued Western capitalism from its most severe crisis.

Economic success, however, created new problems. As manufacturers competed for consumer discretionary income by diversifying, the Keynesian system started breaking down. Its single-purpose machines and standard batches of mass production soon turned into flexible technology based on computers, automation, and robots. Profitable factories bought microelectronic manufacturing processes that quickly shifted to new products. The assembly line's time-consuming model changes were replaced, in the 1980s, by computer-assisted programs that responded immediately to technical innovations and market conditions.

The high wages of unionized workers made it difficult for corporations to finance the transition to automated plants. Corporate debt rose to the point where it threatened profits, and unions were attacked for inhibiting industrial flexibility. Industries that mass-produced standard items travelled to the non-unionized South, and then to less developed regions where land and labor were cheap. High-tech, profitable industries that used programmed automation to manufacture a wide variety of specialty items remained in the U.S., but they needed fewer skilled workers to handle the sophisticated machinery. Unions no longer were needed by well-paid workers in automated factories, and didn't exist where they were most needed. The nation as a whole shifted from goods to service production, where low-paying, unskilled jobs were plentiful. Blue-collar factory workers became a declining percentage of the workforce, while non-unionized service workers increased dramatically. A diminishing sector of skilled and white-collar workers, as well as professionals, gainfully represented traditional middle-class values, but they couldn't compensate for the sharp reductions in aggregate consumer demand.

Capitalism's new technical and occupational structure, with fewer desirable jobs for more workers, generated chronic unemployment and poverty, even for many of the unskilled who were lucky enough to find work. At the other end, a small but growing number of millionaires ate larger bites of the nation's wealth and income. The costs of public safety-net programs spiralled up at the moment when the middle-class tax base was disappearing. Government, however, was still responsible for stimulating private profit and paying the rising social costs of those profits. Something had to give.

President Reagan made sure it wasn't corporations. Supply-side tax cuts depleted public revenues without significantly improving the economy. Productivity grew and jobs were created, but capitalism's cyclical economic recoveries had taken on an ominous profile. New, mostly service jobs paid less than the manufacturing jobs they replaced, and not nearly enough to allow consumption of excess production from automated industries. Corporations used part of their untaxed profits to further automate and streamline production, and inefficient factories closed or laid off workers, further eroding the tax base.

As the tax burden shifted from rich to poor, trickle-down wealth never materialized because only corporations and the wealthy gained new disposable income, and they invested in profitable nonproductive ventures that often created unmanageable long-term debts. Nationwide, Harrington noted in *The Next Left*, savings actually declined. Reagan's assaults on labor weakened unions and lowered salaries to the point where wage freezes and pay-cuts were commonplace. Harrington argued that the brief 1984 recovery was fueled by consumer spending on credit, not increased savings and investment, so rising personal debt threatened working-class families as well as the economy. On the one hand, less grassroots purchasing power created an underconsumption crisis. On the other, growing public, corporate, and consumer debts, and wild speculation among the wealthy, enriched speculators but buried some prestigious businesses.

Public revenues couldn't keep up with the expanding list of needy entitlement recipients. Interest rates remained high because financial markets were worried about the burgeoning supply-side deficits. The overvalued dollar increased imports and worsened unemployment in the beleaguered manufacturing sector. Marginally profitable businesses collapsed, and foreign investors pumped capital into U.S. businesses that would otherwise have gone to more impoverished regions. America's economic fate was now increasingly determined by wealthy foreigners. Reagan's version of laissez-faire economics promoted inequality, poverty, and unemployment at home, and helped reduce the market for U.S. goods abroad. It also imperiled the social wage that had stoked Keynesian prosperity for over forty years.

Bankrupt governments cannibalized their social programs. Austerity struck the most vulnerable, marginalized people, inflaming the crisis by cutting consumer demand for everything but unaffordable social services. The Republican Party shrewdly associated its economic program with popular appeals to family, work, neighborhood, nation, and the joys of "positive thinking," effectively precluding meaningful electoral protest. Image triumphed over substance in the 1984 and 1988 elections. Reagan's so-called recovery, however, proved that even economic upturns now contributed to the general malaise.

Modern capitalism had subverted its internal market, but economists feared that increased public spending and lower taxes would merely inflate the economy by worsening the mounting public debt. With supply-side economics already discredited, politicians were motionless in economic quicksand. Entrepreneurs searched for new markets, internationalizing the economy. As local corporations turned multi-national, and as finance became globalized, national governments could no longer effectively regulate corporations and banks. A kind of international economic anarchy existed within the advanced nations, and between them and the third world. Bad loans, unwise investments, and shady deals propelled the world economic system to the edge of financial collapse. Economic policy was out of public control.

Capitalism's welfare state was based on growth, not redistribution. When the economy turned sour, public officials manufactured canards to placate an overtaxed middle class and disunite the impoverished. They suggested that welfare benefits were enjoyed by people who didn't earn them, and they accented the bureaucratic, rather than the therapeutic, nature of these programs. Welfare, they claimed, fragmented and depersonalized recipients, producing a dependent, lazy underclass. These evils far out-weighed any help the poor and the sick may have received, or any reforms that might improve the system by empowering local communities.

A disproportionately high percentage of welfare recipients, though not a majority, were nonwhites. By attacking welfare, politicians scored points with poor whites, whose fear and anger otherwise might threaten the rich. Racism kept poor workers busy fighting each other and also won elections. Harrington believed that capitalism's crisis was structural rather than episodic, conceding too much to the private sector rather than too little. Any tactics—rational *or* irrational—that reinforced the priority of corporate interests in economic decision-making only worsened an already bad situation.

The welfare state had become too socialist to let capitalism work and too capitalist to permit socialism, and Reagan's free-market cure proved worse than the disease. Behind the populist rhetoric of its so-called "revolution," conservatism sanctioned an unfair distribution of wealth. It wanted an old-fashioned future that was outmoded already, but with communism dying and democratic socialism fast asleep no alternatives existed. Thus, capitalism was experiencing a "slow 1929"[15]: a nondramatic, noncataclysmic structural crisis with frightening consequences.

SOCIALISM REBORN

When the home team wins, people celebrate. No one thinks about the kitchen sink filled with dirty dishes or the unpaid bills throbbing in the desk drawer. Flushed with victory over a communist empire that was disintegrating, Americans ignored Harrington's sobering message: capitalism was collapsing at home the way communism was abroad, and the welfare state was experiencing a crisis like none before. Harrington wasn't vindicated because, although laissez-faire economics had failed, bigotry replaced progress, and socialism dissolved in the hopeless welfare state.

Life was certainly going to change: the question was not "if" but "how." Would capitalism become a corporate dictatorship that only preserved liberal rhetoric? Or would the U.S. democratize production and distribution? Harrington's final project offered democrats an ideology that explained the current crisis and pointed to a just future. Capitalists believed in their system and knew how it worked. Socialism, for Harrington, needed to be redesigned because working people also needed something to believe in that would improve their lives. Marx realized this, and so had the utopians; Harrington now wanted to spread the word.

Two decades after criticizing reductionism, Harrington again acknowledged that workers had material *and* nonmaterial needs; they had to be fed as well as inspired. Harrington's final books—*The Next Left* (1986), *The Long-Distance Runner: An Autobiography* (1989), and *Socialism: Past and Future* (1989)—outlined a "New Socialism" that tied nineteenth-century utopian ethics to Marx's politics. By recovering a forgotten past, it buried the modern left's meager values and its welfare-state mentality. Harrington felt it was a groundbreaking kind of radicalism that could appeal to those in the ideological center, somewhere between the boardrooms and the barricades. The bridge between mainstream America and Harrington's New Socialism was the tiny, hunchbacked, formidable Italian Marxist, Antonio Gramsci, "one of the most fascinating thinkers in the history of Marxism."[16]

Gramsci wrote that cultures survive by exerting "hegemony," or control, over people's ideas. Capitalism, for example, lives in a massive network of bourgeois institutions—schools, churches, political parties, newspapers, media, and private associations—that use ideas to buttress corporate production. Socialists needed to fight bourgeois hegemony in a long and complex "war of position" from which a new hegemonic apparatus would emerge. Gramsci warned that socialist cadres trained only to seize political power would fail miserably, because a state's power included all those cultural institutions through which power relations are mediated. Gramsci's "integral state" embodied coercive or political power to subdue class enemies, and cultural or civil power to subdue dangerous ideas. Socialists had to defeat both the political and civil components of capitalism. Harrington realized that U.S. socialists had never fully joined the civil struggle.

For Gramsci, intellectuals legitimized culture, and therefore were as important for maintaining capitalism as public officials who enacted and executed the law. In books, journals, classrooms, pulpits, and airwaves, intellectuals created the national values that we internalized as children and that later defined us as members of a particular culture—what Gramsci called a "historical bloc." Each historical bloc had its own legitimizing experts. Hence, a historical bloc is an integral state rooted in an organic relationship, not just an alliance, between leaders and masses. Neither can stray too far from the other without the state collapsing.

Gramsci believed that revolutionary intellectuals like Harrington demystified culture by explaining how popular words and symbols represented a historical bloc dominated by capitalists. If successful, they turned good citizens into rebellious workers. This dramatic and complex project required direct communication between workers and intellectuals. By manipulating familiar words, symbols, and emotions, intellectuals plugged into, and critiqued, public culture. Gramsci called these radical thinkers "organic" because they arose from and reflected the needs and values of real working people. National Marxist parties, therefore, needed to pay attention to public culture, and in America this meant surpassing liberalism without annihilating it.

Gramsci speculated that workers participating in factory decision-making, even in a capitalist economy, gradually became enlightened and empowered, and then revolutionary. Harrington also believed that democracy was inherently progressive; as workers took on more responsibilities, even little ones, they gained self-confidence and eventually became socialists. Harrington's moderate political program was thus precisely what Gramsci had in mind when he challenged the Russians and set Italian Marxists on their own nationalist track.

Gramsci also directed socialists away from both violence and reformism, re-established the complex linkages of state and civil society, emphasized the global character of socialism, and reminded activists to change culture, not just the economy. Real workers weren't merely clones of some proletarian stereotype. They even loved their country when doing so was not in their best interests. Gramscian socialists legitimized working-class values and delegitimized the injustices done in their name.

Harrington accused socialists of being preoccupied only with economics or politics, a one-dimensional package that didn't sell. People were often too busy with practical activities and cultural interests to notice or care. Americans needed a new sense of purpose in their everyday affairs that sanctioned a beloved heritage and also helped them live better.

Conservatives already claimed to "own" the future, in Owen Harries's words, to "determine the spirit of the age, the prevailing notions concerning what is possible, inevitable, desirable, permissible, and unspeakable."[17] Ronald Reagan did his part by using myths to consolidate the new conservative consensus in the 1980s. As historian Harvey Kaye noted, he emphasized the virtues of "small-town America," and trumpeted traditional values such as self-control, self-reliance, national pride, weak government, and the free market. His speeches referred to the Pilgrims, Paine, Lincoln, the Founding Fathers, Franklin D. Roosevelt, John F. Kennedy, and other U.S. heroes.[18] He personalized his stories and related them to popular national sentiments, amiably reinforcing the notion that people became poor because of their own shortcomings: they were unmotivated, lazy, dishonest, and stupid. He perpetuated and revitalized the "American dream" that anyone could succeed if he tried hard enough, and had only himself to blame if he didn't. In short, Reagan distorted, harnessed, and manipulated the nation's cultural heritage for his own political gain.

Conservatives then cut medicaid, maternal and child health programs, and funds for community health centers; slashed over \$2 billion from Aid to Families With Dependent Children (AFDC); depleted child nutrition programs in 1981, daycare programs in 1982, and food stamp programs in

1983; eliminated training and employment programs under CETA; and added "workfare" to welfare eligibility, rather than providing jobs. Surveying the wrecked lives of poor people, including some Reaganites, sociologist Ruth Sidel concluded in 1986 that the sophisticated use of tradition and mythology was "perhaps Mr. Reagan's most significant and most pernicious accomplishment."[19]

Harrington conceded the civil, ideological, and cultural aspects of capital's successful class war from above. Conservatives had indeed represented the past in such a way as to reinforce the social order and power structure, and mollify subaltern classes. But he also challenged socialists to learn from the enemy, to embrace public culture—once contemptuously called the superstructure—in order to promote democracy and end inequality. Capitalism had a new class system that was dense and diverse, with yawning cultural gaps separating workers. Economics alone could no longer catalyze social change because workers were not aligned on class issues. Although these "dealigned" workers on balance did better economically if they cooperated rather than competed,[20] they needed a powerful emotional bond.

The depressing facts were certainly indisputable. A high percentage of poor and working Americans were racial and ethnic minorities, women, and the elderly. They became militantly self-conscious, and often bonded exclusively around cultural traditions they shared only with other group members. Each group fought independently for its rights, further weakening an already fractured working class. As issue-oriented activists they saw trees not forests, and ignored the structures of impoverishment.

Social rights are meaningless if people can't afford to live decently, and hard economics always conditions the quality of life. America's hegemonic ideology celebrated competition between selfish individuals and groups. At a time when Americans identified with race, sex, age, ethnicity, and environment more than class, the knowledge that economics counts, for Harrington, "put further strains on a New Deal coalition based on loyalties developed during an era of greater class simplicity and interest."[21] Socialism had failed by preaching from the economic perimeter to people walking straight down the middle—tying racial bigotry, for example, to capitalism, but ignoring the richer and more complex black experience.[22] Traditional socialism was irrelevant, not wrong. Harrington's New Socialism cared about economics without being economistic, and took non-economic groups and issues very seriously because workers also did.

New Socialists needed to plunge head-first into everyday life, defending victims, articulating real suffering, and exploring new political tactics. By demythologizing and then strengthening the mediations linking class and everyday behavior, an organic working class would congeal from the bottom up, each member tempered by consensual loyalties that would nourish a blooming collective consciousness.

Blue- and white-collar unions were still central to Harrington's project because they defended economic rights, but in the 1980s gender, race, ethnicity, ecology, and religion were more politically potent than class. Identity groups were as important as unions; together, they transformed dissatisfied factions into a bonded electoral majority. This was Gramsci's message, and it also became the core of Harrington's mature theory.

THE NEW SOCIALISM

Each thread in Harrington's ethical net represented one part of a new morality, a new world view. Woven together, they mixed culturally diverse workers into the common project of fighting capitalist hegemony in every sphere of life. The New Socialist morality, Harrington warned, was neither an ethical utopia nor a religion, but would encourage people to create a world with more options for personal growth than had ever before existed.[23] Socialism would rise from below as people adjusted to their expanded freedoms.

Civilized societies traditionally have used abstractions to justify elitism: in the Middle Ages, an organic community established by God empowered landed aristocrats; Enlightenment individualism, and its natural laws, elevated capitalists into a new hegemonic elite; and communism recaptured the medieval sense of community, but reduced everything to matter and then justified a barbaric dictatorship. Throughout history, truth always unravelled into domination, and social obedience became a moral absolute. Democratic socialism's fate, on the other hand, indicated that social movements without philosophical principles were insubstantial. Critique alone padded vitae and created media gurus, but didn't mobilize the kind of widespread support that is needed to change a culture.

The problem of philosophically anchoring emancipatory social theory has vexed radicals, particularly those associated with the Frankfurt School, throughout this century.[24] Harrington's solution was to frame the New Socialism in "values rooted in programs that actually change the conditions of life."[25] This "practical idealism" was critical and flexible, nondogmatically challenging the status quo. When different programs were shown to produce better living conditions, the values also changed. Harrington's practical idealism was thus actualized in the give and take of democratic decision-making and empirical inquiry. Ethically and tactically justifiable, it was something democrats could believe in and also use to establish an electoral majority.

The actual substance of Harrington's New Socialism was an ancient principle that had inspired democrats and revolutionaries throughout history, but was never operationalized. Harrington believed that the perennial question of how to reconcile the needs of a just community with those of free individuals could be answered by resurrecting the republican ideal of the citizen, wherein public and private interests were harmonized. Republican government was the common business (*res publica*) of citizens, which they transacted for the common good. Citizens were free, self-governing, and virtuous enough to place the public's welfare above selfish interests. Harrington acknowledged the "immoral foundation" of Athenian democracy, with its heinous practices of slavery and sexism. Why, then, resurrect a tarnished ideal? "Because the Greeks," Harrington answered, "at their best, built a political system in which there was no bureaucracy, no state looming over the citizen, but a culture of participation and social commitment . . . . The forms of Athenian politics, in short, have a value that can be detached from their shameful historical base, particularly when a technological revolution obviates the economic necessity of subordination and exploitation."[26]

Classical republican values richochet through the Roman Empire, the late Middle Ages, and the French, American, and Russian Revolutions. Each historical epoch articulated one moment of the original public-private totality: universal harmony, individual rights, or social commitment. The dialecticians, particularly Marx and the utopians, tried to piece together history's broken unity, but lacked enough resources to sanction the synthesis. Productive capacity could not satisfy individual needs or finance vital social services, so competition, not harmony, worked best. Since public institutions allowed rival interests to check one another, the wealthy could also procedurally block republican initiatives that threatened property rights.

Modernity finally enabled democrats to reclaim their republican legacy. New technologies increased material production dramatically. Liberals, especially in England and the U.S., discovered a social conscience, and Marxists tried to safeguard individual liberty. After its spin through history, republicanism landed in this fertile material and philosophical milieu. The reborn republican ethic of growing and prospering with, not against, others was now reinforced by advanced productivity and a mature democratic tradition. An ethical, multi-class, and decentralized socialism, what Gramsci called a new historical bloc, could now succeed capitalism and communism. Its popularity in nations, moreover, would create a new sense of world citizenship. International solidarity, like republicanism, offered practical solutions to immediate problems, and also, in Harrington's words, strengthened "that oneness of humankind celebrated in the biblical account of the common parents of all human beings."[27] A real synthesis of individualism and collectivism was now possible, and Harrington called it "Socialist Republicanism."[28]

America has its own republican tradition that goes back to Thomas Jefferson. It has surfaced sporadically in domestic struggles for freedom and equality. Politics will decide if this radical tradition of citizenship as a moral value and a basic commitment ever becomes more than what Harrington called "nostalgic rhetoric."[29] Harrington believed, however, that U.S. public life had disintegrated into isolated, disconnected, self-absorbed individuals and groups. Democratic socialism, not liberalism, resembled those "little republics" that Jefferson once said guaranteed liberty. It was part of the nation's ethical conscience, that non-elitist, democratic mentality that Harrington characterized as a "particularly American spirit."[30] The left needed to reclaim this republican sentiment, which had sadly been kidnapped and abused by Reaganites. "I do not think that the Left can afford to leave the civic emotions to the Right," Harrington warned. "In a profound sense, that is our heritage more than theirs."[31]

Socialist republicanism was progressive and indigenous, with roots in traditional American values. By reflecting the collective interests of a free, united people, and advocating popular participation in civic affairs, it was also profoundly patriotic. Jefferson would have called it the rock-solid foundation of U.S. democracy; and Gramsci, the basis of a democratic historical bloc. For Harrington, however, it Americanized socialism and socialized America.

A POLITICAL PROGRAM, PART TWO

Harrington's New Socialism represented a national morality that finally enabled diverse workers and interests to coalesce. This process, for Harrington, was "the work of an historic epoch"[32], not a year or a decade, and socialists had to slowly harness the painful transformations that already were underway. Democratic reforms developed their own momentum, altering what people believed and how they acted. Praxis created theory, and reinforced democratic politics. "The transition to socialism," wrote Harrington, "would be much more protracted and profound than most socialists, including Marx, had thought."[33]

Harrington had once outlined a political program, but hardly anyone noticed. Politics, he realized, needed a "language of sincere and genuine idealism. A politics without poetry will simply not be able to bring together all of the different, and sometimes antagonistic, forces essential to a new majority for a new program."[34] Socialists enhanced productivity and redistributed wealth, and also introduced new, larger possibilities to a pessimistic nation. In Harrington's words, socialists had to "state . . . prejudices boldly"[35] in order to morally rebuild a dispirited, frightened polity. Once Fordism had thrived by combining justice and efficiency. Now socialists also had to catch the public with exciting dreams, not just tactics. Since many workers in the 1980s were neither poor nor class conscious, Harrington's new political program emphasized quality-of-life issues.

High-wage full employment was still the heart of Harrington's domestic agenda and the material prerequisite for democracy. Decent, federally-guaranteed jobs for every citizen, paying from five to seven dollars per hour, would drive up wages in the private sector and increase productivity and efficiency. The loss of marginal jobs from the market was easily outweighed by expanding social consumption. America's decrepit infrastructure, moreover, needed to be rebuilt by thoughtfully expanding public-sector investment. A public rail system, for instance, would create jobs, save energy, and reduce auto pollution. Harrington planned to solve the housing crisis—and also create jobs—by subsidizing interest rates on loans for public or private low- and middle-income housing, letting market rates prevail for investment in expensive housing, capping the deductibility of mortgage interest, and increasing funds for public housing. He wanted to raise morale by reducing the work-week to thirty or thirty-five hours, thereby also increasing the number of workers by about 20 percent. Salaries needn't fluctuate if a portion of the resulting wage increase was in added leisure time rather than money, and another portion in progressive tax reductions. The total would reach forty paid hours, with a small fraction publicly subsidized because increased productivity and reduced unemployment represented a social saving. Since fixed labor costs (e.g., payroll taxes, health benefits, etc.) would rise, Harrington proposed abolishing or reducing payroll taxes by funding these programs through general revenues, and creating a national healthcare system.[36]

If each reform was part of an integrated, long-range plan, Harrington felt that economic growth would not suffer. Employee-related expenses, for example, could be publicly financed by revising the tax code, repealing every Reagan-sponsored tax cut that didn't create jobs and income for poor people, and accelerating military budget cuts. Public assistance going to the aged and children, and to safety-net social programs like health insurance, AIDS research, and childcare services, were adequately fundable only, in Harrington's own words, when full-employment resources "economically and politically permit such decency."[37] Aside from establishing a national welfare minimum, indexed to median income, Harrington would leave the welfare program alone. He predicted that workfare would fail if jobs that offer medical benefits and daycare, and pay significantly more than AFDC and food stamps, were unavailable. As things now stood, workfare just shuttled people from welfare to impoverished work. Harrington's New Socialism offered a humane *and* efficient system of production, not charity.

"The most hallowed populist principle of American society"—that is, progressive taxation—"must be embraced," in Harrington's opinion, to equitably finance economic justice.[38] America's tax burden shifted dramatically during the 1980s from the rich to the middle class and poor. Harrington placed redistribution back on the political hotplate, but rejected new wage or payroll taxes since, in a private economy, these created employment disincentives. France's socialist government nearly went broke when mandated wage hikes depleted private accumulation and investment. Harrington also wanted to cap mortgage interest deductions on median-priced houses; extend the social security tax to include all income; end the hiring disincentives at lower wage scales by exempting the first $4000 of earnings from the social security tax; tax capital gains on inherited stock and large inheritances; regulate inherited voting rights in private enterprises; and raise taxes on annual incomes above $200,000. These policies probably wouldn't antagonize capitalists, and might even earn some business support by financing justice for workers in an economy that, in the short run, would remain capitalist.

Socialism, however, was now much more than merely raising and redistributing money, and creating jobs. Quality was now as important as quantity, and by the mid-1980s Harrington's original full-employment program became, in his words, "qualitatively defined full employment."[39] New jobs had to be meaningful, challenging, and wherever possible engaged with labor-saving technology. So-called smart machines, Harrington claimed, worked better if smart people, laboring creatively, ran them, which might happen when new technology was organized in small-scale, cooperative settings. Laborers needed fulfilling work, not just more jobs, so the economy's character as well as its size had to be upgraded. This ambitious goal became Harrington's precondition for meaningful democratic reforms.

Private corporations investing in useful research and development should be rewarded with tax benefits. Federal and state agencies, financed by public debt that was paid off like any long-term investment, also needed to create high-quality public employment. The nation had to revamp public schools to produce skilled, motivated, and ambitious workers, and citizens prepared to creatively use an expanding block of leisure time. Some wage increases could take the form of sabbaticals, annual leaves for job-related study, that improved the quality of life and also raised productivity. These expanding opportunities for personal growth would accomplish for workers what the post-World War II G.I. Bill of Rights did for veterans.

Workers were expending the equivalent of an additional month of paid labor each year more than they had two decades ago, but for many the extra hours merely slowed a free-fall into poverty.[40] Although working more hours, they earned fewer adjusted dollars and lost valuable leisure time.

Once Harrington would have magnified pertinent economic factors such as shrinking salaries and benefits, inflation, deindustrialization, deunionization, and the need for two-income families. His New Socialism instead emphasized the crisis of time faced by middle-class and poor families, the fact that love alone couldn't keep them together: parents worked so many long hours they rarely had the time or energy just to be parents; simple pleasures like shared vacations were rapidly disappearing from family routines. Conservatives aggravated the crisis with their free-market economic policies but nonetheless used it to their own advantage by blaming government. Harrington wanted socialists to steal the right's pro-family thunder by actually delivering on promises to help working households. Radicalism often burned inside of cherished traditions.

Leisure time had become a quality-of-life issue that played in middle America, and would not go away. Sophisticated twenty-first-century technology would reduce the orbit of necessary labor to less than one-half of a workers' waking hours. In the past, people identified with the work they did. What would our identities become? Would we watch electronic spectacles or create the future? With its traditional hierarchies and bottom-line mentality, capitalism kept us glued to the tube. Socialists needed to suggest a range of new possibilities for using leisure hours creatively. Harrington always favored expanding and improving public education to accomodate every qualified citizen, regardless of wealth. Now he realized that "sending more and more people to college in a society which doesn't create enough jobs requiring the college-educated can be destructive to individuals and wasteful of resources."[41] The U.S. needed better schools and universities, but also physical investments in theaters, athletic fields, fix-it shops, and libraries, as well as increased public support for music, art, poetry, crafts, hobbies, and participatory sports.

If America was to compete successfully in the world market Harrington knew that justice had to enhance, not inhibit, efficiency.[42] On a sinking ship, empowered workers merely supervised their own descent. Thus, cultural enrichment was meaningless without a robust national economy, which required a combination of national initiatives to coordinate and streamline productivity, and local initiatives to democratize the workplace. This two-pronged strategy increased the number of quality jobs, promoted economic growth, and fostered republicanism. Economic democracy could also be a popular platform for mobilizing insecure voters.

Command economies obviously were inefficient and unjust, as were market systems where investments enriched the wealthy. Harrington favored a national industrial policy to subsidize basic industries that had economic and social value, and to uphold global ecological agreements. Local communities, using federal subsidies, could hire experts to negotiate the specifics. Harrington also wanted to establish a national investment bank to raise capital in financial markets with federally guaranteed loans. He hoped that unions would eagerly invest pension funds in this kind of guaranteed, no-risk outlet, and benefit from its activities. The bank would be legally mandated to invest only in ecologically sound projects that developed technology, productivity, and jobs—especially in areas where the rate of return discouraged private investment. "It would not," Harrington added, "be in the business of underwriting corporate takeovers, greenmail, golden parachutes, or any other ingenious device of the paper entrepreneurs."[43]

The nation's economic plan framed local investment and production policies. Harrington still believed that improved morale and increased productivity resulted from worker and community participation in these basic decisions, including plant location. Many of his proposals already were on record. With one eye on quality-of-life issues, he now suggested that federal legislation mandate employee involvement in designing factory technology.[44] He wanted to put teeth into employee stock ownership programs (ESOPs).[45] Corporations had used ESOPs to qualify for government tax subsidies. In return, they marginalized workers by making them individual owners of small amounts of stock with almost no power. Restructured to empower workers instead of managers, Harrington believed that ESOPs promoted democratic economics. Collective profit-sharing arrangements established in Sweden, Holland, and Denmark were models of what ESOPs could become; companies were required to pay a tax in the form of voting stock into a mutual fund controlled by the elected representatives of workers, who would actively participate in the decision-making process and not simply be passive stockholders.[46]

Home-based employment is usually associated with exploitative forms of capitalist production. Harrington, however, felt that working at home actually saved time and money now spent on commuting, and freed workers from the tight discipline of the assembly line or office.[47] It also promoted decentralized communities where jobs, shopping, and financial resources no longer were concentrated far away from residences and schools. All this was possible, however, only if the transition to home work was strictly regulated so that workers weren't left isolated, de-unionized, alienated, and enslaved by a computer. Thoughtfully reformulated, this kind of work might preserve basic union standards and also increase freedom, creativity, and flexibility.

Underlying all of Harrington's proposals for democratizing production was the need to strengthen and expand democratic unions. Union membership had steadily dropped since the 1960s until, in 1989, the percentage of unionized workers was at its lowest point since before the depression.

Harrington attributed this to structural changes in the economy and to reactionary politics.

U.S. corporations moved labor-intensive factories south, computerized others, and invested heavily in the service sector. Unions found their traditional blue-collar constituency replaced by unskilled service employees and educated, well-paid white-collar workers. Even in the best of times, therefore, unions would have suffered, and the last 40 years have been anything but that. Since the Taft-Hartley Act in 1947, workers have found organizing very difficult, and employers have taken full advantage of the permissive legal climate. Management consultants created union-free environments, stunning anti-labor decisions, particularly by the Rehnquist Court, impeded labor activities, and the National Labor Relations Board grew hostile. In other industrial democracies and in the public sector, unions were growing two or three times faster than in the workforce as a whole. Harrington asked liberals and socialists to support labor law reform that would democratize unions and facilitate workplace organizing.[48] A strong, cohesive labor movement decentralized management and redistributed income and wealth, and also promoted full employment and a robust economy. It gained workers a voice and a vote in workplace decisions, thereby organizing people to press toward such worthy goals as national health insurance and legislation regulating capital flight abroad, corporate pollution, junk bonds, and corporate raids. Unions, in short, raised working-class consciousness. Unionization made economic democracy possible, and also introduced socialist republicanism into local communities.

Harrington's New Socialism was, then, a way of living, not an economic doctrine; a quality of life rather than production; a process instead of a concept. Neither a formula nor a legal mode of ownership, socialism, said Harrington, is "a principle of empowering people at the base, which can animate a whole range of measures, some of which we do not even yet imagine."[49] Socialism *is* democracy. Any measure that democratized the system was socialist, even if it privatized production.

The question of whether socialists should nationalize production was for Harrington still unsettled[50], subject to pragmatic discussion and empirical inquiry. If nationalization promoted socialism, it was desirable; if it inhibited workplace democracy and creativity, it was undesirable. However, essential production that required large-scale planning and investments, and couldn't be easily decentralized (e.g., power grids, transportation systems, and communication networks) in Harrington's opinion must be nationalized. Also, their internal structures and their impact on communities and the nation also needed to be socialized, so that workers could make key decisions. If the daily operations of nationalized industries resembled private corporations, the quality of life would not change. Harrington again suggested that workers and community representatives serve permanently on factory boards of directors, where they could influence the national plan.

America would remain a mixed economy, dominated by private business, for the foreseeable future. The fear of public bureaucracies and centralized production was also widespread in the U.S., even among workers. Harrington urged socialists to create exciting new forms of social ownership that socialized production without necessarily nationalizing it.

In small-scale high-tech industries, cooperatives and worker-owned enterprises might work best. Harrington cited the Swedish experiment in establishing wage earner funds.[51] Workers negotiated a profit-sharing agreement with management, and then invested a percentage of the annual profit in Swedish businesses and served on the boards of directors wherever they invested. Independent units of workers soon controlled corporate decisions. An American version, which Harrington called "collective capital formation,"[52] could be financed by pension funds or profit-sharing revenue. It wasn't burdened with the ugly communist legacy often associated with nationalization, and might even appeal to progressive Democrats. It would survive only if it actually stimulated qualitative economic growth and full employment. If it didn't, even socialists would bail out.

Nationalization, then, was not socialism. Nor was socialism necessarily a planned economy, or capitalism a market economy. Harrington once again shocked the left by suggesting that, in certain conditions, markets actually socialized an economy.[53]

Markets always presuppose and reinforce a given distribution of wealth and power. They are amoral mechanisms that won't foster change, and break down when people want new social relationships. In equality, markets are a wonderful device for communicating individual desires. When people are unequal, however, markets exaggerate the desires of the wealthy. Since Americans admire markets, socialists need to make them serve social priorities rather than rich consumers. "The truth is," Woodrow Wilson once said, "we are living in a great economic system, which is heartless."[54] By combining democratic planning with market efficiency, socialism could put heart into a bountiful U.S. economy.

Harrington felt that Marx's ambivalence on the topic of markets crippled the socialist movement.[55] Marx noted the historic tendency of competition to reinforce inequality and monopoly, where corporations no longer were subjected to the discipline of efficiency and workers became the dynamic class. Marx's socialist economy was like a single factory based on hierarchical relations of superiority and subordination, a proletarian monopoly that functioned without effective markets. Marx, however, also believed that socialist politics required a free association of workers and communities based on horizontal relations of equality.

Marx's democratic politics clearly contradicted his centrally planned, hierarchical economy.

Markets, said Marx, occasionally even helped workers. His theory of exploitation, for example, showed how wealthy buyers hire poor workers at a salary that is less than the value they produced. Unfair social conditions, not the markets themselves, trapped workers in this painful agreement. By clarifying the coercive process whereby workers "freely" sold their labor power at a "fair" value that produced more for capital than it cost, Marx suggested that changing the conditions of this wage bargain also changed the market outcome. Marx illustrated this in *Capital* by differentiating absolute and relative surplus value. The former increased profits by extending the work day and prolonging worker exploitation; the latter by cutting the work day, upgrading machinery, and raising productivity. Marx believed that relative surplus value was economically and morally superior to the brutality of absolute surplus value, and he endorsed Britain's Ten Hours Law as a "modest Magna Carta," a significant working class victory over capitalism. A simple reform in the structure of the labor market profoundly altered the meaning of the market economy. Even by partially redistributing social wealth or guaranteeing full employment nations democratized the wage bargain without sacrificing efficiency.

One reading of Marx popular among materialists virtually eliminated markets from consideration. Another, Harrington's, implied that socialist markets needn't resemble markets in capitalism. When Karl Kautsky proclaimed that in socialism workers could not change jobs because labor markets will disappear, he was thus correct *and* incorrect. He accurately cited Marx's critique of market capitalism but ignored Marx's free association of producers.

Kautsky's economism became communist dogma, but was by no means universally accepted. Bukharin, Trotsky, and Preobrazhensky noted the important role markets played in the transition to socialism, especially by stimulating consumer production and weeding out inefficient industries. Other Bolsheviks warned that Stalin's state-run monopoly required a surplus from workers and peasants, which would fetter production and productivity. Communism's economic monopoly had all of the drawbacks Marx ascribed to capitalist monopolies: it was bureaucratic, wasteful, inefficient, and unjust. Also, investment was controlled by a centralized bureaucracy. China under Deng Xiaoping introduced limited market mechanisms in 1979, and again in 1983 and 1992, to stimulate production. The Soviet state monopoly collapsed in 1989 as its leaders were campaigning for the introduction of markets. Harrington agreed with these communists that the choice was simple: "All one needs to do is choose the libertarian Marx over the centralist Marx and then confront reality instead of texts."[56]

Markets also played an important role in the transition to socialism for as long as the demand for resources exceeded supply. In scarcity, socialists needed to be as concerned with efficiency as capitalists were.[57] But socialist efficiency expressed social and global goals, not just private interests. Socialists minimized the input of human and material resources, in public and private sectors, in order to maximize a surplus that alleviated suffering. In today's competitive world market, top-down Old Left egalitarianism hurt rather than helped workers. Taylorism, on the other hand, permitted unfair markets to command the economy. Neither planning nor markets alone was sufficient, but prudently combined, each was indispensible. Even in socialism, however, stubbornly inefficient factories have to close down, and society must provide job retraining, public works employment, job placement, employer subsidies, moving subsidies, and, as a last resort, unemployment compensation. Workers were human beings, not commodities, even when victimized by the labor market.

Informal, decentralized, cooperative efforts were often more efficient than standard bureaucratic procedures, particularly in delivering social services.[58] Recipients became independent and creative, displacing public officials who did not understand life on the dole. Inventive delivery strategies that minimized costs and maximized services also trimmed bloated bureaucracies and delivered more bang for the public buck. Decentralization in the workplace inspired workers to challenge bureaucratic inefficiencies with new strategies informed by their knowledge of the assembly line and the consumer market. Harrington was certain they would make more and better items for less cost than traditional workers. But this required a market modified by democratic planning priorities, where workers minimized costs, maximized production, and then shared in the expanded surplus. "And that," Harrington added, "leads to what must seem to be a very heretical thought for a socialist: that there must be sources of individual and collective gain in this process."[59]

Socialist republicans strive for excellence on moral grounds or because excellence is its own reward, but in scarcity they must also economize inputs and link performance and success. Workers thus needed material incentives to maintain a competitive edge. How, asked Harrington, could socialists eliminate greed if workers were selfish?

"The evidence," he answered, "is ambiguous."[60] Rising living standards in the 1960s purged the greed and inhumanity from competition. In the 1980s, however, the nation became more acquisitive and heartless than ever. Economic democracy might collectivize capital within this competitive market, so that workers in efficient factories prospered and those in inefficient enterprises suffered; inequality would grow instead of diminish.

Harrington conceded that in scarcity, markets reward innovative producers and penalize lazy ones, but in democracies markets can't be sovereign. Socialists had to decide what kind of markets were appropriate, not whether markets were necessary. Later, workers' psychological reactions to socialist markets would become a policy issue affected by political struggles between forces representing both sides of the question. "Making self-interest—including collective self-interest—the instrument of community purpose will be a contradictory, and even dangerous, idea for the foreseeable future," Harrington wrote. "It is also necessary."[61] As schools and public services improved, republicanism spread, and reliable information replaced hucksterism, Harrington felt that consumers would become more intelligent and rational. Real majority rule would then finally prevail in the marketplace, the way it did at the ballot box. In these new circumstances the politics of selfishness would evaporate.

Harrington didn't agree with "market socialists," for whom market relations defined socialism. Harrington's socialist markets efficiently implemented democratic priorities, effectively limiting the anti-social consequences of market rewards and penalties. Losers in this socialist market would not suffer unemployment, hunger, inadequate medical care, substandard housing, or shameful educations. Winners wouldn't be sovereign. In the New Socialism, "the heirs of Karl Marx may well vindicate the hopes of Adam Smith."[62] If and when scarcity was replaced by abundance, then socialist markets, like those in capitalism, would wither away.

8

ASSESSING MICHAEL HARRINGTON

In a paper delivered at a 1965 plenary session of the American Sociological Association's annual meeting, Talcott Parsons dismissed Karl Marx as someone "whose work fell entirely within the nineteenth century . . . . [H]e belongs to a phase of development which has been superceded . . . . [His] predictions about the course of the socio-economic system have been deeply invalidated by the course of events in most advanced industrial societies . . . . [J]udging by the standards of the best contemporary social science . . . Marxian theory is obsolete." Parsons went on to argue that Marxism was elitist, inflexible, and oblivious to "elements of what may be called pluralization." It also incorrectly ignored the state's role in improving living standards and eliminated "ideal and normative factors" from its sterile social science.[1]

An anachronism in 1965, and even more so today, Parsons's critique nevertheless mirrors the kind of mob psychology that has always characterized American anti-socialism. What it comes down to, in the U.S., is a fundamental conflict between two world views: one good, the other evil;

one individualist, the other collectivist; one American, the other un-American. Had it not appeared on its own, orthodox Marxism probably would have been invented by some enterprising U.S. politician. It was a ploy for ambitious patriots, the reverse image of everything America cherished, and also the relic of a failed legacy that even U.S. leftists rejected. Subjectivity, politics, science, gender, race, religion, and family—the flesh of everyday life—were reduced to class and then pulverized beyond recognition. It was as if, by fiat or perhaps through a few decades of political education, orthodoxy believed it could eradicate an entire culture.

Democratic socialists boarded the anti-orthodox bandwagon, where unfortunately passengers did not discriminate between Marxisms. Parsons's critique, shopworn but accurate, entirely disregarded nonorthodox leftism, which unpacked class into its components. A worker filled a slot in production, and also was part of a family, sex, race, religion, ethnic group, neighborhood, government, culture, nation, world-system, and generation. Everyday attitudes existed in this coherent totality, one important, but not determining, aspect of which was the work people did.

Socialists in what Harrington called the Marxian underground plugged into America's rock-solid sense of individualism, its faith in political activism, its commitment to empirical science, and its tolerance of deep, powerful non-economic associations. Mass culture, which communists either couldn't understand or tolerate, became their vehicle for change, the body wherein Marx's radical spirit materialized. By noting the linkages between base and superstructure, and the importance of values, they evoked the frightening spector of a homegrown, popular socialism. This indigenous movement was cast aside by liberals and censured by the mainstream left.

Michael Harrington wove the threads of democratic socialism into a tapestry depicting America's bittersweet legacy of freedom. He carried it from coast to coast, through urban and rural landscapes, into small villages, coal towns, the farmbelt, and polluted megacities. He showed it on television and radio, in newspapers and journals, and in seventeen published books. He toiled to create nation-wide organizations where theory became praxis, and democratic socialism became a real possibility to civic-minded workers and intellectuals. He worked hard and remained optimistic, but never cracked America's compulsive anti-socialism, even when conditions deteriorated in the 1970s and 80s. When Harrington died in 1989, for the general public he was still the best kept secret in town.

Of course, socialists in the U.S. are always shoved to the margins of public life. Harrington, moreover, was dogmatically anti-communist, and never fully regained the trust of the young New Leftists with whom he feuded at the 1962 Students for a Democratic Society meeting at Port Huron, Michigan. So Harrington lacked a natural constituency on the left, particularly after he exited the Socialist Party (SP) in 1972. He wanted, therefore, to join centrist liberals with progressives to build a nationwide electoral coalition for change that, he felt, would slowly and steadily turn left. We have seen that his own name and reputation became associated with his first major publication, the very popular *The Other America*. This book, and to a lesser degree its sequel, *The New American Poverty*, peddled Old Left socialism dressed in New Deal reformism. The former was an imported collectivist ideology based on economic laws that U.S. workers neither understood nor believed. In the 1970s, Harrington himself depicted the latter as old capitalist wine in new bottles. *The Other America* thus unexpectedly impacted the political system in two ways. By helping expand the capitalist welfare state it inflated the system's fiscal problems to the point that New Dealism itself eventually was discredited. And its stale reductionism told anyone who cared that economism simply didn't work, and socialists were dinosaurs.

Harrington's intellectual pilgrimage from economism to dialectics culminated in *The Next Left, The Long-Distance Runner: An Autobiography*, and *Socialism: Past and Future*, wherein, like Gramsci, he challenged socialists to embrace public culture. These last works outlined a New Socialist morality to reach into America's heartland and touch its republican pulse, and a New Socialist politics to gather a progressive electoral majority. This program is Harrington's legacy to socialists in the 1990s and beyond.

LEARNING FROM FAILURE

Harrington was personally responsible for some of his troubles. Although his eloquent prose towered over the turgid work of other leftists, his exuberance galloped wildly. Sections of his books are so overloaded with data, often given without citations, that even sympathetic readers may be exasperated. Also, Harrington refused to edit himself. "I've hardly ever had a thought that I didn't commit to print," Harrington joked in a 1988 *Newsweek* interview.[2] In fact, he often buried salient points in an avalanche of silly predictions.[3] This buckshot strategy delivered too much information; readers painfully cracked open many oysters to find one pearl.

But these are small blemishes on an impressive career—not all of Harrington's foibles are so easily dismissed. A youthful, dynamic, astute, and articulate Harrington was the obvious choice in the 1960s to meld aging socialists and brash New Leftists. A unified left might then have reconfigured the political process, as well as the public's perception of socialism. He didn't accomplish this union however, in part because at the time he could not fathom his own rich ideas. Harrington's bold Americanism had cut both ways; it anchored a formidable theory in a familiar style and syntax, but the Yankee impulse to do something practical instead of thinking abstractly sometimes produced thoughtlessness.

At least since the mid-1960s, when he wrote *Socialism*, Harrington suspected that Marxism's fate was bound to dialectics. Society was a complex and interacting whole "in which the slums of *The Other America* and the mountain sanitorium of *The Magic Mountain* were utterly different and yet parts of a common process."[4] Harrington's books thus constitute an *oeuvre*, not just a string of disparate volumes. Separately, they cover current events, theoretical politics, or cultural criticism. Each book, however, is just one narrow insight into the totality. When we eat freshly baked bread we taste the final product, not flour, water, yeast, and oil, even though each ingredient is necesary and special. Life, Harrington wrote, also was a rich blending of ingredients, and he wanted people to taste its wholeness instead of swallowing each experience separately. His *oeuvre* enriches each book, just as the work one does has a broader meaning in addition to personal experiences. This is why people who only read *The Other America* don't really know what Michael Harrington was about.

Nonetheless, Harrington behaved during the 1960s and '70s as if only the economic problems of unionized blue-collar workers counted, reformist legislation was the left's sole priority, and a small fringe of communists had become diabolical enemies. Meanwhile, the left's precious days of reckoning passed unnoticed by Harrington and his feuding colleagues. Old and new radicals sensed a once-in-a-lifetime opportunity, but bickered like children anxiously awaiting a teacher. When Harrington finally arrived they were gone. Harrington's star was stuck in a reductionist past, and its glow subsided.

In the compulsively unionist, anti-communist world of traditional democratic socialism, Harrington was a breath of fresh air. He opposed the Vietnam War, criticized George Meany, and courted the "new politics" groups in order to broaden socialism's popularity. David McReynolds reflected on the sclerotic U.S. left as Harrington fenced with Shachtman and the SP's old guard in 1972, and accurately termed Harrington a "creative" Marxist, "the kind in short supply these days."[5] Harrington can indeed take credit for modernizing and Americanizing socialism by redefining dialectics and re-tooling an outdated politics. For too many years, however, he couldn't measure up to his own standards, and for someone so attuned to life's complexity and the ties between theory and praxis, he surely should have been more sensitive. In *The Politics at God's Funeral*, Harrington bonded religion and radicalism, opening the left to believers. Socialism, he suggested, would never replace religion because "a finite human movement can [never] satisfactorily answer questions about the infinite."[6] For many years, this absorbing spirituality buried gender, race, and sexual preference in the material interests of unionized workers.

Women, African Americans, lesbians and gays, and young people had all discovered personal dignity during the 1960s. Radical women and blacks particularly were organizing independently, apart from traditional socialist organizations. Standard Old Left answers to "the women question" and "the negro question," which reduced gender and race to economics, were discarded by victims who suffered at least as much because of their gender and/or race as their class. They claimed that Marxism arrogantly subordinated subjectivity to science. As workers *and* as individuals with specific needs, capitalism hurt them. They were socialists because a market economy permanently dominated by white males would forever exploit them economically and culturally, whereas in socialism at least they competed on a level economic field. They focused on transforming families, neighborhoods, bureaucracies, schools, art, entertainment, religion, and recreation. They would not dissolve in an undifferentiated, unionized electoral constituency, nor would they play politics when their game was elsewhere.

Harrington's commitment to the goal of full racial equality went unquestioned, even when he backed the United Federation of Teachers in its struggle with black activists during the 1968 Ocean Hill-Brownsville controversey. But he followed A. Phillip Randolph, not W.E.B.Dubois, and fought to integrate the *class* struggle against exploitation and racism. He questioned radical blacks who, "in the name of a romantic exaltation of the 'power of the people,'" advocated "a decentralist panacea" that ignored "the power of class structures."[7] He often equated what he called "the problem of race" with economic indicators such as structural unemployment and miserable housing,[8] when blacks knew that even a socialist U.S. would treat them as second-class citizens. The Democratic Socialist Organizing Committee (DSOC)'s greatest failure, Harrington admitted in 1974, was its "inability to establish any kind of a presence in the black community."[9] Three years later he inadvertently explained this failure: "Of course, I think that what we've been advocating—full employment and redistribution of wealth and income—are political programs which need to be central to blacks and other minorities."[10] Championing the class interests of black workers by integrating unions and electoral politics got Harrington nowhere. Militants, whose popularity was undeniable, empowered neighborhoods by appealing to black racial and cultural solidarity. DSOC's strategy of working with the Democratic Party, even during the Vietnam War, also meant that Harrington acquiesced to cuts in domestic civil-rights and welfare programs, alienating blacks and depleting DSOC of its few remaining minority recruits. Like Marx and the Communist and Socialist Parties, Harrington mistakenly reduced black suffering to impersonal structures.

African Americans would not transcend their blackness any more than Harrington would his spirituality. From the late-nineteenth-century black preachers through the Harlem Radicals, the African Blood Brotherhood, W.E.B. Dubois, C.L.R. James, Richard Wright, the Black Panthers, and Manning Marable, black socialist intellectuals reiterated one message: American blacks needed distinct ideas and institutions reflecting their own experiences, such as those in the movement for black cultural solidarity. All workers were free only in socialism, but the bonding of blacks had to precede that of workers. Harrington's position that minority races disappear in a generic proletarian electoral bloc was deeply rooted in U.S. socialist history. For many blacks it was insensitive and racist because white American workers had repeatedly supported white capitalists rather than black workers.[11]

The simple-minded notion that socialism automatically eliminated bigotry, that no special programs or strategies were needed, also fractured Harrington's popularity among feminists. No one questioned his or DSOC's commitment to full equality for women. Harrington fought sexism, supported the ERA, recruited women into DSOC, and upheld feminist positions on gender-related issues. But he also emphasized class rather than gender and, until the 1980s, did not understand that feminist values were as basic to socialism as working-class values. At the founding convention of DSOC not one woman speaker was featured, and feminist issues were not even mentioned. Harrington subsequently refused to make abortion a serious campaign issue, although he personally supported a woman's right to choose. Many feminists agreed with DSOC member Suzanne Donovan that "there was no perception of DSOC working in the feminist movement."[12] Harrington once again was trapped in a reductionist legacy.

Feminists believe that the primary social contradiction is between men and women, and women's subordination is caused by the patriarchal system. Orthodox Marxists, however, see the gender issue as a struggle between capitalists and workers. Female subordination is primarily due to a particular social organization based on private property and characterized by elitism. For feminists, sexuality is central; for socialists, it is the class struggle. Predictably, America's orthodox Socialist and Communist Parties rejected feminism.[13]

Radical women chafed at socialism's refusal to confront gender-based oppression. Often called Marxist or socialist feminists, they suggested that feminism and socialism were compatible because each highlighted one aspect of a complex capitalist totality. Many socialist feminists were in Harrington's camp on issues unrelated to gender. Whereas Harrington reduced gender to class, however, they enlarged Marx's mode of production to include not only the means by which people have organized to produce and distribute food, shelter, and clothing, but also the means by which they have organized to produce and distribute sexuality, nurturance, and children. Economic *and* sexual divisions of labor satisfied basic human needs, and neither one alone adequately explained women's oppression in capitalism. Orthodoxy explained the origins and nature of an economic ruling class, thus isolating activities characteristic primarily of males in capitalism and ignoring altogether the issue of a ruling gender. Production actually belonged to this ruling gender, as well as to the ruling class.

Culture, therefore, was bourgeois and masculine. Women were exploited on both levels, but especially by males who traditionally excluded them from the economic sphere. As homemakers, mothers, and wives, they were subjugated by personal relationships to men that society taught them early in life and continually reinforced. They learned to perform without pay the socially necessary work of child-rearing and family care, creating new generations of law-abiding, respectful boys and girls. As consumers rather than producers, they maintained a high level of aggregate demand for commodities, and their untapped economic potential kept male wages low. Women's dependency in this so-called private sphere reinforced the basic features of public life, where men were subjugated by capitalists. Politics was inescapable, and each mode of political subjugation, private and public, froze the masculine, capitalist status quo. Economic production and sexual reproduction, class and gender, were neither identical nor autonomous. The abolition of economic slavery was, therefore, tied to the abolition of gender slavery.

Female activists wanted to transform attitudes as much as institutions, and were especially popular among liberals—just the people Harrington wanted on board. But Harrington was locked into the SP's class perspective. As feminists struggled against patriarchy, Harrington, incredibly, was uncomprehending, and, as he admitted retrospectively, "insensitive to the demands of women . . . . as women, as feminists . . . ."[14] Instead of opening DSOC to feminists and forging alliances with feminist interest groups, Harrington feuded with females who refused to prioritize class.[15] One irate woman in DSOC confronted its white male leaders in 1973, Harrington included, by pointing out that "day care and the Equal Rights Amendment . . . are as basic to women as health care and community control . . . . [Women] reject the view that the concerns of half the population are the concerns of just another 'special interest group' . . . . In many small ways, the DSOC comes close to giving the appearance of being willing to win the support of organized labor at the expense of even those most common and fundamental objectives which all women share."[16] What Harrington learned years earlier at Port Huron about bending in youthful storms, instead of angrily running for cover, obviously had not yet sunk in.

Harrington was equally insensitive during the 1960s and '70s to the non-economic demands of gays, who he offended by refusing to spearhead a floor fight for gay rights that might have diluted his economic initiatives at the 1972 Democratic Convention. "I am against placing . . . gay rights . . . at the center of the Democratic Party platform . . . . [R]aising the 'gay is good' slogan in mainstream politics, at times and in places where the order of the day is building a progressive social majority, is simply counter-productive."[17] More than a decade after Port Huron, he told women, minorities, gays, and liberal professionals that only unions were "rooted in the necessities of working life. They therefore have a stability, a perma-nence, that in this society is denied the other opposition movements, which demand that women or minorities or professionals add a voluntary respon-sibility to their normal, and often exhausting, routine."[18] With more money, facilities, and organizers, unions were clearly more important than other progressive interests. "I am convinced," a confident Harrington noted, "that the working class must be the decisive element in a coalition of the democratic Left because of its unique social and political importance. When I speak of the working class in this fashion, I do not refer to an imag-inary proletariat but primarily (if not exclusively) to the actual and existing organizations of the American workers: first and foremost to the AFL-CIO, then to the UAW, the Teamsters, etc."[19]

Perhaps Harrington was fooled by outrageous events and anticipated a rebellion. Why, he may have thought, be too cute when only an old-fash-ioned political kick was needed. Thus, he ignored mobilized grassroots movements, constricted non-political activities, advocated political and economic centralization, and scolded non-traditional radicals.

Reflecting in 1974 on socialist tactics, Harrington trivialized his later work by declaring "I do not for a moment urge a non-electoral approach to the building of socialist consciousness. . . ."[20] He was obsessed with politi-cal rather than cultural strategies, "for trends do not create new societies; they only make them possible."[21] Being a democrat meant committing to what he called the "precious" principle of "one man, one vote," realigning the Democratic Party, and pulling it left. "In a stratified society," he pointed out, "the people can 'own' the state in only one way: through the political freedom to change its policies and personnel, i.e. through political democ-racy, or one man, one vote."[22] "You are right," Harrington answered an unhappy socialist, "about all the factors operating against an electoral vic-tory for socialism, but omit that these same facts (and others) make a non-electoral strategy even more problematic."[23] Politics, especially coali-tion-building in Congress and in the party system, was Harrington's way of changing capitalist structures. "We believe that the American system does not enshrine any economic doctrine but rather provides a democratic mech-anism for change," he asserted. "We are deeply committed to that democratic system and we see in it the best mechanism for changing the inequities and iniquities of a corporate dominated economy."[24] Harrington himself later portrayed this naively hopeful attitude as "radical utopianism." His early faith in state-run programs poisoned suggestions that socialists also needed to challenge bourgeois culture and struggle outside of the electoral system. Thus he admitted that "My own political interests and instincts tend away from the direct democracy idea. Personally, I am more comfortable working for a political program than for changes in the political process, and I frankly think that too much liberal energy is channeled into process reforms."[25]

Socialist political success certainly is important. Harrington learned this in the SP, which had prioritized political activism and state power. Socialists, however, first must struggle effectively in the political arena against entrenched elites. When they lack wealth, power, and prestige, the capitalist political process always tilts toward tradition and reinforces the status quo. Socialists end up campaigning for reformist millionaires, and the economic benefits of reformism affect only a small fraction of workers. If inflated wages alone caused a revolution of rising worker expectations, it would have materialized in this proletarian elite long ago.

Social change can't be reduced to just one factor. Harrington confessed in 1988 to unreasonably simplifying things "now that gender and race and age and new social strata that had never been imagined in the old scenario are forces in their own right."[26] Always predisposed toward using government to solve social problems, Harrington had crashed into a dilemma. The class structure was differentiated, college-educated professionals were powerful, racial and ethnic consciousness was blooming, and women were redefining exploitation. On the other hand, politics still was important because even quarrelsome workers shared common interests, and prudent public programs could make a difference. "[T]he right to eat in a once segregated restaurant is almost meaningless if you are poor or part of a despised underclass," Harrington noted. "The color of your skin no longer matters, but the color of your money does. So, too, with the ideal of genuine equality for women, respect for the environment, and creating alternatives to military violence throughout the world."[27] "How," he asked, "does one actually practice the politics of a coalition divided into sometimes warring components?"[28]

His answer was to further articulate specificity and establish a common denominator of economic need. A reborn dialectician and "New Socialist," Harrington finally realized during the 1980s that although "the quality of life is crucially affected by the quantity of jobless,"[29] it is affected by other things as well. Socialists had to formulate a unified economic program that didn't trash non-economic agendas. "Indeed," he now warned, "it should be frankly acknowledged that constituencies that join together behind this basic program might fight one another on other issues."[30]

Socialist politics, then, succeeds only when it is part of a large strategy that empowers people culturally, defends progressive special interests, and challenges everyday capitalist values. As non-economic interests mobilize, they will become formidable politically. When they are persuaded that socialist economics creates cultural diversity, they will incite the moribund union movement, and their strength will be multiplied. And when redesigned, Americanized socialist values and programs link them with plain, God-fearing, hard-working people, they will be a democratic majority.

Some feminists, blacks, and gays were saying precisely this during the 1960s and '70s. Until DSOC's Left Caucus forged an alliance with the New American Movement, however, and later the Democratic Socialists of America pledged to fight for realignment and cultural change, as a tactician Harrington was unforgiveably tardy.

When he finally came to his senses and realized that non-economic groups were more than pawns in a proletarian army, a special moment had already passed. Harrington struggled "not simply for the next step, but for the next step in a voyage of ten thousand miles."[31] Unfortunately, at this crucial juncture in U.S. history, he sacrificed the future to an antiquated formula.

WHAT'S LEFT IN AMERICA?

In the 1960s and '70s, a reductionist Harrington and his unionist colleagues helped derail radical feminists, blacks, and gays as they lurched leftward. In one sense, then, he came of age as a socialist more than two decades too late, long after he foolishly jilted embittered young leftists at Port Huron, ridiculed non-economic special interests, and fractured what might have become a powerful union of workers, students, women, and minorities. His belated retribution, however, was to attach U.S. public culture to Marxian critique during the 1980s, in what he called New Socialism. The highlight of Harrington's legacy, in the end, is this thoughtful blending of economics, politics, and culture that, during his life, isolated him from every major constituency on the left, right, and center. If and when the boat that he missed in the early years returns, Harrington's New Socialism may help others jump on board.

Public culture consists of attitudes, beliefs, and institutions that are held communally by a people and influence their social behavior. In the U.S. it includes the liberal democratic package of individualism, pluralism, capitalism, and empiricism. Reasonable people disagree about questions of equity and justice, but not about the fact that most Americans are socialized from cradle to grave to accept this heritage. Rather than either trashing socialism or ignoring reality, Harrington defined a uniquely American radicalism that worked with and through everyday attitudes.

Socialism will vanish when capitalism resolves its serious problems. The likelihood, however, of new economic recessions and new attempts to increase capital accumulation by imposing austerity on workers makes class conflict, even in the U.S., a distinct possibility. Harrington realized that socialism won't be a viable option until it grabs onto nations that are careening from comfortable pasts into uncertainty. Socialism must evoke cherished memories and also deliver dreams. Like all successful political movements, it must become part of public culture before changing it.

In its day, New Deal liberalism plugged a leaking dike that threatened a deluge of class and racial violence. It inspired America to polish a tarnished legacy with creative reforms; it was part of a heritage, yet it also fostered change. With an eloquent helmsman, this liberalism defined four generations of U.S. voters, refashioning the nation's values in a succession of electoral campaigns. But it finally couldn't deliver what it promised, and couldn't afford what it delivered. As the post–World War II liberal coalition fractured during the 1970s, affluent Americans shrewdly tapped festering frustrations. They recast the U.S. social agenda by transforming material woes into moral wedge issues that could win elections for conservatives who didn't want to initiate change. In newspapers, books, churches, movies, television, and on Capitol Hill, they injected laissez-faire capitalism back into America's cultural arteries. In universities, think-tanks, government bureaus, and international organizations, Keynesians gave way to model-building macroeconomists championing market liberalization, deregulation, and privatization. Free-market capitalism once again became part of the body politic, even though it actually turned a bad situation much worse. The dike is leaking again, but no one has explained how an invisible hand can plug the leak—or stop a deluge.

Capitalism still expands and contracts in cyclic bursts. Now, however, each downturn leaves a permanent residue of misery in poor and middle-class neighborhoods, while the benefits of economic growth are shared by a shrinking number of mostly wealthy people. As social programs were privatized by conservatives, economic victims fended for themselves, often unsuccessfully. In urban areas, among minorities, and for groups of migrant laborers, family farmers, miners, and service workers, the prospects increased for civil disorder on the scale of the 1992 Los Angeles riots. These horrible events were incited by the acquittal in nearby Simi County of LA police officers who beat Rodney King, just the kind of serendipitous event—"like the North Carolina sit-ins of 1960 or the women in the SNCC [Student Non-violent Coordinating Committee] a few years later who decided to say no to sexism . . . . [or] Port Huron"[32]—that Harrington guessed would shatter the status quo.

Although people were angry as the gap between rich and poor widened, and as unemployment rose, they were also confused. Conservatives had reattached laissez-faire capitalism to public culture, reclaiming a historical legacy and the allegiance of millions of voters. But studies showed that public opinion still supported some principles and priorities of the liberal Keynesian state. The conservative's electoral victories, in Harvey J. Kaye's opinion, may have been "due more to their adeptness at mobilizing and harnessing popular anxieties, fears, and hopes than their having accomplished a transformation of the political and cultural views and values of the American . . . people."[33]

Scholars in the 1980s and '90s once again, as in the 1970s, discovered dissonance in U.S. culture and danger on the horizon.[34] The dominance of the same capitalist productive relations and values that had thrown parts of the economy into a tailspin in the 1980s created severe social tensions among workers. The system dampened dissent and disingenuously refocused attention away from economic hardships. Instead of rumbling politically, workers turned toward a past that appeared purer with each new dose of conservative hindsight, desperately searching for a wealthy messiah to restore the mythic Golden Age. Competition among a growing number of people for a dwindling number of good jobs bred the desire to eliminate marketplace rivals. Among white males, the vulnerable majority of the workforce, racist and sexist sentiments, which in better times were considered disgraceful, became safety-valves. Lacking rational alternatives to what for many was a desperate situation, scapegoats—e.g., Jews, Catholics, communists, unions, foreigners, politicians—were blamed for the plague of financial disasters among entrepreneurs and farmers. Unemployment and powerlessness gave rise to jingoism and Ramboesque military adventures to restore lost national pride. Personal failure often renewed people's faith in traditional hierarchies; the contentment gained from upholding conventional power structures seemed to more than outweigh their economic heartaches. When frustrations boiled over, the system was cleverly purged by new faces representing the same old ideas and interests.

New victims irrationally blamed old ones, nudging the political center farther to the right. Victimized as wage earners, workers aimlessly dispensed retribution, and absorbed power, wherever they could. Each dose of phony self-respect, however, quickly evaporated in the economic heat, and the nation drifted further from its egalitarian legacy. By 1993, some Democrats were even celebrating trickle-down economics, and wealthy politicians were campaigning "against the system" by working to privatize public resources. Only in America, it seems, can the rich campaign as rebels in a depressed economy by asking poor people to make them richer.

Economic misfortune did not popularize socialism, nor did the nation's crises foster change. Values lagged far behind objective economic indicators because the left, old and new, failed to articulate proletarian hopes and expectations—or even convince workers that capitalism was the problem. It didn't bear witness to the rich experiences of U.S. workers or offer a shared vision of the past and future; and it hasn't attracted the diverse working class that suffers economically and culturally. Where once liberals and now conservatives infiltrated society's conscience, the left still exists in the margins of everyday life.

The Old Left wiped out public culture with collectivist values and harsh tactics. Perceived by many workers as insensitive and authoritarian, it was summarily dismissed, along with its otherwise perceptive capitalist critique. Democrats in the SP traded insurrectionism for a utopian faith in history, and were soon irrelevant. In Harrington's own words, communists were "disastrously wrong," and the SP "vague and merely rhetorical."[35] Old Leftists who believed in something were untrustworthy; those who were trusted didn't know what they believed. No wonder that Old Left socialism went broke in the political marketplace.

New Leftism, to the extent one can generalize about such an amorphous event, believed that ideas were merely political weapons for classes struggling in history. A theory is valuable if strategically effective; otherwise, it is worthless and expendable. The Old Left's philosophy of dialectical materialism was "true" only because it expanded the power of Communist Party (CP) officials. New Leftists wanted people to rebel, and they justified efficacious words or ideas, regardless of content. Action, not reflection, mattered. The revolution could be defended later with ideas that kept workers powerful.

New Leftists in the U.S. were originally inspired by the stream of anticommunist revolts in Eastern Europe, domestic racism, the war in Vietnam, and the cynical economic exploitation of former colonies. They were interested in personal freedom and social justice, but were disillusioned with reactionary trade unions and wanted to replace workers as socialism's vanguard. Rather than emphasizing class relations or institutional change, they defended the legitimate concerns of trans-class constituencies such as women, racial and ethnic minorities, and gays, in an effort to transform everyday life. This program went over well in America, where classlessness, populism, and pluralism were part of public culture.

The New Leftists contested imperialism, racism, sexism, homophobia, and the burgeoning "culture industry." Every aspect of life became "political," even private activities. Without cohesive organizations or competent leaders, political resistance was equated with "doing your own thing," as long as that entailed assaulting the dominant culture. Thus, politics was robbed of any determinate meaning, and the movement became incoherent and undisciplined. New Left slogans like "decentralization" and "participatory democracy" evoked the youth revolt against authority, the black struggle for emancipation, and the U.S.'s legacy of direct democracy. They challenged bureaucratism and, given the movement's fragmentation, also made necessity a virtue.

Galvanizing speeches attracted people who supported "anti-establishment" activities like rent strikes, marches, demonstrations, and boycotts, not for their revolutionary value, but as means of reforming social inequities. These "radicals" were often fellow-travelers working to replace inept officials, change the law, or establish liberal rights and freedoms for political non-participants. Their goals left capitalism untouched. The exuberant movement became a marriage of convenience, with one partner unaware of its liberal bias and the other unwilling to discuss such esoteric nonsense. The basic differences separating rebels and reformists rarely surfaced.

New Leftism, moreover, never really engaged a majority of the American public until its claims regarding the futility of the Vietnam War were borne out. Democrats rejected George McGovern's candidacy, and Republicans opposed everything New Leftism represented. Middle-class professionals questioned the New Left critique of technocracy, and the bourgeoisie feared its anti-capitalism and anti-imperialism. Whites feared black power, workers rejected iconoclasm, and unions didn't care about ending racism and sexism. New Leftists thus identified primarily with the new social movements and the abused "street people" who were largely excluded from the benefits of advanced industrial society. These non-traditional interests, however, never bonded either with each other or with a broader constituency. Each had a particular "experience" of oppression that cut across class lines, hence nursing an interest-group mentality set forth in radical rhetoric. Their versions of liberation lacked any institutional referent and did not require new productive processes. Hip and relevant, New Leftists nonetheless dissolved in "identity politics" and the scripted realities of gender, sexuality, race, and ethnicity. New Leftism's undifferentiated and symbolic attack on "the system" neglected the fact that most victims were actually hard-working, "straight," even religious people who culturally had little in common with outsiders or the dispossessed.

By its original standards, then, New Leftism failed dismally because its accomplishments were ultimately integrated into the commodity structure of capitalism. Youthful activists wanted to radically change middle class values, but had no strategy for radicalizing economic and political institutions. As capitalism reformed, New Leftists were defused and the coalition disbanded. Former members drifted into corporate and professional positions or sought help elsewhere, sometimes in religions or cults. When political movements lack organization, intellectual substance, and a mass base, when they merely manipulate popular symbols in order to unite excited activists, they dissolve as quickly as they coalesce.

The U.S. intellectual left retreated into the academy where, as scholars and teachers, they were disengaged from the public.[36] They deconstructed and discarded not only communism and capitalism, but everything most people took for granted, including everyday language. From ivory-tower pulpits they preached postmodernism, while conservatives outside distorted and ridiculed their cryptic message, and then stole the nation's democratic legacy. Like feuding communist sectarians in the 1930s, left intellectuals were now perched too far above public life to be anything but targets.

CP and SP Old Leftists, in short, neglected the nuts-and-bolts of public life by reducing everything to either economics or electoral politics. This kind of unimaginative strategy might have succeeded if people had only one thing on their minds, or if public debate was restricted to one topic, but it was impotent in advanced industrial societies. The Old Left's legacy is the capitalist critique and socialist political theory that people like Harrington salvaged from the ideological wreakage. New Leftists manipulated popular sentiments to start a process of radical change they mistakenly thought would take on a life of its own. Their lack of critical knowledge, ideals, compassion, and organization made them ill-equipped for the long haul; nonetheless, they demonstrated the enormous power of an emotionally aroused public. And academic leftists revised the scholarly agenda with critiques of capitalism and of racial, patriarchical, and ethnic oppression, but didn't reach into popular experience or touch the public's imagination.

It is impossible and wrong to ignore groups that have been denied a fair share of social resources. For one thing, collectively they represent more than half the population. For another, interest groups often emotionally sustain their members to such an extent that other political organizations no longer can take their place. The experiences of those who share gender, race, sexual preference, or ethnicity not only unveil forms of exploitation that lie below the class struggle, but are also formidable bonding agents. Democrats must build alliances and work cooperatively, or they become irrelevant. History is littered with spent leftist parties that were more concerned with class purity than survival.

New Leftists understood that initial groups may be founded on categories or identities of a trans-class character like race or sex, but they largely ignored universal processes that were fettering production. Old Leftists magnified the big picture without emotionally touching a variegated working class that didn't always understand or even care about economic classes. Harrington spoke to both traditions in a voice neither heard.

From New Leftists, Harrington learned belatedly about women, minorities, young people, and professionals, whose concerns weren't always those of blue-collar workers. Their lives were conditioned as much by unique personal experiences as by income, wealth, or occupation. Harrington, however, also coveted the Old Left's critique of capitalism, its unswerving loyalty to workers, and its unionist tactics, even as he jumped a sinking materialist ship. Class struggle was central to everyday life—even for minorities and women—and subjective experiences of oppression had to be linked to the objective processes of capitalist production. He insisted on advancing the general concerns of working people with material equality, which initially informed the socialist project, even as he struggled in the 1980s to appreciate the particularity of sexual and racial oppression, and defend non-economic groups. Harrington wanted to decentralize public decision-making and empower grassroots interests, but also organize politically, in a realigned Democratic Party, in order to gain national power. The political struggle for socialism, moreover, had become an ideological one, and the path to socialist power ran directly through public culture. Socialists had to reach into America's heartland by appropriating, not opposing, its beloved heritage.

Harrington engaged popular experience and imagination with eloquence, practicality, critical scholarship, and a world-view steeped in Yankee tradition. By widening the socialist umbrella to cover new social movements as well as workers, Harrington spoke clearly to all working people across the gender, racial, and cultural divides, in a language they understood. He also befriended, educated, organized, trained, and inspired young people who went on to distinguished careers in politics, communications, academia, and labor organizing. Surely some of Harrington's ideas will gradually seep into the crevices that have fissured the post-communist left, and socialists then can finally take part in public debate on the nation's future.

Harrington did not just tell people what they wanted to hear. Pluralism and multiculturalism were empty vessels without economic justice. The formal freedom of aroused groups depended on their having jobs, money, and power. For Harrington, socialism was a universal catalyst for the particularisms of gender, race, ethnicity, and sexual preference. Free women, minorities, and gays must have an equal say in the making of significant public decisions, including those regarding investment, production, and distribution, which determine who prospers and who doesn't. Socialism, for Harrington, is a lifestyle where everyone, straight white males included, is free. It is something good and real, something that cannot be deconstructed into oblivion—it *is* democracy. Harrington's politics truly was both democratic and socialist. He supported progressive social movements because they empowered working people and democratized society. When these groups got trapped in identity politics, when they advocated replacing one elite with another, public-be-damned, they no longer were progressive.

After 1989, with the left weak and international communism dying, liberals and even socialists forecasted the death of socialism and the final triumph of capitalism. Robert Heilbroner, for example, who once announced the end of what he called "business civilization," in 1989 wrote in the *New Yorker* that "Less than seventy-five years after it officially began, the contest between capitalism and socialism is over: capitalism has won."[37] The liberal Ralf Dahrendorf boldly stated, "socialism is dead, and . . . none of its variants can be revived."[38] The principles of free-market capitalism "have gripped significant portions of the masses in the East as well as the West," Stanley Aronowitz, a socialist and sociologist, pointed out. "The emergence of these ideas conjoins with the increasingly powerful argument that freedom presupposes a relatively free market, especially for consumer goods."[39] "Few people," the economic historian Joyce Kolko concluded, "any longer even conceive of other than a capitalist future."[40] Francis Fukuyama's *The End of History and The Last Man* (1992)[41] made anti-socialism a cultural icon for the 1990s, thirty-two years after Daniel Bell had convinced the U.S. that ideology—capitalist *and* socialist—had expired.

Popularity is profitable, and scholars, even radical ones, deserve all the success they can get. But perhaps we should remember that prognosticators once heralded history's final curtain in the conformist, consumerist 1950s—then came the 1960s. The Soviet empire was considered immutable, and it suddenly collapsed. Workers in the 1930s and '40s were the backbone of F.D.R.'s New Deal; today many are Reaganites. Harrington resolutely insisted, in word and deed, that capitalism was in crisis, and he chose to play now instead of rooting from beyond left field. He hoped that if and when the time came, socialists would know what to do and how to do it, and they would be taken seriously. They also would have struggled mightily to improve conditions for everyone when others merely complained, which was worthy in itself. In the real world of U.S. capitalism, socialists in the short run will either contend for needed reforms and plug into mainstream cultural values or remain marginalized. Harrington's central message has withstood the test of time.

Indeed, the components of President Clinton's 1992 plurality coalition included the poor, minorities, Catholics, union members, women, liberal professionals, and moderate middle-income groups that Democratic presidential candidates had difficulty attracting in the 1970s and '80s. By reaching toward the middle, Clinton commanded as much loyalty from Democrats as President Bush did from Republicans, and Democrats, even after 1994, still enjoin many voters. On the campaign trail in 1992, Clinton frequently called for a new sense of community to replace the galloping individualism of the Reagan years, evoking what Harrington called the nation's lost republican heritage. Of course, Clinton was a centrist. Middle-class benefits, he implied, will trickle down to the poor, so that, like Social Security and the G. I. Bill, government programs will alleviate poverty by offering benefits to everyone. Harrington wanted Democrats to court the middle classes and directly attack poverty. Still, Clinton's successful tactics show that Harrington was correct in redefining socialism to attract the middle class, not just factory workers, and in working to reconstitute the New Deal coalition around common economic issues. And if political power is finally trickling down to a frustrated middle class-dominated electoral majority, maybe economic power will too. It is, Harrington would say, the first tiny step in a long journey.

An empowered middle class with conservative values won't alter capitalist production. Harrington also critically engaged public culture by having socialists represent popular ideals that were strangled by capitalist productive relations. Socialists must be practical *and* idealistic, walking slowly but steadily into a brighter future. Harrington's long-term strategy for economic and cultural renewal radicalized his politics. Scientists, artists, theologians, labor leaders, professors, intellectuals, philosophers, community leaders, social activists, professionals, as well as factory workers, were advised to solve their own problems. Cumulatively, these small democratic projects congeal into a socialist world view, a new cultural vision, that explains reality, resolves its major problems, and competes for voters. Unlike the hierarchical, centralized Old Left, this is a grassroots project that cultivates many separate interests and respects traditions. Its incremental successes—economic, political, social, cultural—break down barriers that have hindered human cooperation. Eventually, a mobilized working class coalesces, united under shared material interests and divided into cohesive, self-governing associations.

This slow, steady, democratic transformation is what Harrington meant by revolution. Humane values create reforms that can mend ruptured lives. The chasm between fact and value narrows, eventually disappearing altogether. As the nation approaches this horizon, a serendipitous spark—one of the small but painful crises that are now so common—could ignite a democratic firestorm. This will only occur, however, if socialism has already been planted and cultivated in the expectations of decent, patriotic workers. Eventually, Harrington hoped, they would see that socialism fulfilled the American dream, and capitalism, with its glorification of selfishness and inequality, was un-American.

NOTES

INTRODUCTION

1 See Michael Harrington, "Between Generations," *Socialist Review* 17 (May–August 1987): 152.

2 Ibid.

3 James Miller, *Democracy Is In the Streets: From Port Huron to the Seige of Chicago* (New York: Simon and Schuster, 1987), 154

4 Hayden draft, in ibid., 112. A complete copy of Hayden's "Draft Paper for S.D.S. Manifesto, for consideration in convention 11–15 June, F.D.R. Labor Center, Port Huron, Michigan" is housed in NYU's Tamiment Library.

5 Ibid.

6 Harrington, "Betweeen Generations," 153.

7 Ibid. See also Harrington, *Fragments of the Century* (New York: Simon and Schuster, 1972), 132–65; and Kirkpatrick Sale, *SDS* (New York: Random House, 1973).

8 Hayden draft, in Miller, *Democracy Is In the Streets*, 112.

9 See Harrington, "The Mystical Militants," in Irving Howe, ed., *Beyond the New Left* (New York: McCall, 1965), 33–9.

10 Hayden interviewed by the author on 27 November 1984, in Miller, *Democracy Is In the Streets*, 115. All subsequent Harrington quotations in Miller come from this interview.

11 Harrington interviewed by the author, in ibid.

12 Harrington interviewed by the author, in ibid., 111–5.

13 Hayden draft, in ibid., 112.

14 Harrington interview, in ibid., 113.

15 Ibid.

16 Horowitz interviewed by the author, in ibid., 127. Some members of SDS, including Steve Max, argued that Harrington's plan had always been for YPSL to take over SDS, because SDS was out-recruiting YPSL and was not anti-communist enough. This argument is rebutted by Barkan, "Remembering Mike," *Dissent*, 37 (Winter, 1990):105–9. Barkan had opposed Harrington at Port Huron.

17 This and previous quote are from "extensive handwritten notes taken by an SDS member," and are in Sale, 61–4.

18 Spoken by Robert Ross, in Jack Newfield, *A Prophetic Minority* (New York: New American Library, 1966), 134.

19 James Miller, 132–4.

20 Ibid., 140.

21 Newfield, 134.

22 Tom Hayden, "Writing the Port Huron Statement," in Linda Rosen Obst, ed., *The Sixties* (San Francisco: Rolling Stone Press, 1977), 71.

23 See Harrington, "Radicals, Old and New," *New Republic* 153 (3 July 1965): 29.

24 Harrington claims to have apologized to New Left leaders either "within a matter of a month or so" following the convention ["Between Generations," 153], or "within a matter of weeks" [*Taking Sides* (New York: Holt, Rinehart and Winston, 1985), 59].

25 Miller, 135.

26 Harrington, *The Long Distance Runner: An Autobiography* (New York: Henry Holt, 1988), 58.

27 Harrington, "Between Generations," 153.

28 Harrington, *The Long Distance Runner*, 57.

29 Ron Chernow, "An Irresistible Profile of Michael Harrington (You Must Be Kidding)," *Mother Jones* 2 (July 1977): 32. See also the essays written by Barkan and by Paul Berman in "Remembering Mike," 105–9.

30 Hayden to Harrington, 2 April 1981, Harrington Correspondence.

31 Miller, 325.

32 Ibid., 138.

33 Ibid., 139.

Chapter One

1 See the Harrington interview in Ron Chernow, "An Irresistible Profile of Michael Harrington (You Must Be Kidding)," *Mother Jones* 2 (July 1977): 31.

2 Harrington, *Fragments of the Century* (New York: Simon and Schuster, 1972), 64.

3 Ibid.

4 Ibid., 7.

5 Ibid., 65.

6 Harrington, *The Long Distance Runner* (New York: Henry Holt, 1988), 1.

7 Harrington, *Fragments of the Century*, 66.

8 Dan Wakefield, *New York in the Fifties* (New York: Houghton Mifflin, 1992), 130.

9 Harrington, "We Few, We Happy Few, We Bohemians," *Esquire* 78 (August 1972): 102.

10 Harrington quoted in James Miller, *Democracy is in the Streets: From Port Huron to the Siege of Chicago*, (New York: Simon and Schuster, 1987), 37. For more information on Harrington's work in the Fund for the Republic, see Charles Moritz, ed., *Current Biography Yearbook* (New York: Wilson, 1969), 197.

11 Harrington, *Fragments of the Century*, 178.

12 Ibid., 179.

13 Ibid., 94–131.

14 Chernow, "An Irresistible Portrait of Michael Harrington," 28–9.

15 Ronald W. Johnson to Harrington, 4 December 1971, Michael Harrington Correspondence, Democratic Socialists of America Collection, Tamiment Library, New York University.

16 Harrington to Irving Howe, ca. August 1971, Harrington Correspondence.

17 Ibid.

18 See David Spitz to Irwin Suall, 25 April 1972, Harrington Correspondence. Seymour Martin Lipset, "Neo-Conservatism: Myth and Reality," *Society* 25 (July–August, 1988), 29–37, argues that the SDUSA was discredited and misinterpreted by Harrington in order to curry favor with militant New Left students. Lipset also argues that SDUSA was *not* conservative, and remained supportive of New Deal reforms.

19 Harrington, "Forsaking Debs for Nixon: A Call to American Socialists," *Nation* 215 (13 November 1972): 454–5. See Harrington, *Taking Sides* (New York: Holt, Rinehart and Winston, 1985) 106–15, for five of Harrington's articles outlining his revised views on Vietnam. See also "Socialism and Reactionary Anti-Communism," ca. 1973, Harrington Correspondence.

20 Harrington, "Forsaking Debs for Nixon," 455.

21 Ibid.

22 Harrington to SP members, 29 June 1972, Harrington Correspondence.

23 On this, see especially Harrington, "Marxism in America," *New Catholic World* (May–June 1977): 118–21.

24 Harrington to C. Edwin Murphy, 5 September 1974, Harrington Correspondence.
25 Minutes of Democratic Agenda: National Board Discussion, New York, 25 June 1977, Harrington Correspondence.
26 Harrington to William Shanon, 19 June 1974, Harrington Correspondence.
27 Harrington, "The Other American: Michael Harrington," interview by Bill McKibben, *Mother Jones* 13 (July–August 1988): 58.
28 Harrington to Rev. Msgr. George G. Higgins, 4 December 1974, Harrington Correspondence.
29 Harrington, "Toward a Socialist Presence in America," ca. July 1973, Harrington Correspondence.
30 See Chernow, "An Irresistible Portrait of Michael Harrington," 34.
31 Harrington, *The Long Distance Runner*, 65.
32 Ibid., 66. See also Harrington, "Between Generations," *Socialist Review* 17 (May–August 1987): 158.
33 The Second International (1889–1914) was a loose federation of mostly European socialist parties and trade unions that held its congresses every two to four years to debate socialist policy and decide on common actions. When some of its leading parties ignored International policy and voted to support their governments' participation in the First World War, the Second International collapsed. Several attempts in the 1910s to revive it failed, but in 1921 activist socialists from ten parties met in Vienna to constitute the International Working Union of Socialist Parties—the "Vienna Union"—which was nicknamed the "Second-and-a-Half International." In 1923, at a congress in Hamburg, it united with a revived Second International to form the Labour and Socialist International, which died in 1940. It was succeeded in 1951 by the present Socialist International, which represents the aspirations of democratic socialist parties from around the globe. U.S. socialist representatives include Harrington's DSA, the SDUSA, and the Jewish Bund. Aside from articulating the principles of democratic socialism, and organizing meetings, it has supported third world sister parties and helped mediate political disputes in Latin America, the Middle East, and Africa.
34 Harrington and Irving Howe to Shlomo Avineri, 2 November 1976, Harrington Correspondence.
35 Article 12 of the Declaration of Principles of the Socialist International, (London: Socialist International, 1989), p.6.
36 Harry Fleischman, conversation with the author, 26 May 1993.
37 Harrington, *The Long Distance Runner*, 118.
38 Wakefield, *New York in the Fifties*, 320.
39 Harrington, *The Long Distance Runner*, 119.
40 Harrington, *Taking Sides*, 3.
41 Tamar Jacoby, "A Life At the Barricades," *Newsweek* 112 (8 August 1988): 30.
42 Harrington, "The Other American," 56.
43 Harry Fleischman, conversation with the author, 26 May 1993.

44 Harrington, *The Long Distance Runner*, 2.

45 Chernow, "An Irresistible Portrait of Michael Harrington," 31.

46 Harrington, *Taking Sides*, 9.

47 In Harrington, "The Other American," 59.

48 Harrington, *The Long Distance Runner*, 4.

49 Harrington to Leonard Leif, 15 May 1974, Harrington Correspondence.

50 Harrington to Susan Schaeffer, 5 November 1974, Harrington Correspondence.

51 Harrington to Sargent Shriver, 8 September 1982, Harrington Correspondence.

52 James R. Gorman, "Conversation with an Atheist," *Christian Century* 95 (21–28 June 1978): 641. See also Peter Steinfels, James Finn and Patrick Lacefield "A Man Who Made a Difference," *Commonweal* 116 (8 September 1989): 466; Harrington, "The Other American," 59; Chernow, "An Irresistible Portrait of Michael Harrington, 59; and Harrington, *The Long Distance Runner*, 4.

53 See Arthur F. McGovern, *Marxism: An American Christian Perspective* (Maryknoll, NY: Orbis, 1980), 93–105; and Marc Karson, "Catholic Anti-Socialism," in John H.M.Laslett and Seymour Martin Lipset, eds., *Failure of A Dream?* rev. ed. (Berkeley: University of California Press, 1984), 82–102.

54 The legacy of Catholic union leaders includes Peter McGuire, president of the Carpenters' Union and an AFL founder; James O'Connell, a machinist and an AFL founder; folk hero James Larkin; John Fitzpatrick, Chicago packing house and steel union leader; George McNeill and J.P. McDonnell, socialists in the International Labor Union; Terrance Powderly of the Knights of Labor; Phillip Murray and James Carey in the CIO; and Miners' president John McBride.

55 On the CW see: Patrick G. Coy, ed., *A Revolution of the Heart: Essays on the "Catholic Worker"* (Philadelphia: Temple University Press, 1988); Anne Klejment and Alice Klejment, *Dorothy Day and the "Catholic Worker": A Bibliography and Index* (New York: Garland, 1986); William Miller, *A Harsh and Dreadful Love: Dorothy Day and the Catholic Worker Movement* (New York: Liveright, 1973); Mel Piehl, *Breaking Bread: The "Catholic Worker" and the Origin of Catholic Radicalism in America* (Philadelphia: Temple University Press, 1982); and Nancy L. Roberts, *Dorothy Day and the "Catholic Worker"* (Albany: SUNY Press, 1984).

56 Harrington, by telephone reading to ITT, 1980, Harrington Correspondence.

57 The previous quotes are in Harrington, "Religion and Revolution," *Commonweal* 91 (14 November 1969): 203.

58 See Patti Peterson, "The Young Socialist Movement in America from 1905–1940: A Study of the Young Peoples Socialist League," (Ph.D. diss., University of Wisconsin, 1974).

59 On the turbulent history of LID during the 1930s, see Robert Cohen, "Revolt of the Depression Generation: America's First Mass Student Protest Movement, 1929–1940," (Ph.D. diss., University of California at Berkeley, 1987); and Hal Draper, "The Student Movement of the Thirties: A Political

History," in Rita Simon, ed., *As We Saw The Thirties* (Urbana: University of Illinois Press, 1969).

60 See, for example, Harrington's appreciation of Debs and Thomas in Chernow, "An Irresistible Profile of Michael Harrington," 31.

61 Ex-Trotskyists who abandoned Leftism include Saul Bellow, Irving Kristol, Sidney Hook, Harold Lasky, Seymour Martin Lipset, Daniel Bell, William Barrett, Norman Podhoretz, Lionel Abel, and Melvin Lasky. To one degree or another, all were once associated with the "Committee for the Free World," led by Midge Dector and her husband, Norman Podhoretz. Other ex-Trotskyists became liberals. These include Hannah Arendt, Max Eastman, James T. Farrell, Clement Greenberg, Mary McCarthy, Dwight Macdonald, Delmore Schwartz, Diana and Lionel Trilling, Edmund Wilson, Alfred Kazan, Leslie Fiedler, Albert Halper, William Phillips, Harry Roskolenko, and Bernard Wolfe. Not all Trotskyists turned to the right. Those who remained socialists include C.L.R. James, Raya Dunayevskaya, Carl Boggs, Martin Glaberman, and George Novack. See James Burnham and Max Shachtman, "Intellectuals In Retreat," *New International* 5 (January 1939): 4–22. The authors critically describe this anti-Stalinist dynamic, which would eventually envelope them as well.

62 In Constance Ashton Myers, *The Prophet's Army* (Westport, CT: Greenwood, 1957), 14. See also Max Shachtman, "Footnote For Historians," *New International* 4 (December, 1938): 377.

63 Harrington, *Fragments of the Century*, 75. See also Harrington, "What's Left," *New Republic* 159 (21 September 1968): 36.

64 Harrington, "The New Radicalism," *Commonweal* 72 (3 September 1965): 624.

65 See Alan Wald, *The New York Intellectuals: The Rise and Decline of the Anti-Stalinist Left from the 1930s to the 1980s* (Chapel Hill: University of North Carolina Press, 1987), 332. See also 311–34.

66 Howe to Harrington, 17 December 1972, Harrington Correspondence.

67 Howe to Harrington, 29 April 1973, Harrington Correspondence. For a more sympathetic view, see Howe, *A Margin of Hope* (New York: Harcourt, Brace, Jovanovich, 1982).

68 Memorandum from Women's Caucus of DSOC, 14 November 1973, Harrington Correspondence.

69 Arnold Kaufman was a progressive Michigan philosopher who attended the Port Huron Conference and coined the phrase "participatory democracy." On radical liberalism, see Kaufman, *The Radical Liberal* (New York: Atherton, 1968); "A Sketch of a Liberal Theory of Fundamental Human Rights," *Monist* 52 (October 1968): 595–615; "Wants, Needs, and Liberalism," *Inquiry* 14 (Autumn 1971): 210–12; "A Philosophy for the American Left," *Socialist Commentary* (November 1963), 13; "A Strategy for Radical Liberals," *Dissent* 18 (August 1971): 34–52. A complete bibliography is in *Social Theory and Practice* 2 (Spring 1972): 153–9. The best secondary source is Richard Rodewald and Richard Wasserstrom, "The

Political Philosophy of Arnold Kaufman," *Social Theory and Practice* 2 (Spring 1972): 5–32. Howe's contributions to the theory of radical liberalism, which he called "democratic radicalism," include *Steady Work: Essays in the Politics of Democratic Radicalism, 1953–1966* (New York: Harcourt, Brace, and World, 1966) and *The Radical Imagination* (New York: New American Library, 1967).

70 See T. B. Bottomore, "The Social Movements," *Critics of Society; Radical Thought in North America* (New York: Pantheon, 1968), 82–105; Irving Louis Horowitz, *C.Wright Mills: An American Utopian* (New York: Free Press, 1983); and Paul Buhle, *Marxism in the USA* (London: Verso, 1989), 214.

71 Actually, with Paul Jacobs, Harrington had already edited *Labor In a Free Society* (Berkeley: University of California Press, 1959). *Retail Clerks* (New York: Wiley, 1962) was the first book Harrington wrote.

72 Harrington to Ron Veselak, 14 April 1980, Harrington Correspondence.

73 Harrington to Howe, ca. August 1971, Harrington Correspondence.

74 Harrington, *Fragments of the Century*, 182.

75 Ibid., 183.

76 Chernow, "An Irresistible Portrait of Michael Harrington," 34.

77 Harrington to W. H. Ferry, 10 May 1979, Harrington Correspondence.

78 Harrington, *The Long Distance Runner*, 133.

79 Ibid., 141.

80 In Harrington, "The Other American," 58. See also Harrington, *The Long Distance Runner*, 142.

CHAPTER TWO

1 Harry Fleischman, conversation with author, 26 May 1993.

2 Paul Buhle, *Marxism in the USA* (London: Verso, 1989), 251. See also Harvey J. Kaye, *The Powers of the Past* (Minneapolis: University of Minnesota Press, 1991), 26–8.

3 Harrington, *Socialism* (New York: Saturday Review Press, 1970), 5–6. See also ibid., 155 ff.; *Accidental Century* (New York: Macmillan, 1965), 114; and *The Twilight of Capitalism* (New York: Simon and Schuster, 1976), 33–4.

4 Harrington quoted in Marion Long, "Paradise Tossed: Visions of Utopia," *Omni* 10 (April, 1988): 103. This is an interview with Harrington concerning his views on utopia.

5 From a Marxian tract entitled "False Brothers," quoted in Harrington, *Socialism*, p.7. Harrington offers a short history of nineteenth-century anti-socialist socialism in ibid., 65–70.

6 Harrington, *Socialism*, 37.

7 Harrington and Deborah Meir, *Theory, Life and Politics* (New York: Institute for Democratic Socialism, 1977), 6.

8 Harrington, *Socialism*, 63. See also Harrington, "Old Working Class, New Working Class," *Dissent* 19 (January, 1972): 153.

9 Harrington, *Twilight of Capitalism*, 36.

10 Harrington, *Socialism*, 48.

11 See ibid., 50 ff.

12 Sidney Hook, *Towards The Understanding of Karl Marx* (New York: John Day, 1933), 300.

13 Harrington, *Socialism*, 52.

14 E.g., "A social formation never goes under before all the productive powers are developed which it can possibly contain; new higher production relationships never appear in place before all the material conditions of their existence have matured in the womb of the old order." Harrington believed that Marx knew this statement contradicted facts Marx himself cited elsewhere showing that there was no unilinear progress in history. See Harrington, *Twilight of Capitalism*, 39–40.

15 Ibid., 39.

16 Harrington, *Socialism*, 87, quoting Marx, *A Contribution to the Critique of Political Economy*.

17 Harrington, *Twilight of Capitalism*, 46.

18 Ibid., 42.

19 See ibid., 45.

20 Ibid., 13.

21 The Hegelians included Labriola, Lukacs, Korsch, Gramsci, Luxemburg, Pannekoek, Gorter, Jaures, and, more recently, Marcuse and the mid-career Kolakowski; and the phenomenologists included Enzo Paci, the Vietnamese Tran Duc Thao, Sartre, Merleau-Ponty, Karel Kosik, and others.

22 Arthur Schlesinger, ed., *Writings and Speeches of Eugene V. Debs* (New York: Heritage, 1948), 111.

23 Debs, "Unionism and Socialism," in Eugene V. Debs, *Debs: His Life, Writings, and Speeches* (Chicago: Kerr, 1908), 138.

24 Ibid., 136.

25 David A. Shannon, *The Socialist Party of America* (New York: Macmillan, 1955), 12.

26 Louis Boudin, *The Theoretical System of Karl Marx in the Light of Recent Criticism* (Chicago: Kerr, 1912), 180.

27 Louis Fraina, *Revolutionary Socialism: A Study in Socialist Reconstruction* (New York: Communist Press, 1918), 76. See also Fraina, "Problems of American Socialism," *The Class Struggle* 2 (February 1919), 46–7.

28 See Fraina, "The Future of Socialism," *New Review* 3 (January 1915): 7–20; and "Socialism and Psychology," *New Review* 3 (May 1915): 12.

29 In this spirit, Fraina joined the staff of *Modern Dance* magazine to explain how bourgeois repression was being contested by joyous men and women moving freely in America's dance halls. Fraina's editorials are reprinted in "The Modern Dance," *Cultural Correspondence* 6–7 (Spring 1978), pp 22–45.

30 See Louis Boudin, "Exit the Socialist Party," n.d., Louis Boudin Papers, Columbia University.

31 Fraina, *Revolutionary Socialism*, 210.

32 See Lewis Corey [Fraina], *The Unfinished Task: Economic Reconstruction for Democracy* (New York: Viking, 1942), especially 5–6, 127–36, 205 ff.

33 Hook, 6. See also 7–32.

34 Ibid., 114. See also Hook, "The Meaning of Marxism," *The Modern Quarterly* 4 (1930): 430–5; and *From Hegel to Marx: Studies in the Intellectual Development of Karl Marx* (New York: Reynal and Hitchcock, 1936), 33.

35 See Hook, "The Scope of Marxian Theory," *American Socialist Monthly* 7 (1936): 30. The passage to pragmatism is traced in Hook's later works: *The Hero In History* (New York: John Day, 1943), *Marx and the Marxists* (New York: Van Nostrand, 1955), and *Reason, Social Myths and Democracy* (New York: John Day, 1940).

36 Harrington, *The Politics at God's Funeral: The Spiritual Crisis of Western Civilization* (New York: Holt, Rinehart and Winston, 1983), 9.

37 Harrington, *Twilight of Capitalism*, 21. See also 15 ff.

38 Ibid., 60, quoting from Marx, *Grundrisse*. See also *Twilight*, 22–7.

39 See ibid., 149 ff.

40 Harrington, *Socialism*, 108.

41 Harrington, *Twilight of Capitalism*, 60. The lighting metaphor is taken from Marx's 1857 "Introduction" to *The Critique of Political Economy*. See also Harrington, "Marxism in America," *New Catholic World* 220 (May-June 1977): 118–21.

42 Harrington was not a structuralist, even though he admired Althusser's formulation of the dialectic, and especially of the role of economic relationships therein. Althusser argued that economics is "determinant in the last instance," although it may not be "dominant" in a given social formation. Harrington, however, felt that Althusser overemphasized the role played by the capitalist system, and ignored facts and human praxis. Althusser also believed in two Marx's: one young and idealistic, the other old and scientific. Harrington, we have seen, rejected this dichotomy.

43 Harrington, *Twilight of Capitalism*, 75.

44 Ibid., 103.

45 For example, it magnified Marx's and Engels' careless assertion in *The German Ideology* that "the basis of all history" can be explained by analyzing the "actual production process, and the forms of exchange which are part of this mode of production and produced it." If this is taken at face value, then Marx and Engels had tried to explain all of human history on the basis of a social reality unique to capitalism. Marx, in Harrington's view, later—in *Capital*—clarified that his propositions are only the most general abstractions, and that capitalism, a system that is qualitatively different from all previous systems, is the focus of his attention. See *Twilight of Capitalism*, 87.

46 Ibid., 73.

47 Ibid., 80.

48 Harrington, *Socialism*, 82.

49 Ibid., 83.

50 Harrington, "Comment," in John H. M. Laslett and Seymour Martin Lipset, eds., *Failure of A Dream?*, rev. ed. (Berkeley, CA: University of California Press, 1984), 525.

51 Harrington also rejected G. A. Cohen's technological determinism for ignoring the internal, dialectical link between technological growth and worker exploitation. Neither "caused" the other, and a qualitative growth in technology doesn't automatically cause a similar growth in exploitation. If technological growth alone caused socialism, why did capitalism begin long before the industrial revolution began? And why aren't developed economies now socialist? For Harrington, human relationships, not machines, are decisive. See especially Harrington, *Twilight of Capitalism*, 94–9; and *Socialism*, 9.

52 Ibid., 355.

53 Harrington, *Twilight of Capitalism*, 30. Marx's statement is in the "Introduction" to *The Critique of Hegel's Philosophy of Right*.

54 See Harrington and Meir, *Theory, Life, and Politics*, 9.

55 Harrington, *Twilight of Capitalism*, 192.

56 Ibid., 194.

57 Ibid., 195. Harrington criticized Erich Fromm for duplicating orthodoxy's reductionism by tipping this delicate dialectical balance in an idealist direction.

58 Ibid., 196.

59 Ibid., 200.

CHAPTER THREE

1 *The New American Poverty* (New York: Holt, Rinehart and Winston, 1984) was intended to update and enrich the analysis of poverty in *The Other America: Poverty in the United States* (New York: Macmillan, 1962).

2 In 1959, Harrington and Paul Jacobs edited *Labor in a Free Society* (Berkeley: University of California Press, 1959), an anthology of commentaries on the state of the union movement in America. His first authored book was *The Retail Clerks* (New York:Wiley, 1962), which traced the history of American retail workers and their unions. Neither noticeably impacted U.S. culture.

3 See, for example, "Marxist Literary Critics," *Commonweal* 71 (11 December, 1959): 324–6; and "Labor in the Doldrums," *Commonweal* 71 (11 March 1960), 643–6.

4 Harrington, *Taking Sides: The Education of A Militant Mind* (New York: Holt, Rinehart and Winston, 1985), 80.

5 Harrington, *The New American Poverty*, 8.

6 Harrington, *Taking Sides*, 80–1. The title actually came from a long 1960 piece in *Commentary*, also called "The Other America," in which Harrington referred to "The good America, the decent America, that survives even in the age of mass culture."

7 Harrington, "The Other American: Michael Harrington," interview by Bill McKibben, *Mother Jones* 13 (July-August, 1988): 58.

8 In Ron Chernow, "An Irresistible Profile of Michael Harrington (You Must Be Kidding)," *Mother Jones* 2 (July 1977): 30.

9 Harrington, "The Other American," 58.

10 Ibid.

11 The term is from Peter Townsend, *Poverty in the United Kingdom* (Berkeley: University of California Press, 1979). Harrington's definition of poverty is directly derived from Townsend, and indirectly from T.H.Green's distinction between positive and negative freedom. Harrington argues that poverty is, in effect, a denial of positive freedom.

12 Harrington, *The Other America*, 179.

13 Ibid., 162.

14 Ibid., 9.

15 The details of this procedure are in Harrington, "Hiding The Other America," *New Republic* 176 (26 Feb. 1977): 15–7.

16 See especially Harrington, "The Politics of Poverty," in Irving Howe, ed., *The Radical Papers* (Garden City, NY: Doubleday, 1966), 122–43; and Harrington, *Toward a Democratic Left: A Radical Program for a New Majority* (New York: Macmillan, 1968), esp. 56 ff.

17 Harrington, *The New American Poverty*, 1.

18 Ibid., 8.

19 These figures, and those to follow, are from Harrington and Mark Levinson, "The Perils of a Dual Economy," *Dissent* 32 (Fall 1985): 417–26. Harrington's data echoes those compiled by people like Barry Bluestone and Robert Kuttner.

20 See Harrington, "Willful Shortsightedness on Poverty," *Dissent* 33 (Winter 1986), 19.

21 Harrington, *The New American Poverty*, 40–1.

22 Ibid., 140.

23 Ibid., 193–5.

24 Ibid., 196–204.

25 Ibid., 206.

26 See ibid., 206–16.

27 These included Shaker villages, Zoar and Amana settlements, Owenite communities, Fourieristic phalanxes, and several unattached efforts such as Adin Ballou's Hopedale, Bronson Alcott's Fruitlands, Etienne Cabet's Icaria, and John Humphrey Noyes's Oneida. See Morris Hillquit, *History of Socialism in the United States*, rev. ed. (New York: Funk and Wagnalls, 1910), 21–134; David Harris,

Socialist Origins in the United States (Assen, Netherlands: Van Gorcum, 1966), 1–7; Albert Fried, ed., *Socialism in America* (New York: Doubleday, 1970), 6–10; and Philip Foner, *American Socialism and Black Americans* (Westport, CT: Greenwood, 1977), 3–4.

28 See Charles Sotheran, *Horace Greeley and Other Pioneers of American Socialism* (New York: Humboldt, 1892); H. S. Foxwell, introduction to *The Right to the Whole Produce of Labor* by Anton Menger (London: Macmillan, 1899); A.M.Simons, *Social Forces in American History* (New York: Macmillan, 1911); and Harold Laski, *The American Democracy* (New York: Viking, 1948).

29 See Paul Buhle, *Marxism in the USA* (London: Verso, 1989), 29–31; Howard H. Quint, *The Forging of American Socialism* (Columbia.: University of South Carolina Press, 1953), 6–12; Theodore Draper, *The Roots of American Communism* (New York: Viking, 1957), 11–4; Harris, 8–13; and John Diggins, *The Left in the Twentieth Century* (New York: Harcourt, Brace, Jovanovich, 1973), 54 ff.

30 See Patrick Renshaw, *The Wobblies* (New York: Doubleday, 1967), esp. 53. See also L. Glenn Seretan, *Daniel DeLeon: The Odyssey of An American Marxist* (Cambridge, MA: Harvard University Press, 1979); Diggins, 66; and Harvey Klehr, "Daniel DeLeon" in *Biographical Dictionary of Marxism*, ed. Robert A. Gorman (Westport, CT: Greenwood, 1986), 90–2.

31 See Staughton Lynd, *Intellectual Origins of American Radicalism* (New York: Pantheon, 1968) and Norman Pollack, *The Populist Response to Industrialist America* (Cambridge, MA: Harvard University Press, 1962).

32 In 1904, the first national platform of the SP stated that socialism should not be "a theory imposed upon society for its acceptance or rejection." Instead, it is "the interpretation of what is, sooner or later, inevitable. Capitalism is already struggling to its destruction." Proceedings, National Convention of the Socialist Party, Chicago, Illinois, 1–6 May 1904, 308.

33 See James Weinstein, *The Decline of Socialism in America* (New York: Vintage, 1967), 22; Daniel Bell, *The Cultural Contradictions of Capitalism* (New York: Basic Books, 1976), 99; Draper, 41; Diggins, 60; and David A. Shannon, *The Socialist Party of America* (New York: Macmillan, 1955), 5.

34 Harvey Klehr, *The Heyday of American Communism* (New York: Basic Books, 1984), 4.

35 Harrington, "The Virtues and Limitations of Liberal Democracy," *Center Magazine* 14 (March–April, 1981): 51.

36 Ibid., 53.

37 Harrington, *Socialism: Past and Future* (New York: Arcade, 1989), 14.

38 Harrington, *The Accidental Century* (New York: Macmillan, 1965), 22.

39 Ibid., 29–35.

40 Ibid., 17.

41 Ibid., 92.

42 See ibid., 115–43, 229–38.

43 Ibid., 146. See 146–75, 341.

44 Ibid., 174.

45 Ibid., 229.

46 Emphasizing maladroit institutions and personalities, unfavorable economic conditions, politics, and the cultural hegemony of liberalism.

47 Harrington, *Socialism* (New York: Saturday Review Press, 1970), 122–7. See also "A Socialist's Centennial," *New Republic* 192 (7 January 1985): 16–8. See also Weinstein, viii, and Phillip Foner, "Socialism and American Trade Unionism," in *Failure of a Dream?*, rev. ed., eds. John H.M. Laslett and Seymour Martin Lipset (Berkeley: University of California Press, 1984), 156.

48 See Harrington, *Socialism*, 109–10 and 130–1; "Marxism in America," *New Catholic World* 220 (May–June 1977): 118–21; and *Taking Sides*, 18, 166.

49 Werner Sombart, *Why Is There No Socialism in the US?* (1906; reprint, White Plains, NY: International Aptitudes and Sciences Press, 1976); Selig Perlman, *A Theory of The Labor Movement* (New York: A.M. Kelley, 1928). See also Eric Foner, "Why Is There No Socialism in the United States?" *History Workshop Journal* 17 (Spring 1984); Sean Wilentz, "Against Exceptionalism: Class Consciousness and the American Labor Movement, 1790–1920," with critiques by Nick Salvatore and Michael Hanagan, and a reply by Wilentz, *International Labor and Working Class History* 26–7 (1984–5); Walter Galenson, "The American Labor Movement Is Not Socialist," *American Review* 1 (Winter 1961); Marc Karson, *American Labor Unions and Politics, 1900–1918* (Boston: Beacon Press, 1965), 286; Lipset, *Continental Divide* (New York: Routledge, 1990), xiv, 8, 10; and Irving Howe, *Socialism and America* (San Diego, CA: Harcourt, Brace, Jovanovich, 1985).

50 See Harrington, *Socialism*, 5. See also Harrington, "Toward Legalizing Revolution," *Current* 122 (October 1970): 28–31.

51 Kriege contended that poverty could be eliminated by giving every worker a plot of land. See Harrington, *Socialism*, 111–8.

52 Harrington, *Toward a Democratic Left*, 278.

53 Ibid., 280. For the roots of this idea, see Harrington, "The Other America," *Commonweal* 62 (27 May 1960): 224.

54 Sombart, 112.

55 Ibid., 20.

56 Patricia Cayo Sexton, *The War on Labor and the Left* (Boulder, CO: Westview, 1991), 36.

57 Harrington, *Socialism*, 119. See 118–9, where Harrington describes the bloody strikes and working-class political movements preceding World War II.

58 K. Edwards, *Strikes in the U.S., 1881–1974* (New York: St. Martin's, 1981), 235.

59 Ibid., 250–1. See also 252–69.

60 Harrington, "Voting the Lesser Evil," in *Taking Sides*, 143. First published in *Commentary* 45 (April 1968): 22.

61 Harrington, "Say What You Mean— Socialism," in *Taking Sides*, 167. First published in *Nation* 218 (25 May 1974), 648–51.

62 Harrington, "The Virtues and Limitations of Liberal Democracy," 50.

63 See Harrington, *Toward a Democratic Left*, 298; "Between Generations," *Socialist Review* 17 (May–August 1987): 157; and "Getting Restless Again," *New Republic* 181 (1 September 1979): 15.

64 Harrington, "The New Radicalism," *Commonweal* 82 (3 September 1965): 627.

65 Harrington, "Youth and the Labor Movement," (address to meeting of AFL-CIO, University of Illinois, Urbana, 4 December 1971), 5, DSA Collection, Michael Harrington Correspondence, Tamiment Library, New York University.

66 Harrington, *Fragments of the Century* (New York: Simon and Schuster, 1972), 63.

CHAPTER FOUR

1 Paul Buhle, *Marxism in the U.S.A.* (London: Verso, 1987), 249.

2 Harrington first used the term "socialist capitalism" in *Socialism* (New York: Saturday Review Press, 1970). Thereafter, he used this term and "post-industrialism" interchangeably.

3 See Harrington, *The Twilight of Capitalism* (New York: Simon and Schuster, 1976), 210–20.

4 Both statements, taken from the *Manifesto*, are quoted in ibid., 208. See also Harrington, "'Post-Industrial Society' and the Welfare State," *Dissent* 23 (Summer 1976): 244–52.

5 Quoted in Harrington, *Toward A Democratic Left: A Radical Program for a New Majority* (New York: Macmillan, 1968), 30. See also 30–50 and "The Politics of Poverty," in *The Radical Papers*, ed. Irving Howe (Garden City, NY: Doubleday, 1966), 130–9.

6 Harrington, *Decade of Decision* (New York: Simon and Schuster, 1980), 28.

7 Ibid., See also *Socialism*, 199–204.

8 See Samuel Bowles and Herbert Gintis, *Democracy and Capitalism* (New York: Basic Books, 1986), 57–8.

9 Barbara Ehrenreich, *Fear of Falling* (New York: Pantheon, 1989), 121–2. See also Mike Davis, *Prisoners of the American Dream* (London: Verso, 1986), 126–7 ff.

10 See Patricia Cayo Sexton, *The War on Labor and the Left* (Boulder, CO: Westview, 1991).

11 Harvey J. Kaye, *The Powers of the Past* (Minneapolis: University of Minnesota Press, 1991), 59. President Carter's comments are in ibid.

12 Anthony King, "Overload: Problems of Governing in the 1970s," *Political Studies* 23 (Summer 1975): 284–96; Jürgen Habermas, *Legitimation Crisis* (Boston: Beacon, 1975); Alan Wolfe, *The Limits of Legitimacy* (New York: Free Press, 1977); Daniel Bell, *The Cultural Contradictions of Capitalism* (New York: Basic Books,

1976); Samuel Brittan, "The Economic Contradictions of Democracy," *British Journal of Political Science* 5 (Fall 1975): 129–59; Robert Nisbet, *The Twilight of Authority* (New York: Oxford, 1975); and Michael Crozier, Samuel Huntington, and Joji Watanuki, *The Crisis of Democracy* (New York: New York University Press, for the Trilateral Commission 1975).

13 Harrington, *Twilight of Capitalism*, 224 ff. See also *Toward A Democratic Left*, 106–10.

14 The following figures are from Harrington, *Twilight of Capitalism*, 267– 92; *The New American Poverty* (New York: Holt, Rinehart and Winston, 1984), 89–93; "The Big Lie About the Sixties," *New Republic* 173 (29 November 1975): 15–9; and Alfred L. Malabre, Jr, "Economic Roadblock: Infrastructure Neglect,"*Wall Street Journal*, 30 July 1990, A1, which compares social spending in the U.S. to other industrialized nations from 1970 to 1990.

15 Harrington, "The Big Lie About the Sixties," 18.

16 Harrington, *Twilight of Capitalism*, 306.

17 On the differences between social democracy and democratic socialism see the first chapter of *Socialism*; "Why We Need Socialism in America," *Dissent* 17 (May 1970): 316–20; and "Soaking the Poor," *Commonweal* 97 (20 October 1972): 57.

18 See Harrington, "The Politics of Poverty," 139; and *Toward A Democratic Left*, 30.

19 Harrington, "The Virtues and Limitations of Liberal Democracy," *Center* 14, no. 2 (March–April 1981): 53.

20 Ibid., 54.

21 Marx, *Selected Correspondence* (Moscow: International, n.d.), 125.

22 See Marx, *Capital* (Moscow: International, 1975) 1: 278–9.

23 See Marx, *On Revolution*, ed. Saul K. Padover (New York: McGraw-Hill, 1971), 34, 116–7, 235, 343, 350; *The Poverty of Philosophy* (New York: International, 1963), 172; and Marx and Engels, *The Civil War in the U.S.* (New York: International, 1961), 139–40.

24 Marx, *Capital*, 1: 326.

25 See Morris Hillquit, *Socialism in Theory and Practice* (New York: Macmillan, 1919), 1–9; *Socialism Summed Up* (New York: Fly, 1912), 34; Hillquit and John Ryan, *Socialism: Promise or Menace?* (New York: Macmillan, 1917), 88–102, 133. John Spargo, *Applied Socialism* (New York: Huebsch, 1912), 18; *Karl Marx: His Life and Work* (New York: Huebsch, 1910), 325–6; *Sidelights on Contemporary Socialism* (New York: Huebsch, 1911), 52. Victor Berger, "Real Social Democracy," in *Berger's Broadsides* (Milwaukee: Social Democratic Publishers, 1912), 3.

26 Spargo, *Applied Socialism*, 337.

27 Berger quoted in Joseph R. Conlin, *Big Bill Haywood and the Radical Union Movement* (Syracuse: Syracuse University Press, 1969), 35.

28 Harrington, "Private Profit and the Public Good," ca. 1980, p.3, Michael Harrington Correspondence, DSA Collection, Tamiment Library, New York University.

29 Harrington, *Twilight of Capitalism*, 307.

30 Ibid., 310.

31 Harrington, "Why We Need Socialism in America," 265.

32 Internal, intraclass disputes among capitalists pit large capitalists against small; MNC's against national corporations; old money against parvenus; and smart capitalists against stupid ones.

33 Harrington, *Twilight of Capitalism*, 206–7.

34 Harrington criticized Domhoff's popular instrumentalist view of the state for crudely ignoring the subtleties of capitalist politics. See *Twilight of Capitalism*, 313–9.

35 Harrington, *Toward A Democratic Left*, 14.

36 Harrington, *Socialism*, 344.

37 Harrington, *Decade of Decision*, 320–1. See also "Our Proposals for the Crisis," *Dissent* 22 (Spring, 1975): 102.

38 See David Vogel, *Fluctuating Fortunes* (New York: Basic Books, 1989), 145; and Leonard Silk and David Vogel, *Ethics and Profits* (New York: Simon and Schuster, 1976), 57–8.

39 Bennett Harrison and Barry Bluestone, *The Great U-Turn* (New York: Basic Books, 1988), 51.

40 Vogel, 193–213; and Kim McQuaid, *Big Business and Presidential Power* (New York: Morrow, 1982), 284–306.

41 See Peter Steinfels, *The Neoconservatives* (New York: Simon and Schuster, 1979), and S. Blumenthal, *The Rise of the Counter Establishment* (New York: Times Books, 1986), esp. 122–65.

42 See especially Harrington, *Toward A Democratic Left*, 101–5, 125–7, 142–50; *Socialism*, 303-6; *Decade of Decision*, 171–5, 204–20, 247–53, 280–3; *The Accidental Century* (New York: Macmillan, 1965), 280–3; *The New American Poverty*, 238–51; "A Path for America: Proposals from the Democratic Left," *Dissent* 29 (Fall 1982): 417–9; "Welfare Capitalism in Crisis," *Nation* 219 (28 December 1974), 691–3; "Our Proposals for the Crisis," 101. Harrington's housing proposals, which stressed innovative strategies of public investment in housing, are in Harrington, Richard Appelbaum, and Peter Drier, "A Faded Dream: Housing in America," *Dissent* 31 (Winter 1978): 21–4.

43 Harrington, *Decade of Decision*, 211. See also "Social Retreat and Economic Stagnation," *Dissent* 26 (Spring 1979): 132.

44 Harrington, *The New American Poverty*, 237.

45 Ibid., 240.

46 See Richard Freeman, "On the Divergence of Unionism Among Developed Countries," Working Paper 2817 (New York: National Bureau of Economic Research, January 1989), x.

47 See Harrington, "A Path for America," 423; "What Is Socialism," *Current* 207 (November 1978): 21–4; and "The Virtues and Limitations of Liberal Democracy," 50–3.

48 Harrington called this "collective profit sharing." See "Social Retreat and Economic Stagnation," 134.

49 Harrington called this the President's "Report on the Future." See *Toward A Democratic Left*, 110–8. In *The Other America*, xxvi, Harrington called for an "Office of the Future" attached to the Presidency, and a Joint Congressional Committee on the Future to receive, debate, and modify or adopt the White House suggestions. The broad perspective of this "Report on the Future" would be operationalized in the target dates and quantities of what Harrington termed (adopting A. Phillip Randolph's phrase) a "Freedom Budget." The latter would present a timetable for abolishing poverty and achieving full employment over a period of ten years. See *Toward A Democratic Left*, 123–4.

50 Ibid., 121–3; *Decade of Decision*, 204–7; "I Am Not a Marxist, I Am Marx," *Nation* 213 (27 December 1971): 694–6; and "Grass-Roots Needs," *Nation* 218 (19 January 1974): 68.

51 Harrington, "Private Profit and the Public Good," 4.

52 See Harrington, "Our Proposals for the Crisis," 103–4; *Decade of Decision*, 138–9; and "Full Employment and Socialist Investment," *Dissent* 25 (Winter 1978): 125–36.

53 Harrington, "A Path For America," 419. See also "Social Retreat and Economic Stagnation," 134.

54 Harrington, "Our Proposals for the Crisis," 104; "Full Employment and Social Investment," 125–30; and *Decade of Decision*, 140.

55 Harrington, "Private Profit and the Public Good," 4.

56 See Harrington, "What Socialists Would Do In America—If They Could," *Dissent* 25 (Fall 1978): 440–52. See also *Socialism*, 297.

57 Harrington, "Our Proposals for the Crisis," 104.

58 Ibid. See also "How to Reshape America's Economy," *Dissent* 23 (Spring 1976): 119–23; and "Our Proposals for the Crisis," 101. Harrington also suggested possibly nationalizing at least one of the major agricultural export concerns to encourage farmers to grow the greatest possible food yield in order to drive prices down at home and use excess supply to feed the hungry at home and abroad. See "Welfare Capitalism in Crisis," 686–93.

59 Harrington, "Full Employment and Socialist Investment," 132. See also "Economic Planning: Promises and Pitfalls," *Dissent* 22 (Fall 1975): 315–8.

60 See Harrington, "What Socialists Would Do In America," *Dissent* (1978), in *Taking Sides: The Education of A Militant Mind* (New York: Holt, Rinehart and Winston, 1985), 212.

61 Harrington, "Private Profit and the Public Good," 13.

62 Harrington, "Economic Planning: Promises and Pitfalls," 317. Harrington gave mixed reviews to America's non-profit sector, including TVA. Particularly prior to the 1980s, Harrington felt that they were partially successful in democratically controlling corporate power. On this, see "Why We Need Socialism in America," 263;

Socialism, 300; "Our Proposals for the Crisis," 102; "Jobs For All," *Commonweal* 103 (30 January 1976): 77; "Two Cheers for Socialism," *Harper's Magazine* 253 (October 1976): 70–2; and "Full Employment and Socialist Investment," 133.

63 See Harrington, *Socialism*, 303; and "What Socialists Would Do in America," *Dissent*, 440–52.

64 Ibid., 210.

65 Ibid., 217 ff.

66 Ibid.

67 Ibid., 219.

68 Harrington, "What Socialists Would Do In America," 440. See also Harrington, "Toward Legalizing Revolution," *Current* 122 (October 1970): 30; *Toward A Democratic Left*, 44–7; and Harrington, Peter Camejo, Jack Barnes, Stanley Aronowitz, Carl Haessler, and George Breitman, *The Lesser Evil?: The Left Debates The Democratic Party and Social Change* (New York: Pathfinder Press, 1977), 34.

CHAPTER FIVE

1 The following figures are based on CBO data published in 1976. See also Harrington, "A Path for America, Proposals from the Democratic Left," *Dissent* 29 (Fall 1982): 405–7.

2 Eric Olin Wright, *Class, Crisis, and the State* (London: New Left Books, 1978), 9.

3 Fred Block, "Marxist Theories of the State in World System Analysis," in *Social Change in the Capitalist World Economy*, ed. Barbara Hockey Kaplan (Beverly Hills: Sage, 1978), 33.

4 Theda Skocpol and Ellen Kay Trimberger, "Revolutions and the World-Historical Development of Capitalism," in Hockey Kaplan, 128. See also Skocpol et. al., *Bringing The State Back In* (Cambridge: Cambridge University Press, 1985), and Skocpol, "Political Response to Capitalist Crisis: Neo-Marxist Theories of the State and the Case of the New Deal," *Politics and Society* 10 (Spring, 1981): 200.

5 On tactical issues, see Block, "Beyond Relative Autonomy," in *Socialist Register*, Ralph Miliband and John Saville, ed., 1980, 240; Skocpol, "Bringing the State Back In," in Skocpol et al., 15–27; and Trimberger, *Revolution From Above* (New Brunswick, NJ: Transaction, 1978).

6 See Paul Sweezy, *The Theory of Capitalist Development* (New York: Oxford University Press, 1942); and Sweezy and Paul Baran, *Monopoly Capitalism* (New York: Monthly Review, 1966).

7 Ernest Mandel, *Marxist Economic Theory* (London: Merlin, 1962); and *Late Capitalism* (London: New Left Books, 1975).

8 James O'Connor, *The Fiscal Crisis of the State* (New York: St. Martin's, 1973), 7.

9 Ibid., 101.

10 Ibid., 7. See also 150.

11 Ibid., 9. See also 40, 179, 221.

12 See especially Harrington, *The Twilight of Capitalism* (New York: Simon and Schuster, 1976), 317 ff.

13 Ibid., 323.

14 Ibid., 322. See also 323–32.

15 Ibid., 321.

16 Ibid., 320.

17 Harrington, *Decade of Decision* (New York: Simon and Schuster, 1980), 108.

18 Michael Crozier, Samuel Huntington, and Joji Watanuki, *The Crisis of Democracy* (New York: New York University Press, 1975), 9. Huntington wrote the essay "The United States," and part of the introduction.

19 An enormous primary and secondary literature now surrounds liberation theology. For an overview and pertinent bibliography see the essay in my *Biographical Dictionary of Neo-Marxism* (Westport, CT: Greenwood, 1987), 260–3.

20 See James H. Cone, *Black Theology and Black Power* (New York: Seabury, 1969); *A Black Theology of Liberation* (New York: Lippincott, 1970); and *God of the Oppressed* (New York: Seabury 1975). See also Cornel West, *Prophecy Deliverance* (Philadelphia; Westminster, 1982).

21 Daniel Bell, *The Cultural Contradictions of Capitalism* (New York: Basic Books, 1976), 28.

22 Ibid., 12–3.

23 Ibid., 170.

24 Ibid., 29.

25 Ibid., 282.

26 Harrington, *The Politics at God's Funeral: The Spiritual Crisis of Western Civilization* (New York: Holt, Rinehart and Winston, 1983), 1.

27 Ibid., 4. Recent studies have shown that although a growing number of people identify themselves as religious, their social behavior has become more opportunistic. See also the data from "The Impact of Belief," a report commissioned by the Connecticut Mutual Life Insurance Co., in Harrington, *The Politics at God's Funeral*, 174–87. See also 187–96.

28 Ibid., 6.

29 Ibid., 34.

30 Ibid., 33.

31 Ibid., 35–47.

32 Ibid., 47–8.

33 The metaphor of religion as the "opiate of the masses" was originally used by Bruno Bauer.

34 Marx, "Contributions to the Critique of Hegel's Philosophy of Right," in *Karl Marx: Early Writings* (New York: Vintage, 1974), 244. Interestingly, the next sentence reads "It is the opium of the people."

35 Marx, *Critique of the Gotha Program* (Moscow: Progress, 1971), 29.

36 Marx, *Capital* (Moscow: International, 1975), 1: 79. See also "The Decay of Religious Authority," in *Reader in Marxist Philosophy* , edited by Howard Selsam and Harry Martel (New York: International, 1963), 240; Helmut Gollwitzer, *The Christian Faith and the Marxist Critique of Religion* (New York: Scribner's, 1970), esp. 1; and Delos McKown, *The Classical Marxist Critiques of Religion* (The Hague: Martinus Nijhoff, 1975), 94–121.

37 Harrington, *The Politics at God's Funeral*, 51.

38 Ibid., 82. See also Harrington, "Conversation with an Atheist," interview by James R. Gorman, *Christian Century* 95 (21 June 1978): 641–4; *Fragments of the Century* (New York: Simon and Schuster, 1972), 227; *Twilight of Capitalism*, 163; and *The Long Distance Runner: An Autobiography* (New York: Henry Holt, 1988), 242. Many Marxists have argued in favor of linking religion and Marxism. See my "Marxism and Theology in Liberal America," *Politics, Culture, and Society* 3(Summer 1990): 463–84.

39 Harrington, *The Politics at God's Funeral*, 206–18.

40 Ibid., 211.

41 See Harry Magdoff, *The Age of Imperialism* (New York: Monthly Review, 1969), and *Imperialism: From the Colonial Age to the Present* (New York: Monthly Review, 1978). What follows is in *The Age of Imperialism*, 30–40.

42 Paul A. Baran, *The Political Economy of Growth* (New York: Monthly Review, 1957).

43 See especially Immanual Wallerstein, *The Modern World-System* (New York: Academic, 1974); *The Capitalist World Economy* (London: Cambridge University Press, 1979); *The Modern World-System II* (New York: Academic, 1980); and *The Politics of the World Economy* (Cambridge: Cambridge University Press, 1984).

44 See Walter LaFeber, "The Last War, the Next War, and the New Revisionists," *Democracy* 1 (January 1981): 93–103; Theodore Draper, "Neoconservative History," *New York Review of Books*, 16 January 1986, 5–15; Jonathan Alter, "A New War Over Yalta," *Newsweek*, (28 April 1986): 49; and Harvey J. Kaye, *The Powers of the Past* (Minneapolis: University of Minnesota Press, 1991), 91.

45 See William Appleman Williams, *The Tragedy of American Diplomacy* (New York: Dell, 1972), and *Contours of American History* (New York: Norton, 1989).

46 Harrington, *The Vast Majority: A Journey To the World's Poor* (New York: Simon and Schuster, 1977). See also "Problems and Paradoxes of the Third World," *Dissent* 24 (Fall 1977): 379–89. This article summarizes the basics of development theory, and refers to the work done by Amin, Emmanuel, Furtado, and Frank.

47 Harrington to Howard Bray, 21 April 1976, Michael Harrington Correspondence, DSA Collection, Tamiment Library, New York University.

48 Harrington, *The Vast Majority*, 108–41. See also Harrington, "American Power in the Twentieth Century," in *A Dissenter's Guide to Foreign Policy*, ed. Irving Howe (New York: Praeger, 1968), 9–64.

49 Harrington to Howard Bray, 26 March 1976, Harrington Correspondence.

50 Wallerstein, *The Politics of the World Economy*, 157.

51 Harrington, *The Vast Majority*, 20.

52 Fernando H. Cardoso and Enzo Faletto, *Dependency and Development in Latin America* (Berkeley: University of California Press, 1979).

53 See Harrington, *Socialism* (New York: Saturday Review Press, 1970) 216–22; *The Vast Majority*, 195; and *The New American Poverty*, 223–4.

54 Harrington, *The Vast Majority*, 75. See also *Socialism*, 216, and 222–49; *Toward a Democratic Left: A Radical Program for a New Majority* (New York: Macmillan, 1968), 210–2; and *Socialism: Past and Future* (New York: Arcade, 1989), 62. In "American Power in the Twentieth Century," Harrington critiques Mao's aborted efforts at building socialism in impoverished China. In *Socialism*, 155–69, Harrington traces the evolution of orthodox Marxism through Lenin and Kautsky to show how it ignored Marx's admonition that socialism couldn't be built on poverty.

55 See Harrington, *The Vast Majority*, 227, and *Socialism*, 309–13.

56 See Harrington, *The Vast Majority*, 99, 226; "Toward a New Socialism," *Dissent* 36 (Spring 1989): 153–63; *Socialism: Past and Future*, 169; and *The Long Distance Runner*, 172–3.

57 See Harrington, *The Vast Majority*, 195–203 and 228–30; *Socialism*, 135–43; "American Power in the Twentieth Century," 52–5; and *Socialism: Past and Future*, 154 ff.

58 Willy Brandt, introduction to *North-South: A Programme for Survival*, report of the Independent Commission on International Development Issues, (Cambridge, MA: MIT Press, 1980), 18.

59 Harrington, *Toward a Democratic Left*, 174. See also 159–75; "American Power in the Twentieth Century, 14–8; and *Socialism: Past and Future*, 161–6.

60 Harrington, *Toward a Democratic Left*, 178. See also ibid., 184–5; "American Power in the Twentieth Century," 21; *The Vast Majority*, 254; and *Socialism: Past and Future*, 145. The following brief phrase is in *Socialism*, 324.

61 Article 99. The Declaration of Principles of the Socialist International, (London: Socialist International), p27.

62 Harrington, *The Vast Majority*, 220.

63 See ibid., 233.

64 On this, see Harrington, *Toward a Democratic Left*, 219–34; "American Power in the Twentieth Century," 45–61; *Socialism*, 328–36; and *Socialism: Past and Future*, 179 ff.

65 Harrington, "The Virtues and Limitations of Liberal Democracy," *Center Magazine* 14 (March-April 1981): 53.

66 See Harrington, *Toward a Democratic Left*, 186–96; *Socialism*, 310–8; and "American Power in the Twentieth Century," 62–4.

67 Harrington, *The Next Left* (New York: Henry Holt, 1986), 192.

68 Harrington, "The First Steps—And a Few Beyond," *Dissent* 35 (Winter, 1988): 54–5.

69 Harrington, *The Next Left*, 192.

70 And even with regard to oil, Harrington felt that the U.S. could nicely adapt to losing its ownership of third world oil, although some private American oil companies might suffer. See *Toward a Democratic Left*, 192–5.

71 See Harrington, "American Power in the Twentieth Century," 36–40; and *Toward a Democratic Left*, 201–6.

72 Article 7. The Declaration of Principles of the Socialist International, (London: Socialist International, 1989), p3.

CHAPTER SIX

1 See Harrington, *Decade of Decision* (New York: Simon and Schuster, 1980), 287–9.

2 Karl Marx, *Capital*, 3 vols. (New York: International, 1967), 3:886.

3 Ibid. Marx made the same points in his *Theories of Surplus Value*, ed. Karl Kautsky. (Stuttgart: Dietz, 1905–10).

4 See the pertinent work of Maurice Zeitlin, especially *Classes, Class Conflict and the State* (Cambridge: Winthrop 1980).

5 E. P. Thompson, *The Making of the English Working Class* (New York: Vintage, 1963), 11.

6 Eric Olin Wright, *Classes* (London: Verso, 1985), 285.

7 The following statistics are taken from many public and non–public sources, including: U.S. Congress Joint Economic Committee, *The Concentration of Wealth in the United States: Trends in the Distribution of Wealth among American Families*, 99th Congress, 2nd Session, July 1986; Bureau of the Census, "Living in Poverty," (Washington, D.C., 1988); Ravi Batra, *The Great Depression of 1990* (New York: Simon and Schuster, 1987); Frank Levy, *Dollars and Dreams: The Changing American Income Distribution* (New York: Basic Books, 1988); "The Vanishing Middle Class and Related Issues: A Review of Living Standards in the 1970s and 1980s," *PS* 20 (Summer 1987): 650–5; Barbara Ehrenreich, "Is the Middle Class Doomed?" *New York Times Magazine*, 7 September 1986, 44–64; Ruth Sidel, *Women and Children Last* (New York: Viking, 1992); Sidney Carroll and Herbert Inhaber, *How Rich is Too Rich? Income and Wealth in America* (New York: Praeger, 1992); and Kevin Phillips, *Boiling Point: Republicans, Democrats, and the Decline of Middle Class Prosperity* (New York: Random House, 1993). When data is taken from other sources, they are noted in the text.

8 See Wright, 285, and Wright and Joachin Singelmann, "Proletarianization in the Changing American Class Structure," *American Journal of Sociology*, 88 (Supplement, 1982): 176–209. Wright's data updated and confirmed Harrington's assertions in *Socialism* (New York: Saturday Review Press, 1970), 352–7, and in *Decade of Decision*, 299–301.

9 Patricia Cayo Sexton, *The War on Labor and the Left* (Boulder, CO: Westview, 1991), 13.

10 Ibid., 14–15.

11 See Richard B. Freeman, "Why Are Unions Fairing Poorly in NLRB Representative Elections?" in *Challenges and Choices Facing American Labor*, ed. Thomas A. Kochan (Cambridge, MA: MIT Press, 1985), 59.

12 In "Worker Rights to Organize and Bargain," AFL-CIO *News* (8 October 1988): 7.

13 Ibid., 6 July 1985: 5.

14 Sexton, 15.

15 Harrington, *Fragments of the Century* (New York: Simon and Schuster, 1972), 219.

16 See Harrington, *Socialism*, 352–3, and "Old Working Class, New Working Class," *Dissent* 19 (Winter, 1972): 152.

17 Ibid., 151. See also *Socialism*, 354–7; and *The Long Distance Runner: An Autobiography* (New York: Henry Holt, 1988), 194.

18 Harrington, *Decade of Decision*, 299–301.

19 Harrington refers to educated youth as the third component of the working class in *Socialism*, 362, and *Fragments of the Century*, 212–4. In "Youth and the Labor Movement" (address to meeting of unionized workers, University of Illinois, Urbana, 4 December 1971), 15, DSA Collection, Michael Harrington Correspondence, Tamiment Library, New York University, Harrington acknowledges that young people have potential for the labor movement, but in themselves don't comprise a class.

20 Harrington, "The New Class and the Left," *Society* 16 (January 1979): 24. See also *The Twilight of Capitalism* (New York: Simon and Schuster, 1976), 208–35.

21 Harrington, *The Retail Clerks* (New York: Wiley, 1962), esp. 1–6 and 84–6.

22 Harrington, *Toward A Democratic Left* (New York: Macmillan, 1968), 265. 263–6, and *Socialism*, 359–61.

23 Harrington, "The New Class and the Left," *Society*, 26. See also "Old Working Class, New Working Class," 160–61; and "The New Class and the Left," in *The New Class?*, ed. B. Bruce-Briggs (New Brunswick, NJ: Transaction, 1979), 128–9.

24 Harrington, "The New Class and the Left," *Society*, 27; and "The New Class and the Left," in Briggs, 130.

25 Harrington, *Toward A Democratic Left*, 270.

26 See Harrington, "The New Class and the Left," *Society*, 29–30; and *Toward A Democratic Left*, 265–6.

27 Ibid., 268–9. See also chapter 13 of David T. Bazelon, *Power in America: The Politics of the New Class* (New York: New American Library, 1967).

28 Harrington, *Toward A Democratic Left*, 297. The term was first used by Norman Podhoretz, "Laureate of the New Class," *Commentary* 54 (December 1972): 4. For data on the percentage increase of professional and technical workers in the nation's labor force, see Harrington, *The Next Left* (New York: Henry Holt, 1986), 181 ff.

29 Ibid.

30 Harrington, *The Long Distance Runner*, 69.

31 The first quote is in Dan Wakefield, *New York in the Fifties* (New York: Houghton Mifflin, 1992), 141; and the second is in Harrington, *The Long Distance Runner*, 71.

32 See Harrington, *Fragments of the Century*, 91 ff.

33 Harrington, "Radical Strategy: Don't Form a Fourth Party; Form a New First Party," *New York Times Magazine* (13 September 1970): 128. See also *Decade of Decision*, 303–6; *The Accidental Century* (New York: Macmillan, 1965), 302; and *Toward A Democratic Left*, 246 ff.

34 Harrington, "Say What You Mean—Socialism," in *Taking Sides: The Education of a Militant Mind* (New York: Holt, Rinehart, and Winston, 1985), 159–67. First published in *Nation* 218 (25 May 1974). See also *The Long Distance Runner*, 94.

35 Harrington, "Toward a Socialist Presence in America," ca. July 1973, Harrington Correspondence.

36 Harrington, "Say What You Mean—Socialism," 165.

37 Harrington to June Magyre, 2 January 1975, Harrington Correspondence.

38 Harrington, *Toward A Democratic Left*, 270.

39 Harrington, "Don't Form a Fourth Party," 135.

40 Harrington, "Voting the Lesser Evil," *Commentary* 45 (April 1968): 30.

41 Harrington, Peter Camejo, Jack Barnes, Stanley Aronowitz, Carl Haessler, and George Breitman, *The Lesser Evil? The Left Debates the Democratic Party and Social Change* (New York: Pathfinder, 1977), 13.

42 Harrington, *Toward A Democratic Left*, 274.

43 Harrington, *The Long Distance Runner*, 116. See also "The New Class and the Left," in Briggs, 131.

44 Harrington, *The Long Distance Runner*, 116.

45 See Democratic Socialists of America, *The New Socialists: An Official Pamphlet* (1984); "Socialists Examine the Two Souls of Liberalism," *The Democratic Left* 5 (March 1977): 6–7; *The Long Distance Runner*, 15–7; John Judis, "Democratic Socialists Move Left," in *These Times* (28 February 1979): 4; and Denise S. Akey, ed., *Encyclopedia of Association*, 16th ed. (Detroit: Book Tower, 1981) 1:1028.

46 In Judis, "Democratic Socialists Move Left," 5. C.f. a similar critique by Irving Howe, quoted in Alan Wald, *The New York Intellectuals* (Chapel Hill: University of North Carolina Press, 1987), 333.

47 Minutes of the DSOC National Board Meeting, New York City, 1–2 March 1975, Harrington Correspondence.

48 Harry Boyte, "Reunion On the Left," *Progressive*, June 1975, 9–10. Boyte was a leader of NAM.

49 Anonymous in NAM to Harrington, 10 January 1974; and Harrington to Harry Boyte, 7 September 1974, Harrington Correspondence.

50 See Harrington, *The Long Distance Runner*, 17 ff; and "Between Generations," *Socialist Review* 17 (May–August 1987): 152–8.

CHAPTER SEVEN

1 Harrington, *Socialism: Past and Future* (New York: Arcade, 1989), 19–28.

2 Ibid., 22.

3 Ibid., 25.

4 Harrington, "Is There Socialism After France? in *Taking Sides* (New York: Holt, Rinehart and Winston, 1984), 233–48; and "Mitterand's Term: A Balance Sheet," *Dissent* 34 (Winter 1987): 82–92.

5 Harrington, *Socialism: Past and Future*, 28.

6 Ibid., 29–37.

7 Harrington based the following argument on Martin Buber's *Paths in Utopia* (Boston: Beacon Press, 1966). See *Socialism: Past and Future*, 37–8.

8 Engels reiterated this point in letters published during the 1890s, and in the 1895 preface to the new edition of Marx's *Class Struggles in France* (Berlin: Dietz, 1895).

9 Harrington, *Socialism: Past and Future*, 43.

10 Ibid., 49.

11 Ibid., 80–90.

12 Ibid., 110.

13 For a detailed explanation of the conservative accusations, see ibid., 122–6; *The Next Left* (New York: Henry Holt, 1986), 50–69; and *Fragments of the Century* (New York: Simon and Schuster, 1972), 232–43.

14 See Harrington, *Socialism: Past and Future*, 126–8; and *The Next Left*, 13–46, 71–95.

15 Harrington, *The Next Left*, 16.

16 Harrington, "Wrestling With the Famous Spector," *Nation* 214 (28 February 1972): 277–8. See also *Socialism* (New York: Saturday Review Press, 1970), 176; *Socialism: Past and Future*, 246; and Antonio Gramsci, *Selections From the Prison Notebooks*, ed. and trans. by Quinton Hoare and Geoffrey Nowell Smith (New York: International, 1971). See also such excellent secondary sources as Anne Sassoon, *Gramsci's Politics* (NY: St. Martin's,1980), Chantal Mouffe, *Gramsci and Marxist Theory* (London: Routledge and Kegan Paul, 1979), Christine Buci-Glucksmann, *Gramsci and the State* (London: Lawrence and Wishart, 1979), Guiseppe Fiori, *Antonio Gramsci* (London: New Left, 1970), Alistair Davidson, *Antonio Gramsci* (London: Herlin, 1977), J.M.Cammett, *Antonio Gramsci and the Origins of Italian Communism* (Palo Alto, CA: Stanford U Press, 1967), Joseph V. Femia, *Gramsci's Political Thought* (Oxford: Oxford Univ Press, 1981), and Carl Boggs, *Gramsci's Marxism* (London: Pluto, 1976). Gramsci's central notion of hegemony, not his Hegelianism, impressed Harrington. See Harrington, "Wrestling With the Famous Spector," *Nation*, 278.

17 Owen Harries, "A Primer for Polemicists," *Commentary* 70 (September 1984): 57. Harries was an American conservative and a Fellow at the Heritage Foundation. He and Norman Podhoretz had signalled that conservatives were intent on winning the ideological battle between liberalism and conservatism. See also Robert Dallek, *Ronald Reagan: The Politics of Symbolism* (Cambridge, MA: MIT Press, 1984), esp. 1–4, for an analysis of Reagan's use of myth.

18 See Harvey J. Kaye, *The Powers of the Past* (Minneapolis: University of Minnesota Press, 1991), 95.

19 Ruth Sidel, *Women and Children Last* (New York: Viking, 1990), 22.

20 Harrington now applies the word "dealigned," formerly used to describe the party system, to describe workers. See *Socialism: Past and Future*, 255–62.

21 Harrington, *The Next Left*, 183.

22 See, for example, Harrington's "The Economics of Racism, " *Commonweal* 74 (7 July 1961): 367–70. Compare this to later writings on this issue—e.g., "A Case For Jackson," *Dissent* 35 (Summer 1988): 262–4—which accented the need for social-ists to focus on black experiences and black mobilization.

23 Harrington, *Socialism: Past and Future*, 266.

24 See my *Neo–Marxism: The Meanings of Modern Radicalism* (Westport, CT: Greenwood, 1985).

25 Harrington, *Socialism: Past and Future*, 272. The following phrases are also found here.

26 Ibid., 276.

27 Ibid., 273.

28 Ibid., 273 ff.

29 Harrington, *The Next Left*, 190.

30 Ibid. A reaction to the Hartzian thesis regarding the liberal quality of America has recently formed around the republicans Bernard Bailyn, J. G. A. Pocock, and Gordon Wood.

31 Ibid., 191. See also Harrington, "A Socialist's Centennial," *New Republic* 192 (7 January 1985), 16–8.

32 Harrington, *Socialism: Past and Future*, 150.

33 Ibid., 253.

34 Harrington, *The Next Left*, 187.

35 Ibid., 143.

36 Harrington, "If There is a Recession—and If Not," *Dissent* 32 (Spring 1985): 142. See also Harrington, "The First Steps—And a Few Beyond," *Dissent* 35 (Winter 1988): 53 ff.; and *The Next Left*, 167–73.

37 Harrington, "Progressive Economics for 1988," *Nation* 242 (3 May 1986): 617. See also "The First Steps—And a Few Beyond," *Dissent*, 47–54.

38 Ibid., 46. See also *The Next Left*, 164 ff.

39 Harrington, "The First Steps—And a Few Beyond," 50. See also *The Next Left*, 144; "If There is a Recession—and If Not," 139–144; and Marion Long, "Paradise Tossed - Visions of Utopia," *Omni* 10 (April 1988): 103.

40 See Juliet B. Schor, *The Overworked American* (New York: Basic Books, 1992). See also Harrington, *Socialism: Past and Future*, 215–6.

41 Harrington to John Simmons, 9 February 1979, DSA Collection, Michael Harrington Correspondence, Tamiment Library, New York University.

42 Harrington, "Toward a New Socialism," *Dissent* 36 (Spring 1989): 153–63.

43 Harrington, "The First Steps—And a Few Beyond," 49. See also *Socialism: Past and Future*, 201. Harrington called investment to create only profit "casino capitalism." (ibid., 208).

44 Harrington, *The Next Left*, 155–6.

45 Harrington, "The First Steps—And a Few Beyond," 52.

46 See Harrington, "Private Profit and the Public Good," ca. 1980, Harrington Correspondence.

47 Harrington, *The Next Left*, 150 ff.; and *Socialism: Past and Future*, 203.

48 Harrington, "The First Steps—And a Few Beyond," 52.

49 Harrington, *Socialism: Past and Future*, 196–7.

50 Ibid., 196 ff.

51 Ibid., 200–2.

52 Ibid., 210–1.

53 Ibid., 218–34; "Markets and Plans," *Dissent* 36 (Winter 1989): 56–70. See also *Decade of Decision* (New York: Simon and Schuster, 1980), 188.

54 Quoted in Lewis Lapham, *Money and Class in America* (New York: Ballantine, 1988), 42.

55 Harrington, *Socialism: Past and Future*, 220 ff., and "Markets and Plans," 57–62.

56 Harrington, *Socialism: Past and Future*, 223.

57 Ibid., 239, and "Markets and Plans," 66.

58 Harrington, *Socialism: Past and Future*, 240 ff., and "Markets and Plans," 67 ff.

59 Harrington, *Socialism: Past and Future*, 243.

60 Harrington, "Markets and Plans," 68.

61 Ibid., 68. See also *Socialism: Past and Future*, 246–7, and "What Socialists Would Do In America," (1978), in *Taking Sides: The Education of a Militant Mind* (New York: Holt, Rinehart and Winston, 1985), 217. This article was originally published in *Dissent*, 25 (Fall 1978), 440-52.

62 Harrington, *Socialism: Past and Future*, 219.

CHAPTER EIGHT

1 The paper was published in Talcott Parsons, *Sociological Theory and Modern Society* (New York: Free Press, 1967). The quotes are on 135, 109–10, 132, 113, 123.

For a similar point of view, see Clinton Rossiter, *Marxism: The View From America* (New York: Harcourt, Brace, and World, 1960), 7–8.

2 Tamar Jacoby, "A Life at the Barricades," Interview in *Newsweek*, 8 August 1988, 30.

3 In 1958 ("Is There a Political Novel?" in *Taking Sides: The Education of a Militant Mind* [New York: Holt, Rinehart and Winston, 1985], 42–53), Harrington predicted that the novel was finished as an art form. Throughout the 1970s, Harrington foresaw a growing radicalism among students on campuses and among workers in factories. See, for example, "Toward Radical Revolution—Is President Nixon Leading The Way?" *Current* 137 (February 1972): 37–43; "Getting Restless Again," *New Republic* 181 (1 September 1979): 12–5; and Minutes of the DSOC National Board, New York City, 16 May 1978 and 10–11 June 1978, DSA Collection, Michael Harrington Correspondence, Tamiment Library, New York University. In the 1980s, Harrington predicted that America would turn left, with socialists playing a leading role, "somewhere between 1986 and 1992." *Taking Sides*, 60. See also *The Next Left* (New York: Henry Holt, 1986), 1, 16–7.

4 Harrington, *The Long Distance Runner: An Autobiography* (New York: Henry Holt, 1988), 227.

5 McReynolds to Harrington, 3 March 1972, Harrington Correspondence.

6 Harrington, *The Long Distance Runner*, 8.

7 Harrington, "When Ed Koch Was Still a Liberal," *Dissent* 34 (Fall 1987): 597. See also *The Long Distance Runner*, 41–7, and Dwight McDonald, "An Open Letter to Michael Harrington," *New York Review of Books* (5 December 1968): 48–9.

8 See, for example, Harrington, "The Economics of Racism," *Commonweal* 74 (7 July 1961): 367–71; and Harrington, Letter to the Editor, *New York Times*, 22 February 1978.

9 Harrington to Martin and Anne Peretz, 24 May 1974, Harrington Correspondence.

10 Harrington to Julian Bond, 17 March 1977, Harrington Correspondence.

11 See my "Black Neo–Marxism in Liberal America," *Rethinking Marxism* 4 (Winter 1989): 118–40. See also Sally Miller, "The Socialist Party and the Negro, 1901–1920," *Journal of Negro History* 56 (July 1971): 220–9; Ira Kipnis, *The American Socialist Movement, 1898–1912* (Westport, CT: Greenwood, 1968), 130–3; Philip Foner and James S. Allen, eds., *American Communism and Black Americans* (Philadelphia: Temple University Press, 1987), 94–103; David Shannon, *The Socialist Party of America* (New York: Macmillan, 1955), 57 ff; James Weinstein, *The Decline of Socialism in America* (New York: Vintage, 1967), 63–74; and Wilson Record, *The American Negro and the CP* (New York: Atheneum, 1951), 100.

12 Minutes of the DSOC National Board Meeting, New York City, 10–11 June 1978, Harrington Correspondence.

13 See Mari Jo Buhle, *Women and American Socialism* (Urbana: University of Illinois Press, 1981), especially 246–87; Joan Landes, "Feminism and The Internationals," *Telos* 49 (Fall 1981): 117–26; Lise Vogel, "Questions on the Women

Question," *Monthly Review* 31 (June 1979): 39–59; Vida Scudder, "Women and Socialism," *Yale Review* 3 (April 1914): 459; Sally Miller, "Women in the Party Bureaucracy," in *Flawed Liberation: Socialism and Feminism*, ed. Sally Miller (Westport, CT: Greenwood, 1981), 13–35; and M. Jane Slaughter, "Feminism and Socialism," *Marxist Perspectives* 2 (Fall 1979): 32–6.

14 Harrington, *The Long Distance Runner*, 27.

15 See Harrington, "When Ed Koch Was Still a Liberal," 599.

16 Memorandum from Women's Caucus of the DSOC, 14 November 1973, Harrington Correspondence.

17 Harrington, Letter to the Editor, *Boston Globe*, 13 November 1974.

18 Recounted in Harrington, *The Long Distance Runner*, 100.

19 Harrington to National Committee Members and Alternates of the Majority Tendency of the Socialist Party, 18 May 1971, Harrington Correspondence.

20 Harrington, "Say What You Mean—Socialism," 1974, in *Taking Sides*, 165. First published in *Nation* 218 (25 May 1974): 648-51.

21 Harrington, "American Power in the Twentieth Century," in *A Dissenter's Guide To Foreign Policy*, ed. Irving Howe (New York: Praeger, 1968), 49. See also 62.

22 Harrington, *Taking Sides*, 120 ff.

23 Harrington to Jessica Tice, 8 July 1980, Harrington Correspondence.

24 Harrington to Robert Keim, 22 July 1975, Harrington Correspondence.

25 Harrington to Barb Pequet, 30 January 1979, Harrington Correspondence.

26 Harrington, *The Long Distance Runner*, 35.

27 Harrington, "Towards a New Socialism," *Dissent* 36 (Spring 1989): 162.

28 Harrington, *The Long Distance Runner*, 35.

29 Harrington to "Politicks," 5 December 1977, Harrington Correspondence.

30 Harrington, "A Path For America: Proposals From the Democratic Left," *Dissent* 29 (Fall 1982): 423.

31 Harrington, *Fragments of the Century* (New York: Simon and Schuster, 1972), 225.

32 Harrington, "Between Generations," *Socialist Review* 17 (May–August 1987): 158.

33 Harvey J. Kaye, *The Powers of the Past* (Minneapolis: University of Minnesota Press, 1991), 123.

34 See, for example, Paul Kennedy, *The Rise and Fall of the Great Powers* (New York: Random House, 1987); George Will, *Suddenly: The American Idea Abroad and at Home, 1986–90* (New York: Free Press, 1992); Robert Nisbet, *The Present Age: Progress and Anarchy in Modern America* (New York: Harper and Row, 1988); and Philip Mattera, *Prosperity Lost* (New York: Addison-Wesley, 1990).

35 Harrington, *Socialism: Past and Future* (New York: Arcade, 1989), 278.

36 On this, see Russell Jacoby, *The Last Intellectuals* (New York: Basic Books, 1987).

37 Robert Heilbroner, "The Triumph of Capitalism," *New Yorker* (31 January 1989): 98–109.

38 Ralf Dahrendorf, *Reflections on the Revolution in Europe* (New York: Times Books, 1990), 42.

39 Stanley Aronowitz, "On Intellectuals," in *Intellectuals: Aesthetics, Politics, Academics*, ed. Bruce Robbins (Minneapolis, MN: University of Minnesota Press, 1990), 5.

40 Joyce Kolko, *Restructuring the World Economy* (New York: Pantheon, 1988), 347.

41 (New York: Free Press, 1992). It was originally published as "The End of History," *The National Interest* 16 (Summer 1989): 3–18.

NOTES

Bibliography

Primary Sources

Books

Harrington, Michael, and Jacobs, Paul eds. *Labor in a Free Society*. Berkeley: University of California Press, 1959.

Harrington, Michael. *The Retail Clerks*. New York: Wiley, 1962.

_____. *The Other America: Poverty in the United States*. New York: Macmillan, 1962.

_____. *The Accidental Century*. New York: Macmillan, 1965.

_____. *Toward a Democratic Left: A Radical Program for a New Majority*. New York: Macmillan, 1968.

_____. *Socialism*. New York: Saturday Review Press, 1970.

_____. *Fragments of the Century*. New York: Simon and Schuster, 1972.

_____. *The Twilight of Capitalism*. New York: Simon and Schuster, 1976.

_____, Peter Camego, Jack Barnes, Stanley Aronowitz, Carl Haessler, and George Breitman. *The Lesser Evil? - The Left Debates the Democratic Party and Social Change*. New York: Pathfinder Press, 1977.

_____ Harrington, Michael and Deborah Meir. *Theory, Life and Politics*. New York: Institute for Democratic Socialism, 1977.

_____. Harrington, Michael *The Vast Majority: A Journey to the World's Poor*. New York: Simon and Schuster, 1977.

_____. *Decade of Decision*. New York: Simon and Schuster, 1980.

_____. *The Politics at God's Funeral: The Spiritual Crisis of Western Civilization*. New York: Holt, Rinehart and Winston, 1983.

_____. *The New American Poverty*. New York: Holt, Rinehart and Winston, 1984.

_____. *Taking Sides: The Education of a Militant Mind*. New York: Holt, Rinehart and Winston, 1985.

_____. *The Next Left*. New York: Henry Holt, 1986.

_____. *The Long-Distance Runner: An Autobiography*. New York: Henry Holt, 1988.

_____. *Socialism: Past and Future*. New York: Arcade, 1989.

Articles

Harrington, Michael. "Marxist Literary Critics." *Commonweal* 62 (11 December 1959): 324–26.

_____. "Labor in the Doldrums." *Commonweal* 62 (11 March 1960): 643–6.

_____. "The Other America." Commonweal 62 (27 May 1960): 220–8.

_____. "The Economics of Racism." *Commonweal* 74 (7 July 1961): 367–70.

_____. "Marx Versus Marx." *New Politics* 1 (Fall 1961): 24–33.

_____. "American Contradiction." *Commonweal* 77 (4 January 1963): 381–4.

_____. "The Mystical Militants." In *Beyond the New Left*, ed. Irving Howe, 33–9. New York: McCall, 1965.

_____. "Radicals Old and New." *New Republic* 153 (3 July 1965): 29.

_____. "The New Radicalism." *Commonweal* 82 (3 September 1965): 623–27.

_____. Introduction to *A Prophetic Minority* by Jack Newfield. New York: New American Library, 1966.

_____. "The Politics of Poverty." In *The Radical Papers*, ed. Irving Howe, 122–43. Garden City, NY: Doubleday, 1966.

_____. "American Power in the Twentieth Century." In *A Dissenter's Guide to Foreign Policy*, edited by Irving Howe, 9–64. New York: Praeger, 1968.

_____. "Voting the Lesser Evil." *Commentary* 45 (April 1968): 22.

_____. "Wisdom and Unwisdom." *New Republic* 159 (20 July 1968): 24–5.

_____. "What's Left." *New Republic* 159 (21 September 1968): 34.

_____. "Art and Politics." *Commentary* 46 (November 1968): 116–9.

_____. "Who Are the True Redeemers." *New Republic* 160 (12 April 1969): 25–7.

_____. "The Role of Compensatory Justice." *Current* 110 (September 1969): 50–1.

_____. "Religion and Revolution." *Commonweal* 91 (14 November 1969): 203–4.

_____. "Betrayal of the Poor." *Atlantic*, January 1970, 71–4.

_____. "Whatever Happened to Socialism?" *Harper's*, February 1970, 99–105.

_____. "Why We Need Socialism in America." *Dissent* 17 (May 1970): 315–22.

_____. "Radical Strategy: Don't Form a Fourth Party, Form a New First Party." *New York Times Magazine*, 11 October 1970, 28–9.

_____. "Toward Legalizing Revolution." *Current* 122 (October 1970): 28–31.

_____. "McCarthyism, Angela Davis, and the Berrigans." *Dissent* 18 (June 1971): 291–6.

_____. "The Misfortune of 'Great Memories': Historical Remarks on the Paris Commune." *Dissent* 18 (October 1971): 375–9.

_____. "Mr. Nixon's Reactionary Revolution." *Commonweal* 95 (26 November 1971): 199–202.

_____. "I Am Not a Marxist, I am Marx." *Nation* 213 (27 December 1971): 694–6.

_____. "Old Working Class, New Working Class." *Dissent* 19, no. 1 (January 1972): 148–59.

_____. "Toward Radical Revolution - Is President Nixon Leading the Way." *Current* 137 (February 1972): 37–43.

_____. "Wrestling With the Famous Spector." *Nation* 214 (28 February 1972): 277–8.

_____. "Last Bourgeois." *Nation* 214 (17 April 1972): 506–7.

_____. "We Few, We Happy Few, We Bohemians." *Esquire*, August 1972, 99–103.

_____. "Soaking the Poor." *Commonweal* 97 (20 October 1972): 57–60.

_____. "Forsaking Debs for Nixon: A Call to American Socialists: Letter of Resignation as National Co-chairman of the Socialist Party-Democratic Socialist Federation, 23 October 1972." *Nation* 215 (13 November 1972): 454–5

_____. "Negative Landslide." *Nation* 215 (27 November 1972): 518–21.

_____. "To Think Again." *Nation* 216 (5 March 1973): 293–4.

_____. "The Welfare State and Its Neoconservative Critics." *Dissent* 20 (Fall 1973): 398–405.

_____. "Grassroots Needs." *Nation* 218 (19 January 1974): 68.

_____. "Say What You Mean—Socialism." *Nation* 218 (25 May 1974): 648–51.

_____. "Old Working Class, New Working Class." *Dissent* 21 (Spring 1974): 328–43.

_____. "The Oil Crisis - Socialist Answers." *Dissent* 21 (Spring 1974): 139–42.

_____. "A Collective Sadness." *Dissent* 21 (Fall 1974): 486–91.

_____. "Welfare Capitalism in Crisis." *Nation* 219 (28 December 1974): 686–93.

_____. "Our Proposals for the Crisis." *Dissent* 22 (Spring 1975): 101–4.

_____. "Economic Planning - Promises and Pitfalls." *Dissent* 22 (Fall 1975): 315–8 .

_____. "The Big Lie About the Sixties." *New Republic* 173 (29 November 1975): 15–9.

_____. "Planning for Social Change." *Social Policy* 6 (November 1975): 49–52.

_____. "A New Crisis of Capitalism." *Dissent* 22 (Winter 1975): 5–10.

_____. "Full Employment." In *Annual Report*, National Bureau of Economic Research. Washington, D.C.: 1976.

_____. "Jobs for All." *Commonweal* 103 (30 January 1976): 73–7.

_____. "How to Reshape America's Economy." *Dissent* 23 (Spring 1976): 119–23.

_____. "Post-Industrial Society and the Welfare State." *Dissent* 23 (Summer 1976): 244–52.

_____. "On the 1976 Election." *Dissent* 23 (Fall 1976): 325–8.

_____. "Two Cheers for Socialism." *Harper's* 253 (October 1976): 68–72.

_____. "July in January?" *New Republic* 176 (22 January 1977): 60.

_____. "Hiding The Other America." *New Republic* 176 (26 February 1977): 15–7.

_____. "Old Comrades Meet." *Harper's* 254 (February 1977): 26–8.

_____. "Socialists Examine the Two Souls of Liberalism." *Democratic Left* 5 (March 1977): 6–7.

_____. "Marxism in America." *New Catholic World* 220 (May 1977): 118–21.

_____. "A Status Quo Economy." *Harper's* 255 (September 1977): 34–5.

_____. "Problems and Paradoxes of the Third World." *Dissent* 24 (Fall 1977): 379–89.

_____; Harrington, Michael, Richard Appelbaum; and Peter Drier. "A Faded Dream: Housing in America." *Dissent* 31 (Winter 1978): 21–4.

_____. Harrington, Michael "Socialism Reborn in Europe." *New Republic* 178 (11 March 1978): 19–22.

_____. Harrington, Michael. "Conversation With an Atheist." Interview by Gorman, James R. *Christian Century* 95 (21 June 1978): 641–4.

_____. "For a Socialist Democracy." *Current* 207 (November 1978): 21–4.

_____. "Full Employment and Socialist Investment." *Dissent* 25 (Winter 1978): 125–36.

_____. "What Socialists Would Do in America—If They Could." *Dissent* 25 (Fall 1978): 440–52.

_____. "The New Class and the Left." *Society* 16 (January 1979): 24–30.

_____. "To the Disney Station." *Harper's* 258 (January 1979): 35–39.

_____. "Social Retreat and Economic Stagnation." *Dissent* 26 (Spring 1979): 131–4.

_____. "Nuclear Power and Corporate Priorities." *Dissent* 26 (Summer 1979): 278–80.

_____. "Getting Restless Again." *New Republic* 181 (1 September 1979): 12–5.

_____. "The New Class and the Left." In *The New Class?* edited by B. Bruce-Briggs, 123–38. New Brunswick, NJ: Transaction, 1979.

_____. "The PLO and the Democratic Left." *Commonweal* 107 (18 January 1980): 10–3.

_____. "The Virtues and Limitations of Liberal Democracy." *Center Magazine* 14 (March–April 1981): 50–3.

_____. "A Path for America: Proposals from the Democratic Left." *Dissent* 29 (Fall 1982): 405–24.

_____. "Americans in Limbo." *Harper's* April 1983, 48–53.

_____. "Paradise or Disintegration." *Commonweal* 110 (4 November 1983): 585–9.

_____. "A Socialist's Centennial." *New Republic* 192 (7–14 January 1985): 16–8.

_____. "Crunched Numbers." *New Republic* 192 (28 January 1985): 7.

_____. "If There is a Recession—and If Not." *Dissent* 32 (Spring 1985): 139–44.

_____, Harrington, Michael and Mark Levinson. "The Perils of a Dual Economy." *Dissent* 32 (Fall 1985): 417–26.

_____. Harrington, Michael. "Willful Shortsightedness on Poverty." *Dissent* 33, no. 1 (Winter 1986): 19. First published in *New York Times*, 9 Setpember 1985, Op-Ed Section.

_____. "Progressive Economics for 1988." *Nation* 242 (3 May 1986): 601.

_____. "Mitterand's Term: A Balance Sheet." *Dissent* 34 (Winter 1987): 82–92.

_____. "Between Generations." *Socialist Review* 17 (May-August 1987): 152–8.

_____. "When Ed Koch was Still a Liberal." *Dissent* 34 (Fall 1987): 595–602.

_____. "The First Steps—And a Few Beyond." *Dissent* 35 (Winter 1988): 44–55.

_____. "A Case For Jackson." *Dissent* 35 (Summer 1988): 262–4.

_____. Harrington, Michael. "The Other American: Interview with Michael Harrington." Interview by Bill McKibbon. *Mother Jones* 13 (July-August 1988): 40–58 passim.

_____. "Markets and Plans." *Dissent* 36 (Winter 1989): 56–70.

_____. "Toward A New Socialism." *Dissent* 36 (Spring 1989): 153–63.

Unpublished Manuscripts, Correspondence, and Letters

Harrington, Michael. Correspondence. DSA Collection. Tamiment Library, New York University.

SECONDARY SOURCES:

Books

Akey, Denise S., ed. *Encyclopedia of Association*, 16th ed. Detroit: Book Tower, 1981.

Baran, Paul A. *The Political Economy of Growth*. New York: Monthly Review, 1957.

Batra, Ravi. *The Great Depression of 1990*. New York: Simon and Schuster, 1987.

Bazelon, David T. *Power in America: The Politics of the New Class*. New York: New American Library, 1967.

Bell, Daniel. *The Cultural Contradictions of Capitalism*. New York: Basic Books, 1976.

Berger, Victor. *Berger's Broadsides*. Milwaukee: Social Democratic Publishers, 1912.

Blumenthal, S. *The Rise of the Counter Establishment*. New York: Times Books, 1986.

Bottomore, T. B. *Critics of Society: Radical Thought in North America*. New York: Pantheon, 1968.

Boudin, Louis. *The Theoretical System of Karl Marx in the Light of Recent Criticism*. Chicago: Kerr, 1912.

Bowles, Samuel and Herbert Gintis. *Democracy and Capitalism*. New York: Basic Books, 1986.

Bruce-Briggs, B., ed. *The New Class?* New Brunswick, NJ: Transaction, 1979.

Buhle, Mari Jo. *Women and American Socialism*. Urbana: University of Illinois Press, 1981.

Buhle, Paul. *Marxism in the USA*. London: Verso, 1987.

Cardoso, Fernando H. and Enzo Faletto. *Dependency and Development in Latin America*. Berkeley: University of California Press, 1979.

Carroll, Sidney and Herbert Inhaber. *How Rich is Too Rich? Income and Wealth in America*. New York: Praeger, 1992.

Cone, James H. *Black Theology and Black Power*. New York: Seabury, 1969.

_____. *A Black Theology of Liberation*. New York: Lippincott, 1970.

_____. *God of the Oppressed*. New York: Seabury, 1975.

Conlin, Joseph R. *Big Bill Haywood and the Radical Union Movement*. Syracuse: Syracuse University Press, 1969.

Coy, Patrick G., ed. *A Revolution of the Heart: Essays on the Catholic Worker*. Philadelphia: Temple University Press, 1988.

Crozier, Michael; Samuel Huntington; and Joji Watanuki. *The Crisis of Democracy*. New York: New York University Press for the Trilateral Commission, 1975.

Dahrendorf, Ralf. *Reflections on the Revolution in Europe*. New York: Times Books, 1990.

Dallek, Robert. *Ronald Reagan: The Politics of Symbolism*. Cambridge, MA: MIT Press, 1984.

Davis, Mike. *Prisoners of the American Dream*. London: Verso, 1986.

Democratic Socialists of America, The. *The New Socialists: An Official Pamphlet*. New York: DSA, 1984.

Diggins, John P. *The Left in the Twentieth Century*. New York: Harcourt Brace Jovanovich, 1973.

Draper, Theodore. *The Roots of American Communism*. New York: Viking, 1957.

Edwards, P. K. *Strikes in the U.S., 1881–1974*. New York: St. Martin's, 1981.

Ehrenreich, Barbara. *Fear of Falling*. New York: Pantheon, 1989.

Foner, Philip. *American Socialism and Black Americans*. Westport, CT: Greenwood, 1977.

Foner, Philip and Allen, James S., eds. *American Communism and Black Americans*. Philadelphia: Temple University Press, 1987.

Fraina, Louis. [Corey, Lewis]. *Revolutionary Socialism: A Study in Socialist Reconstruction*. New York: Communist Press, 1918.

Fraina, Louis. [Corey, Lewis]. *The Unfinished Task: Economic Reconstruction for Democracy*. New York: Viking, 1942.

Fried, Albert, ed. *Socialism in America*. New York: Doubleday, 1970.

Fukuyama, Francis. *The End of History and the Last Man*. New York: Free Press, 1992.

Gollwitzer, Helmut. *The Christian Faith and the Marxist Critique of Religion*. New York: Scribner's, 1970.

Gorman, Robert A. *Neo-Marxism: The Meanings of Modern Radicalism*. Westport, CT: Greenwood, 1985.

_____, ed. *Biographical Dictionary of Marxism*. Westport, CT: Greenwood, 1986.

_____, ed. *Biographical Dictionary of Neo-Marxism*. Westport, CT: Greenwood, 1987.

Gramsci, Antonio. *Selections From the Prison Notebooks*. Ed. and trans. by Quinton Hoare and Geoffrey Nowell Smith. New York: International, 1971.

Habermas, Jürgen. *Legitimation Crisis*. Boston: Beacon, 1975.

Harris, David. *Socialist Origins in the United States*. Assen, Netherlands: Van Gorcum, 1966.

Harrison, Bennett and Bluestone, Barry. *The Great U-Turn*. New York: Basic Books, 1988.

Hillquit, Morris. *History of Socialism in the United States*. Rev. ed. New York: Funk and Wagnalls, 1910.

_____. *Socialism Summed Up*. New York: Fly, 1912.

_____. Hillquit, Morris and John Ryan. *Socialism - Promise or Menace?* New York: Macmillan, 1917.

_____. Hillquit, Morris. *Socialism in Theory and Practice*. New York: Macmillan, 1919.

Hook, Sidney. *Towards The Understanding of Karl Marx*. New York: John Day, 1933.

_____. *From Hegel to Marx: Studies in the Intellectual Development of Karl Marx*. New York: Reynal and Hitchcock, 1936.

Horowitz, Irving Louis. *C. Wright Mills: An American Utopian*. New York: Free Press, 1983.

Howe, Irving, ed. *Beyond the New Left*. New York: McCall, 1965.

_____. *Steady Work: Essays in the Politics of Democratic Radicalism, 1953–1966*. New York: Harcourt, Brace and World, 1966.

_____, ed. *The Radical Papers*. Garden City, NY: Doubleday, 1966.

_____. *The Radical Imagination*. New York: New American Library, 1967.

_____. *A Dissenter's Guide to Foreign Policy*. New York: Praeger, 1968.

_____. *A Margin of Hope*. New York: Harcourt Brace Jovanovich, 1982.

_____. *Socialism and America*. San Diego, CA: Harcourt Brace Jovanovich, 1985.

Jacoby, Russell. *The Last Intellectuals*. New York Basic Books, 1987.

Kaplan, Barbara Hockey, ed. *Social Change in the Capitalist World Economy*. Beverly Hills: Sage, 1978.

Karson, Marc. *American Labor Unions and Politics, 1900–1918*. Boston: Beacon, 1965.

Kaufman, Arnold. *The Radical Liberal*. New York: Atherton, 1968.

Kaye, Harvey J. *The Powers of the Past*. Minneapolis: University of Minnesota Press, 1991.

Kennedy, Paul. *The Rise and Fall of the Great Powers*. New York: Random House, 1987.

Kipnis, Ira. *The American Socialist Movement, 1898–1912*. Westport, CT: Greenwood, 1968.

Klejment, Anne and Klegment, Alice. *Dorothy Day and the Catholic Worker: A Bibliography and Index*. New York: Garland, 1986.

Klehr. Harvey. *The Heyday of American Communism*. New York: Basic Books, 1984.

Kochan, Thomas A., ed. *Challenges and Choices Facing American Labor*. Cambridge, MA: MIT Press, 1985.

Kolko, Joyce. *Restructuring the World Economy*. New York: Pantheon, 1988.

Lapham, Lewis. *Money and Class in America*. New York: Ballantine, 1988.

Laski, Harold. *The American Democracy*. New York: Viking, 1948.

Laslett, John H. M. and Lipset, Seymour Martin, eds., *Failure of a Dream?* ed. Berkeley: University of California Press, 1984.

Levy, Frank. *Dollars and Dreams: The Changing American Income Distribution*. New York: Basic Books, 1988.

Lipset, Seymour Martin. *Continental Divide*. New York: Routledge, 1990.

Lynd, Staughton. *Intellectual Origins of American Radicalism*. New York: Pantheon, 1968.

Magdoff, Harry. *The Age of Imperialism*. New York: Monthly Review, 1969.

————. *Imperialism: From the Colonial Age to the Present*. New York: Monthly Review, 1978.

Mandel, Ernest. *Marxist Economic Theory*. London: Merlin, 1962.

————. *Late Capitalism*. London: New Left Books, 1975.

Marx, Karl. *Selected Correspondence*. Moscow: International, n.d.

————. Marx, Karl and Friedrich Engels. *The Civil War in the U.S.* New York: International, 1961.

————. Marx, Karl. *The Poverty of Philosophy*. New York: International, 1963.

————. *Critique of the Gotha Program*. Moscow: Progress, 1971.

————. *On Revolution*. Ed. Saul K. Padover. New York: McGraw-Hill, 1971.

————. *Early Writings*. New York: Vintage, 1974.

————. *Capital*. 3 vols. Moscow: International, 1975.

Mattera, Philip. *Prosperity Lost*. New York: Addison-Wesley, 1990.

McGovern, Arthur F. *Marxism: An American Christian Perspective*. Maryknoll, NY: Orbis, 1980.

McKown, Delos P. *The Classical Marxist Critiques of Religion*. The Hague: Martinus Nijhoff, 1975.

McQuaid, Kim. *Big Business and Presidential Power*. New York: Morrow, 1982.

Miller, James. *Democracy Is In The Streets: From Port Huron to the Siege of Chicago*. New York: Simon and Schuster, 1987.

Miller, Sally, ed. *Flawed Liberation: Socialism and Feminism*. Westport, CT: Greenwood, 1981.

Miller, William. *A Harsh and Dreadful Love: Dorothy Day and the Catholic Worker Movement*. New York: Liveright, 1973.

Myers, Constance Ashton. *The Prophet's Army*. Westport, CT: Greenwood, 1957.

Newfield, Jack. *A Prophetic Minority*. New York: New American Library, 1966.

Nisbet, Robert. *The Twilight of Authority*. New York: Oxford University Press, 1975.

————. *The Present Age: Progress and Anarchy in Modern America*. New York: Harper and Row, 1988.

Obst, Linda Rosen, ed. *The Sixties*. San Francisco: Rolling Stone Press, 1977.

O'Connor, James. *The Fiscal Crisis of the State*. New York: St. Martin's, 1973.

Parsons, Talcott. *Sociological Theory and Modern Society*. New York: Free Press, 1967.

Perlman, Selig. *A Theory of the Labor Movement*. New York: A.M. Kelley, 1928.

Phillips, Kevin. *Boiling Point: Republicans, Democrats, and the Decline of Middle Class Prosperity*. New York: Random House, 1993.

Piehl, Mel. *Breaking Bread: The "Catholic Worker" and the Origin of Catholic Radicalism in America*. Philadelphia: Temple University Press, 1982.

Pollack, Norman. *The Populist Response to Industrialist America*. Cambridge, MA: Harvard University Press, 1962.

Quint, Howard H. *The Forging of American Socialism*. Columbia: University of South Carolina Press, 1953.

Record, Wilson. *The American Negro and the CP*. New York: Atheneum, 1951.

Renshaw, Patrick. *The Wobblies*. New York: Doubleday, 1967.

Report of the Independent Commission on International Development Issues. *North-South: A Programme for Survival*. Cambridge, MA: MIT Press, 1980.

Robbins, Bruce, ed. *Intellectuals: Aesthetics, Politics, Academics*. Minneapolis: University of Minnesota Press, 1990.

Roberts, Nancy L. *Dorothy Day and the "Catholic Worker."* Albany, NY: SUNY Press, 1984.

Rossiter, Clinton. *Marxism: The View From America*. New York: Harcourt, Brace, and World, 1960.

Sale, Kirkpatrick. *SDS*. New York: Random House, 1973.

Schlesinger, Arthur, ed. *Writings and Speeches of Eugene V. Debs*. New York: Heritage, 1948.

Schor, Juliet B. *The Overworked American*. New York: Basic Books, 1992.

Selsam, Howard and Harry Martel, eds. *Reader in Marxist Philosophy*. New York: International, 1963.

Seretan, L. Glenn. *Daniel DeLeon: The Odyssey of An American Marxist*. Cambridge, MA: Harvard University Press, 1979.

Sexton, Patricia Cayo. *The War on Labor and the Left*. Boulder, CO: Westview, 1991.

Shannon, David A. *The Socialist Party of America*. New York: Macmillan, 1955.

Sidel, Ruth. *Women and Children Last*. New York: Viking, 1992.

Silk, Leonard and David Vogel. *Ethics and Profits*. New York: Simon and Schuster, 1976.

Simon, Rita, ed. *As We Saw The Thirties*. Urbana: University of Illinois Press, 1969.

Simons, A. M. *Social Forces in American History*. New York: Macmillan, 1911.

Skocpol, Theda et. al. *Bringing The State Back In*. Cambridge: Cambridge University Press, 1985.

Sombart, Werner. *Why Is There No Socialism in the U.S.?* 1906. Reprint, White Plains, NY: International Aptitudes and Sciences Press, 1976.

Sotheran, Charles. *Horace Greeley and Other Pioneers of American Socialism*. New York: Humboldt, 1892.

Spargo, John. *Karl Marx: His Life and Work*. New York: Huebsch, 1910.

_____. *Sidelights on Contemporary Socialism*. New York: Huebsch, 1911.

_____. *Applied Socialism*. New York: Huebsch, 1912.

Steinfels, Peter. *The Neoconservatives*. New York: Simon and Schuster, 1979.

Sweezy, Paul. *The Theory of Capitalist Development*. New York: Oxford University Press, 1942.

_____, and Paul Baran. *Monopoly Capitalism*. New York: Monthly Review, 1966.

Thompson, E. P. *The Making of the English Working Class*. New York: Vintage, 1963.

Townsend, Peter. *Poverty in the United Kingdom*. Berkeley: University of California Press, 1979.

Trimberger, Ellen Kay. *Revolution From Above*. New Brunswick, NJ: Transaction, 1978.

Vogel, David. *Fluctuating Fortunes*. New York: Basic Books, 1989.

Wakefield, Dan. *New York in the Fifties*. New York: Houghton Mifflin, 1992.

Wald, Alan M. *The New York Intellectuals: The Rise and Decline of the Anti-Stalinist Left from the 1930s to the 1980s*. Chapel Hill: University of North Carolina Press, 1987.

Wallerstein, Immanual. *The Modern World-System*. New York: Academic, 1974.

_____. *The Capitalist World Economy*. Cambridge: Cambridge University Press, 1979.

_____. *The Modern World-System II*. New York: Academic, 1980.

_____. *The Politics of the World Economy*. Cambridge: Cambridge University Press, 1984.

Weinstein, James. *The Decline of Socialism in America*. New York: Vintage, 1967.

West, Cornel. *Prophecy Deliverance*. Philadelphia: Westminster, 1982.

Will, George. *Suddenly: The American Idea Abroad and at Home, 1986–90*. New York: Free Press, 1992.

Williams, William Appelman. *The Tragedy of American Diplomacy*. New York: Dell, 1972.

_____. *Contours of American History*. New York: Norton, 1989.

Wolfe, Alan. *The Limits of Legitimacy*. New York: Free Press, 1977.

Wright, Eric Olin. *Class, Crisis, and the State*. London: New Left Books, 1978.

_____. *Classes*. London: Verso, 1985.

Articles

Alter, Jonathan. "A New War Over Yalta." *Newsweek*, 28 April 1986, 49.

Aronowitz, Stanley. "Future of Socialism." *Current* 162 (May 1974): 32–4.

Barkan, Joanne. "Remembering Mike." *Dissent* 37 (Winter 1990): 105–9.

Boyte, Harry. "Reunion On the Left." *Progressive* (June 1975): 9–10.

Brittan, Samuel. "The Economic Contradictions of Democracy." *British Journal of Political Science* 5 (Fall 1975): 129–59.

Burnham, James and Max Shachtman. "Intellectuals In Retreat." *New International* 5 (January 1939); 4–22.

Chernow, Ron. "An Irresistible Profile of Michael Harrington (You Must Be Kidding)." *Mother Jones* 2 (July 1977): 28–60 passim.

Draper, Theodore. "Neoconservative History." *New York Review of Books*, 16 January 1986, 5–15.

Ehrenreich, Barbara. "Is the Middle Class Doomed?" *New York Times Magazine*, 7 September 1986, 44–64 passim.

Foner, Eric. "Why Is There No Socialism in the United States?" *History Workshop Journal* 17 (Spring 1984): 143–65.

Fraina, Louis. "The Future of Socialism." *New Review* 3 (January 1915): 7–20.

————. "Socialism and Psychology." *New Review* 3 (May 1915): 1–15.

————. "Problems of American Socialism." *Class Struggle* 2 (February 1919): 40–7.

Fukuyama, Francis. "The End of History." *The National Interest* 16 (Summer 1989): 3–18.

Galenson, Walter. "The American Labor Movement Is Not Socialist." *American Review* 1 (Winter 1961): 104–23.

Gorman, Robert A. "Black Neo-Marxism in Liberal America." *Rethinking Marxism* 4 (Winter 1989): 118–40.

————. "Marxism and Theology in Liberal America." *Politics, Culture, and Society* 3 (Summer 1990): 463–84.

Harries, Owen. "A Primer for Polemicists." *Commentary* 70 (September 1984): 51–63.

Heilbroner, Robert. "The Triumph of Capitalism." *New Yorker*, 31 January 1989, 98–109.

Hook, Sidney. "The Meaning of Marxism." *Modern Quarterly* 4 (Spring 1930): 426–35.

————. "The Scope of Marxian Theory." *American Socialist* 7 (July 1936): 15–34.

Jacoby, T. "A Life at the Barricades." *Newsweek*, 8 August 1988, 30.

US Congress Joint Economic Committee. "The Concentration of Wealth in the United States: Trends in the Distribution of Wealth Among American Families." (July 1986).

Judis, John. "Democratic Socialists Move Left." *In These Times*, 28 February 1979, 4.

Kaufman, Arnold. "A Philosophy for the American Left." *Socialist Commentary* 14 (November 1963): 111–22.

————. "A Sketch of a Liberal Theory of Fundamental View of Human Rights." *Monist* 52 (October 1968): 595–615.

————. "A Strategy for Radical Liberals." *Dissent* 18 (August 1971): 34–52.

————. "Wants, Needs, and Liberalism." *Inquiry* 14 (Autumn 1971): 210–2.

King, Anthony. "Overload: Problems of Governing in the 1970s." *Political Studies* 23 (Summer 1975): 284–96.

LaFeber, Walter. "The Last War, the Next War, and the New Revisionists." *Democracy* 1 (January 1981): 93–103.

Landes, Joan. "Feminism and The Internationals." *Telos* 49 (Fall 1981): 117–26.

Levy, Frank. "The Vanishing Middle Class and Related Issues: A Review of Living Standards in the 1970s and 1980s." *Political Studies* 20 (Summer 1987): 650–5.

Lipset, Seymour Martin. "Neoconservatism: Myth and Reality." *Society* 25 (July-August 1988): 29–37.

Long, Marion. "Paradise Tossed - Visions of Utopia." *Omni* 10 (April 1988): 36–108 passim.

McDonald, Dwight. "An Open Letter to Michael Harrington." *New York Review of Books,* 5 December 1968, 48–9.

Miller, S. "Poverty of Socialist Thought." *Commentary* 62 (August 1976): 31–7.

Miller, Sally. "The Socialist Party and the Negro, 1901–1920." *Journal of Negro History* 56 (July 1971): 220–9.

Podhoretz, Norman. "Laureate of the New Class." *Commentary* 54 (December 1972): 4.

Radosh, Ronald and Michael Harrington. "An Exchange." *Partisan Review* 56 (Winter 1989): 65–85.

Rodewald, Richard and Richard Wasserstrom. "The Political Philosophy of Arnold Kaufman." *Social Theory and Practice* 2 (Spring 1972): 5–32.

Scudder, Vida. "Women and Socialism." *Yale Review* 3 (April 1914): 459.

Shachtman, Max. "Footnote For Historians." *New International* 4 (December 1938): 377.

Skocpol, Theda. "Political Response to Capitalist Crisis: Neo-Marxist Theories of the State and the Case of the New Deal." *Politics and Society* 10 (Spring 1981): 187–205.

Staff. "Michael Harrington." *New Republic* 199 (18 July 1988): 12.

Steinfels, Peter; James Finn and Patrick Lacefield. "A Man Who Made A Difference: Michael Harrington in Our History." *Commonweal* 116 (8 September 1989): 466–70.

United States Census Bureau. "Living in Poverty." (31 August 1988).

Vogel, Lise. "Questions on the Women Question." *Monthly Review* 31 (June 1979): 39–59.

Wilentz, Sean. "Against Exceptionalism: Class Consciousness and the American Labor Movement, 1790–1920." With critiques by Nick Salvatore and Michael Hanagan, and a reply by Wilentz, *International Labor and Working Class History.* 26–7 (1984–5).

Wright, Eric Olin and Joachin Singelmann. "Proletarianization in the Changing American Class Structure." *American Journal of Sociology* 88 (Supplement, 1982): 176–209.

Unpublished Manuscripts

Boudin, Louis. "Exit the Socialist Party," n.d., Louis Boudin Papers, Columbia University.

Cohen, Robert. "Revolt of the Depression Generation: America's First Mass Student Protest Movement, 1929–1940," Ph.D. diss. University of California, Berkeley, 1987.

Peterson, Patti. "The Young Socialist Movement in America from 1905–1940: A Study of the Young Peoples Socialist League," Ph.D. dissertation, University of Wisconsin, 1974.

INDEX

Debs, Eugene V., 11, 16, 38, 39-40, 63
Declaration of Independence, 62
Dector, Midge, 90, 196 n.61
degenerated workers' state, Trotsky's theory of, 18
DeLeon, Daniel, 63-4
Dellinger, Dave, 4
Dellums, Ron, 9
deMan, Henri, 75
Democratic Party, 9
Democratic Plan, Harrington's theory of, 92-3
democratic socialism, 80-1
Democratic Socialist Federation (DSF), 5
Democratic Socialist Organizing Committee (DSOC), 6, 7, 8, 144-6, 177-82 passim
Democratic Socialists of America (DSA), 8, 145-6, 182
Deng Xiaoping, 170
Denitch, Bogdan, 15, 144-5
Dependency Theory, 115-6
dialectical materialism, 30, 35-6
dialectics, 42-7, 176
dictatorship of the proletariat, 34-5, 85
Dissent, 7, 19, 20
dominant economic class, 28
Donovan, Suzanne, 178
Dubois, W.E.B., 177, 178
Dunayevskaya, Raya, 196 n.61
Dylan, Bob, iii

Eastman, Max, 16, 196 n.61
Economic Opportunity Act of 1964, 54-5
Economics Security Council, 122
economism, 30, 34-5, 46
Edwards, P.K., 70

efficiency, and socialist economics, 166-7
Ehrenreich, Barbara, 8, 78
Eighteenth Brumaire of Louis Bonaparte (Marx), 84, 126
Elster, Jon, 102
empiricism, 43-4, 48
Employee Stock Ownership Programs (ESOPs), 167
The End of History and the Last Man (Fukuyama), 189
Engels, Friedrich, 30-1, 35-6, 85, 126
exceptionalism, in the U.S., 68-71

Fabian socialists, 63
Faletto, Enzo, 118
Falwell, Jerry, 90
Farrell, James T., 196 n.61
feminism, 178-9
feminization of poverty, 60
Fiedler, Leslie, 196 n.61
finance capital, 114
First International, 62
fiscal crisis of the state, O'Connor's theory of, 105-6
Fitzpatrick, John, 195 n.54
Flacks, Richard, ix
Fleischman, Harry, vi, 9
Ford, Henry, 154
Fourth International, 17
Fraina, Louis, 11, 40-1
Frank, Andre Gunder, 115, 118
Frankfurt School, 161
Freedom Budget, Harrington's theory of, 207 n.49
Friedman, Milton, 66, 91
Fromm, Eric, 200 n.57
Fukuyama, Francis, 189
full employment, 91-2, 164
fundamentalism, 110

Preobrazhensky, Evgeny Alexeyevich, 170
productive relations, 28

INDEX

Trotsky, Leon, 16, 170
Trotskyism, 16-18
Twilight of Capitalism (Harrington), 45, 79-81 passim

unions, in the U.S., 167-8
United Federation of Teachers (UFT), 177
Universities and Left Review, iii
unthinking socialization, Harrington's theory of, 66
urban violence, 59
utopian socialism, in the U.S., 62-3, 152
utopian spirit, 68-9

vagabond poor, 59
The Vast Majority (Harrington), 116-24 passim
Vienna Union, 194 n.33
Vietnam War, 5, 6, 56
Village Independent Democrats, 140
VISTA, 54
Von Hayek, Frederick, 91
Voting Rights Act (1965), 55

wage earner funds, in Sweden, 169
wages: in Harrington's post-capitalist system, 96-7; in the U.S., 128-30
Wakefield, Dan, 2, 10